A splendid book comprising nine essays contributed to a seminar celebrating the long, distinguished career of Richard Broome. It brings together valuable reflections on the writing of Aboriginal history over the last forty years with often sparkling new work from young scholars who now follow in Richard's pioneering steps.

Henry Reynolds, FASSA, FAHA
Honorary Research Professor, University of Tasmania

This book provides a vivid, balanced and fitting tribute to a passionate scholar of Aboriginal history.

Whether discussing a massacre, a missionary, a boxer or an activist, Richard Broome's quest to position Aboriginal people at the forefront of Australian history has left an immeasurable legacy.

In this compelling collection, an accomplished and diverse set of authors contributes a critique of why, under the weight of colonialism, attempts to forge a mutual understanding could never be enough.

Ann McGrath, AM, FASSA, FAHA
Kathleen Fitzpatrick Laureate Fellow, Australian National University

CONFLICT, ADAPTATION, TRANSFORMATION

Richard Broome and the practice
of Aboriginal history

Edited by Ben Silverstein

ABORIGINAL
STUDIES PRESS

First published in 2018
by Aboriginal Studies Press

© in the collection, Ben Silverstein, 2018

© in individual chapters, held by the contributors, 2018

All rights reserved. No part of this book may be reproduced or transmitted in any form or by any means, electronic or mechanical, including photocopying, recording or by any information storage and retrieval system, without prior permission in writing from the publisher. The Australian *Copyright Act 1968* (the Act) allows a maximum of one chapter or 10 per cent of this book, whichever is the greater, to be photocopied by any educational institution for its education purposes provided that the educational institution (or body that administers it) has given a remuneration notice to Copyright Agency Limited (CAL) under the Act.

The opinions expressed in this book are the authors' own and do not necessarily reflect the view of AIATSIS or ASP.

Aboriginal and Torres Strait Islander people are respectfully advised that this publication contains names and images of deceased persons, and culturallysensitive information.

Aboriginal Studies Press is the publishing arm of the Australian Institute of Aboriginal and Torres Strait Islander Studies.

GPO Box 553, Canberra, ACT 2601
Phone: (61 2) 6246 1183
Fax: (61 2) 6261 4288
Email: asp@aiatsis.gov.au
Web: www.aiatsis.gov.au/asp/about.html

 A catalogue record for this book is available from the National Library of Australia

ISBN: 9781925302530 (pbk)
ISBN: 9781925302547 (ebook: pdf)
ISBN: 9781925302554 (ebook: epub)
ISBN: 9781925302561 (Kindle)

Typeset in Goudy Old Style by Amity Raymont, Australia

Printed in Australia by SOS Printing, Australia

Cover image: 'Land lost, land stolen, treaty' 2016, Marlene Gilson (Wadawarrung), Purchased 2017, City of Melbourne Art and Heritage Collection © Courtesy of the artist. Photographer: Patrick Rodriguez.

AIATSIS acknowledges the funding support of the Department of the Prime Minister and Cabinet (PM&C).

Foreword

As a scholar, a teacher, and a colleague Richard Broome is renowned for an openness and generosity that sets him apart. In our field of historical studies he is one of the giants. A review of any undergraduate Australian Aboriginal History curriculum reveals the impact of his intellectual career. Here, nestled amongst the enviable list of monographs, are journal articles and book chapters that range from Aboriginal boxing to a national survey on Aboriginal history, to careful empirical studies of frontier violence and dispossession, to organisational history and stories of activism, to a close and careful study of the Aboriginal history of Victoria. The central hallmark of these works is an exploration of Aboriginal agency and a desire to see the complexity of the past in terms other than 'black and white'. One admirable aspect of Richard's work in Aboriginal history has been its iterative nature. Subsequent editions of his influential books have not been merely updated but rather he has used these as opportunities to reflect on his own historical processes as well as disciplinary advances. Each expanded edition has provided a new visionary approach to the topic.

For two decades now, in my teaching, students have described Richard's work as challenging and revealing, alive and illuminating. Such achievement is no mean feat, but more importantly it is rare because many academic authors are singularly research focussed and their capacity to explain the past is often mired in convoluted academic concepts, and relies on impenetrable language and expression. As a true educator Richard has valued and prided himself on teaching, and his written works are similarly engaging. It is unsurprising that these works have enjoyed significant sales and reach.

Students, particularly, find useful the way Richard's work deals with intersubjectivity and intersectionality, and how Australian history and Aboriginal history are connected, interdependent and mutually reinforcing. In Richard's histories all Australians can find a narrative they can connect to, be they newcomers, settlers, or Indigenous people. In so doing they will find that, through Richard's writing, Aboriginal agency, action and positionality move from the fringes to a central and indeed highly visible locale. In my recent work I developed a model of attenuated agency which owes itself to a reading and re-reading of Richard's work, while

Foreword

recognising the limitations of discussions of agency, particularly as they apply in a settler-colonial setting. Attenuated agency recognises that in the settler-colonial setting Aboriginal people exercised choice wherever and whenever they could; however, their decisions were inevitably attenuated by their circumstances.[1]

Richard's most recent work on the Victorian Aborigines Advancement League of Melbourne demonstrates his commitment to Aboriginal engagement, close archival research and the documenting of community activism. Presented with a mountainous collection of organisational documents, he set about not merely analysing, researching and writing up, he also undertook the enormous task of properly cataloguing, collating and depositing these unique materials. The employment of Aboriginal research assistants and liaison with the State Library of Victoria ensured that the collection was safely housed and its cultural as well as its historical value was acknowledged.

The one book that I almost invariably ask my doctoral students to review is, perhaps surprisingly, Richard's local history study *Coburg: Between Two Creeks*. Local history is, I assure them, an oft derided and neglected historical terrain. Local history is perceived as small history, as it were. However, in the hands of a master historian, who sees national, transnational and global trends, local history becomes history writ large. There is usually a little puzzlement that I would suggest this text yet, without failure, the students recognise it as a demonstration of how history can be crafted and how a nuanced study can be achieved. And, as I expect it to, it inspires them.

The chapters that follow are an apt testament to a career that has spanned more than four decades. Richard Broome's sustained energy and commitment over that time is evident in a prodigious intellectual output and, perhaps more importantly, a legacy of doctoral supervisions who have gone on to have their own brilliant careers. Although he may have retired from an employed position, he is anything but retiring and no doubt there is much more to come of this fine scholar and generous mentor.

Lynette Russell

Contents

Foreword by Lynette Russell	v
List of Illustrations	viii
Acknowledgements	ix
Contributors	x

1 Voyaging with hope: Richard Broome and the ethics of Aboriginal history
   Ben Silverstein — 1

2 Aboriginal agents, victims and voyagers: Richard Broome's contribution to the debate about the frontier wars in Victoria
   Lyndall Ryan — 18

3 On Paternalisms and Aboriginal Agency: From missions to neoliberal policy in the work of Richard Broome and Noel Pearson
   Claire McLisky and Ben Silverstein — 38

4 The philosophy, opinions and inspiration of Jack Johnson
   John Maynard — 63

5 Nyungar domains: Reading Gyalliput's geography and mobility in the colonial archive
   Tiffany Shellam — 80

6 'Memoirs of an Aboriginal Woman' by Theresa Clements: Reflections on my great grandmother's life
   Julie Andrews — 96

7 Aboriginal education, meritocratic scholarships and the Country Women's Association of NSW 1962–1972
   Jennifer Jones — 122

8 A different courage: 'Radical Hope' and the continuous strand of Aboriginal agency in Victoria
   Richard Broome — 140

9 How do you teach Aboriginal history?
   Maxine Briggs — 159

Appendix — Richard Broome's publications on Aboriginal history	173
Notes	178
References	208

List of Illustrations

Richard Broome at La Trobe University, 2000 — 8

'Gyalliput's sketch', 1833 — 88

Theresa Clements (née Middleton), 1955, Coburg, Melbourne — 97

Figure 6.1. Theresa Clements' family tree — 98

Theresa Clements (née Middleton) with her sister Christina Patten (née Middleton) holding Patten baby, 1905 — 104

Figure 6.2. Map of Victoria and southern New South Wales — 106

Theresa Clements and her daughters, c.1916 — 115

Theresa Clements, her daughters and granddaughters, 1955, Coburg, Melbourne — 117

Note on Language:

In the course of historical description and analysis, this book engages with a number of terms describing Aboriginal people that were in frequent use in the nineteenth and twentieth centuries. These terms are reproduced as they appear in the historical record. Readers should be aware that this unfortunately means reproducing words and phrases that are both damaging and offensive in the text that follows.

Acknowledgements

Richard Broome retired from La Trobe University in December 2012 and was appointed Professor Emeritus in May 2014. To mark the occasion, we organised a symposium in his honour, titled *Writing and Teaching Aboriginal History*, held at La Trobe University in Melbourne on 20 February 2014. Generously sponsored by the History Department of La Trobe University, the symposium was conceived and organised by Katie Holmes, Diane Kirkby, Adrian Jones, and I, and Tracey Banivanua Mar helped shape its focus. Nellie Green, manager of Indigenous Student Services, also provided helpful advice and organising support.

The symposium was attended by almost 100 scholars and community members, including colleagues and collaborators, members of Richard's family and friends. Most of the chapters in this volume were first prepared for that event. A number of other scholars delivered presentations at the symposium, including Genevieve Grieves, Jessica Horton, Ingrid Purnell, Mark Rose, and Leonie Stevens, but for various reasons their papers were not able to be included here. Crystal McKinnon and Patrick Wolfe chaired sessions and contributed to the lively discussions that took place.

Thanks to Rachel Ippoliti, Frances Glavimans, the Publishing Advisory Committee, and the team at Aboriginal Studies Press for their work on this volume, and thanks as well to the two anonymous referees whose comments were helpful in revising the manuscript and bringing it together. I am grateful to Marlene Gilson for her generosity in allowing us to use her artwork as the cover image.

Throughout his career, Richard has been a source of both knowledge and encouragement for other historians, a role he continues to fulfil today. He has been a consistently engaged and committed historian. I hope this book is a fitting reflection of his generosity, astute commentary, and pathbreaking scholarship.

Ben Silverstein

Contributors

Julie Andrews is descended from the Wurundjeri people of Melbourne and the Yorta Yorta tribe near the borders of Victorian and New South Wales along the Murray River. She is a member of the Dhulanyagan family clan of the Ulupna people. Julie has been teaching Aboriginal Studies for approximately 10 years and has extensive experience in policy and Indigenous higher education. She is convenor of Aboriginal Studies at La Trobe University where she teaches the first year Discovery subject HUS1ABS: Introduction to Aboriginal Australia and an on-country subject titled Encountering Aboriginal Victoria: Parallel Systems of Knowledge.

Maxine Briggs has worked for more than 35 years in a variety of community and government jobs that served the Aboriginal community, as well as working with Aboriginal reggae/rock band No Fixed Address in the late 1970s. Since then she has spent time in both the public service and in grassroots community organisations, and co-founded the Koori Arts Collective. She has been researching Aboriginal history in the holdings of collecting institutions, especially Museum Victoria, since the early 1980s, and in 2007 joined the State Library of Victoria to work on indexing the recently transferred Aboriginal Advancement League collection. She has been the Koori Librarian since 2010 and has implemented an Indigenous knowledge system called the Cultural Permissions Program, an operating system for the management of Indigenous materials in the State Library of Victoria.

Richard Broome, Emeritus Professor of History at La Trobe University, taught there for almost 30 years after tutoring at the universities of Sydney and Melbourne. He also spent five years as a commissioned historian. His varied research interests have covered the local, regional and national sphere. He has written books and articles on immigration, religious history, local history, sports history, popular culture, biography and especially Aboriginal history. The last theme was the focus of most of his articles, a Year 12 text, and six of his 13 major books, two of which have won prizes. His book *Aboriginal Australians* has appeared in four editions over 35 years, the last a complete rewrite with sales of more than 60,000 copies. A fifth edition will appear in 2019. His work has focused on cross-cultural engagement, with an emphasis on Aboriginal negotiation, agency and the capacity for Aboriginal self-empowerment. Although clear-sighted about the disastrous effects of dispossession on Aboriginal families, communities and culture, and the extent of violence on the Australian frontier, his work points to Aboriginal people's status as 'voyagers' as well as 'victims' – to quote the terms of his notable 1994 article in the *Journal of Australian Studies*. His latest book in the field was *Fighting Hard* (2015) and his most recent book is *Naga Odyssey* (2017) a colonial story told with Visier Sanyü. He is currently completing an environmental and social history of mallee country in southern Australia with three colleagues.

Jennifer Jones is a Senior Lecturer in Interdisciplinary Studies at La Trobe University. Her second book *Country women and the colour bar*, which examines Aboriginal branches of the Country Women's Association of NSW from 1956 to 1972, is published by Aboriginal Studies Press. Jennifer's research interests include Indigenous Australian history and biography, Indigenous Australian literature, cross-cultural collaboration, rural and religious history and histories of education.

John Maynard is a Worimi Aboriginal man from the Port Stephens region of New South Wales. He is currently chair of Aboriginal History at the University of Newcastle and director of the Purai Global Indigenous and Diaspora Research Studies Centre. He has held several major positions and served on numerous prominent organisations and committees including deputy chairperson of the Australian Institute of Aboriginal and Torres Strait Islander Studies (AIATSIS). He was the recipient of the Aboriginal History (ANU) Stanner Fellowship 1996, the New South Wales Premiers Indigenous History Fellow 2003, an Australian Research Council Postdoctoral Fellow 2004, the University of Newcastle Researcher of the Year for 2008 and 2012, and the Australian National University Allan Martin History Lecturer 2010. In 2014 he was elected a member of the prestigious Australian Social Sciences Academy. Professor Maynard's publications have concentrated on the intersections of Aboriginal political and social history, and the history of Australian race relations. He is the author of several books, including *Aboriginal Stars of the Turf, Fight for Liberty and Freedom, The Aboriginal Soccer Tribe, Aborigines and the Sport of Kings, True Light and Shade: An Aboriginal Perspective of Joseph Lycett's Art* and *Living with the Locals – Early Indigenous Experience of Indigenous Life*.

Contributors

Claire McLisky is a descendant of Scottish, English and Irish settlers who was raised and currently lives on Bundjalung land in northern New South Wales. Claire is an honorary research fellow at both Griffith University and the University of Copenhagen, and researches and writes alongside looking after her two young children. Her work investigates the histories of eighteenth- and nineteenth-century Christian missions to indigenous peoples and their ongoing legacies. From 2012 to 2015 she held a postdoctoral fellowship at the University of Copenhagen, uncovering the emotional economies of early colonial missions to indigenous peoples in Australia and Greenland. Her PhD research considered the history of Maloga Mission in New South Wales, Australia. She is the editor of a recent special issue of *The Journal of Social History*, 'Colonial Christian Missions and their Legacies' (March 2017), and the co-editor of the following: a special issue of *Social Sciences and Missions*, with Kirstie Close-Barry (Fall 2017); *Emotions and Christian Missions: Historical Perspectives*, with Karen Vallgårda and Daniel Midena (Palgrave Macmillan, 2015); and *Creating White Australia*, with Jane Carey (University of Sydney Press, 2009). She has also published articles and book chapters on humanitarianism, settler colonialism, and the role of emotions in Christian missions.

Lynette Russell is an anthropological historian specialising in nineteenth-century Australian history. All of her work is interdisciplinary, combining history, archaeology and material culture studies. Her long-term research focus has been on Aboriginal responses to colonialism and Aboriginal agency. She is the author or editor of twelve books, numerous articles and book chapters. She is director of the Monash Indigenous Studies Centre and node director of the Centre for Australian Biodiversity and Heritage. Her current research examines Aboriginal zoological knowledge and Indigenous science.

Lyndall Ryan is Conjoint Research Professor in the Centre for the History of Violence at the University of Newcastle, Australia. Her most recent books include *Tasmanian Aborigines: A History Since 1803* (2012), and the co-edited collection with Philip G. Dwyer, *Theatres of Violence Massacre, Mass Killing and Atrocity throughout History* (2012). She currently holds two Australian Research Council (ARC) Discovery Grants, one for frontier violence in Australia 1788 to 1960, and the other for violence and intimacy in the settler societies in the Anglo-Pacific rim 1830 to 1930, and is completing an online digital map of Aboriginal massacre sites across Australia.

Tiffany Shellam is Senior Lecturer in History at Deakin University. She is the author of *Shaking Hands on the Fringe: Negotiating the Aboriginal World at King George's Sound* (UWAP 2009) and publishes on the history of encounters between Aboriginal people and Europeans in the contexts of exploration, early settlement and mission stations in the nineteenth century.

Ben Silverstein is a Postdoctoral Fellow in History at the University of Sydney. He completed his PhD at La Trobe University in 2012, and subsequently taught Australian Aboriginal History there, taking over the course Richard Broome had first taught in 1977. He has published work on sovereignties, settler colonialism, and colonial government, and his book, titled *Governing Natives: Indirect Rule and Settler Colonialism in Australia's North*, is forthcoming with Manchester University Press.

CHAPTER 1

Voyaging with hope
Richard Broome and the ethics of Aboriginal history
by Ben Silverstein

Across several of his works, Richard Broome has recorded that the first contact between Aboriginal and non-Aboriginal people in Victoria – the state where he has made his home – took place in February 1802. Under the command of Lieutenant John Murray, the brig *Lady Nelson* entered Port Phillip Bay and five of the crew landed near what is now Sorrento, greeting and dancing with 18 or 20 Boonwurrung men on the beach; Murray described this as a 'friendly intercourse'. Though the Boonwurrung exchanged spears, a stone axe, and a basket for the travellers' shirts, mirrors, and a steel axe, it remained a wary and distrustful encounter. The sailors would not demonstrate their guns, claiming they were merely walking sticks, and the Boonwurrung refused to point the intruders in the direction of water, instead insisting on being given European goods, including the sailors' clothes. The meeting, which Broome casts as a 'bloody shambles', climaxed when a party of Boonwurrung men attacked the Europeans who, in turn, fired muskets and cannons from the ship: in Murray's words, 'teach[ing] them by fatal experience the effect of our walking sticks'.

More promisingly, when the French ship *Naturaliste* landed in April of that year, the second-in-command Pierre Bernard Milius was able to move beyond that initial mistrust when encountering a group of Boonwurrung men who looked down and called to him from the top of a cliff. Understanding them to be inviting him to leave his clothing at the base, he removed his socks and shirt and began climbing, receiving guidance from those above. In the final moments of his ascent he affected a helplessness with the intention of 'supplicat[ing] them to save me'. His pleas unanswered, he pulled himself to the top of the cliff where he was asked to, and did, hand over his pantaloons and shoes. The Boonwurrung men examined his body and 'appeared very satisfied to see that my form resembled theirs'; they made movements he mimicked and 'manifested their joy by laughing'. What is crucial here, for Broome, is that Milius was able to establish a relationship by affecting a genuine vulnerability. He 'stripped off his clothes to reveal his common humanity'. He 'sang and danced to earn their trust'. In many ways, this moment reveals what lies at the heart of the relationships between Aboriginal and non-Aboriginal people that Richard Broome has sought to narrate through his historical practice. Not in its actual denouement, as the Boonwurrung 'fled in dismay' when Milius' companion joined him on the clifftop. But in its glimpsed promise of a common humanity, its recognition of the self as fundamentally akin to and vulnerable to the other, its negotiating search for mutual comprehension, this episode represents that which is most keenly valued in Broome's writing and teaching of Aboriginal history.

When we gathered at La Trobe University in February 2014 to mark and celebrate Richard Broome's career, speaker after speaker emphasised the importance of these themes of generosity, openness, and an insistence on placing Aboriginal people at the centre of our historical focus. These themes, we all knew, have been fundamental to both the substance and the practise of his scholarship. Though his work has changed conceptually over the course of a long career, there have been some fundamental constants. He has consistently sought out encounters characterised by equality, moments where we might find a wilful rejection of the determining force of colonialism. In so doing, he has embedded in Aboriginal history a longing for the possibility of equal relations, of mutual good behaviour, of a coming together of individuals in ways not constituted by colonialism.

In this desire to transcend colonial relations his work bears a similarity to that of his longtime La Trobe colleague Inga Clendinnen, for whom the re-reading of early Australian 'cross-cultural' contact reveals a history of British sensitivity to Aboriginal legal and customary practice.

But where Clendinnen was so moved by glimpses of common humanity that she seemed often to wish just relationships into existence, imbuing men like Arthur Phillip or Watkin Tench with heroically altruistic ambitions and motives, Broome has retained an awareness of the fundamental injustice that attended the British invasion of Australia. He has rarely confused a promise with its redemption, instead emphasising a sense of equality as an aspiration for Aboriginal historical subjects. For him, hope is to be found in the creative imaginations of Aboriginal people who have sought to craft new ways to live in and shape the colonial world into which they were thrust.

This volume reflects contributions to the symposium held in Richard's honour in February 2014, where we spoke extensively of his influence on the way we teach and research Aboriginal history. His contribution to normalising the presence of Aboriginal agency at the heart of Australian history is no small achievement. In exploring and building on this historiographical emphasis on recuperating Aboriginal agency as a response to colonial dominance, the chapters in this collection discern and critique a number of the historical models that have made this project feasible in successive frontier and mission eras. Lyndall Ryan describes Broome's contributions to frontier historiography, particularly focusing on the Victorian frontier wars to trace the complicated trajectory of his attempts to describe the nature and extent of violence. In his diverse representations of Aboriginal people on the frontier, Ryan notes, Broome has complicated the story of colonialism in difficult ways; she makes the vital point that an emphasis on agency both enables and constrains our historical understanding of the frontier. In the following chapter, Claire McLisky and I turn to examine Broome's transformative understanding of mission 'paternalism'. Alongside Noel Pearson's early writing on the topic, Broome's work on understanding paternalist mission relations as a site of Aboriginal agency deserves greater attention. It can help us to conceptualise paternalism as an object of Aboriginal action and tell stories of possibility amid constraint, where Aboriginal mission residents worked with and alongside missionaries to shape paternalist relationships. Broome's conception of paternalism, it is argued, has much to tell us about the ways mission nostalgia has influenced Aboriginal policy over the past decade, and could be the basis for a more nuanced understanding of what is at stake in debates over relationships between Aboriginal and non-Aboriginal peoples.

These chapters demonstrate the capacity of Broome's conceptual models to challenge the ways we understand Australian (and) Aboriginal histories. Inspired by his insistence on reading archives for evidence of Aboriginal agency, the following chapters put his models into practice in new contexts to tell nuanced stories of the ways Aboriginal people in the nineteenth and twentieth centuries both engaged with others and made their own histories. John Maynard argues that telling stories of Aboriginal engagements with boxing — whether as participants or as inspired onlookers — can be an effective way of writing an active Aboriginal presence into Australian history. Broome's focus throughout his career on boxers has been one way of refusing to confine Aboriginal people to an archaic position in the national story, instead assuming the Aboriginal achievement of modernity and putting Aboriginal action at the heart of Australian history. Maynard's study of African-American heavyweight Jack Johnson's 1907 and 1908 visits to Australia takes Johnson seriously as both a gifted physical fighter and an influential black philosopher of race, civilisation, and colonialism. This emphasis is the basis for Maynard's argument that one of the benefits of attending to popular pursuits like boxing is in enabling historians to uncover unexpected practices, relationships, and connections.

Inspired by Richard's teaching on the complicated meanings of Aboriginal country, Tiffany Shellam re-thinks relationships between Aboriginal and non-Aboriginal people through the story of a map sketched by Mineng Nyungar man Gyalliput in 1833 that resides in the National Archives in London. Shellam describes the conditions of its production as a performance to Gyalliput's interlocutor and as a way of telling his story both to the man before him as well as to a distant authority in London. Through Shellam's account, we get a densely layered sense of Aboriginal people acting to shape their world through the men with pens and paper in front of them, engaging with British power but not determined by it. Julie Andrews explores another crucial Aboriginal source: the memoirs of Theresa Clements from Maloga Mission who has left a legacy of extraordinary influence over contemporary Victorian Aboriginal politics, demonstrating the possibilities of Aboriginal agency. Broome has emphasised the importance of Aboriginal memoir and family history in providing us with a richer Australian history, and here Andrews reads her great-grandmother's story to revise our understandings of mission life, of the tenacity and resilience of Koori families, of the experience of child removal, and of the processes of land settlement in Victoria.

Jennifer Jones turns to a little-studied chapter of the history of the NSW Country Women's Association to describe the challenges faced by Aboriginal secondary school students in the 1960s. Examining two students in particular, her account of the expectations and demands they faced throws their struggles to persist and resist into relief. These are people who found and fought for education, and who shaped it for their own circumstances, confounding expectations to ensure they deployed their talents for community. Underlying such accounts is an appreciation of the myriad ways Aboriginal people have practised cultural and political continuity amidst social change, articulating new ways of being Aboriginal in the nineteenth and twentieth centuries. Broome has described these practices as evidence of 'radical hope', a concept he has borrowed from the American philosopher Jonathan Lear to make sense of dynamic contemporary articulations of Indigenous tradition. Here he describes the way 'radical hope' helps to trace Victorian Aboriginal activism from Billibellary in the 1840s through to the Aboriginal Advancement League that, in 2017, celebrated its 60th year of operation. The League, he ultimately argues, continues a tradition established in the earliest years of British invasion of not just surviving but developing new and vibrant ways of being Aboriginal in a world where so much had been destroyed.

And finally, in a more personal piece, Maxine Briggs locates Broome's work as part of a broader effort to overturn the histories that bolster terra nullius, to engage with the colonial archive to write honest histories that more fully and truthfully include Aboriginal people. Inspired by this practice, she provides us with an account of her own life in a range of community settings, from Cummeragunja Mission on the banks of the Murray River through an assimilationist education system and on to a range of community organisations. In each of these sites, Briggs emphasises cultural practice and describes Koori commitments to community and to nationhood. In her current role as Koori Librarian at the State Library of Victoria, as a custodian of archives, Briggs has played a significant role in transforming the ways we engage with records of heritage – not as inert objects but as living subjects – connected to community, reflecting Aboriginal survival and a basis for cultural revival that Broome might understand as evidence of 'radical hope'. Briggs presents the compelling suggestion that a new way of understanding Aboriginal history, through an Aboriginal world view, could transform Australia and create new relations between people that might, I think, aspire to an ethics of engagement Richard would hope for.

This ethics takes shape through Broome's practice of history through a consistent, committed, and measured engagement with the question of 'How ought I to relate to another?' The rest of this chapter is concerned largely with the way Broome has posed and responded to questions of the subject that prefigure this ethical problem: 'Who am I, who ought I to be? And who is the other to whom I relate?' His responses take shape through an engagement with the themes identified above which underlie the contributions to this collection. On one hand his work values those like Milius who were prepared to open themselves up, making themselves vulnerable to Aboriginal people. On the other he has described Aboriginal subjects who emerge as voyagers in his work throughout the 1990s, and as bearers of 'radical hope' in his work from the mid-2000s onwards. These are practices of historical representation that consciously present Aboriginal people as exemplifying a fundamental and recognisable humanity. It is the play of these Aboriginal and non-Aboriginal subjects that makes possible the establishment of ethical relations as an alternative to those relations generated by a determining colonialism. In this introductory chapter, in celebrating Broome's contribution to the vitality and importance of Aboriginal history today, I focus on the way that Broome has placed Aboriginal subjects as agents at the heart of Australian history as a way not only of demonstrating the possibility for a new national dispensation but also, as a practice of writing and teaching, as itself a practice of ethical history.

Knowing ourselves

Though I had learnt from his work for some years previously, I first met Richard when enrolling as a postgraduate student in history at La Trobe University in 2008. He was then serving as head of department and I was struck immediately by his generosity and openness and by the distinctively welcome humanity that characterised his approach to younger colleagues. In the uneven and often unpredictable context of a history department at a modern neoliberal university, Richard personally took care to ensure that we postgraduate students were valued and supported throughout our candidatures. Some years later, in the months following Richard's retirement, I was appointed to coordinate and teach the undergraduate subject Australian Aboriginal History, working from Richard's meticulous notes and carefully chosen texts to continue a longstanding teaching tradition. This was a course Richard had run for the first time in 1977 when he took a three-year appointment at La Trobe, taking over from John Hirst what was the first history unit devoted to Aboriginal–European encounters in an Australian university. Running continuously since then in various forms, Australian Aboriginal History at La Trobe University stands as a testament to decades of Richard's work, linking his pioneering research with the classroom to give generations of students a sense of the shared nature of the Australian past. It was, and remains, a course that insists on centralising Aboriginal experiences of the past, approaching an Australian history by presenting Aboriginal people as vital historical subjects whose lives must be considered fairly and with great empathy.

It was in his first years of teaching this subject that Broome began to research in Aboriginal history, beginning with a study of professional Aboriginal boxers that he carried out by interviewing these fighters, their trainers, and managers in Victoria, New South Wales, and Queensland. At this point, few works of Aboriginal history had been published. Bill Stanner had spoken in 1968 of the 'Great Australian Silence', a silence that had prevailed among historians throughout the twentieth century and which was only beginning to be broken by undergraduate subjects like Richard's. Charles Rowley began publishing his three-volume history with *The Destruction of Aboriginal Society* in 1972, while Peter Biskup, and Raymond Evans, Kay Saunders and Kathryn Cronin published their

Richard Broome at La Trobe University, 2000. © Lindsey Howe, La Trobe University. Photograph courtesy of Richard Broome.

state-based works on Western Australia (1973) and Queensland (1975) respectively. This 1975 work focused intently on Aboriginal resistance, establishing violence at the heart of Australian history but also insisting on a historical practice that valued Aboriginal action and agency. Bob Reece had published *Aborigines and Colonists* in 1974, an equally nuanced work that covered two decades of the history of colonial NSW. Working in similar ways, Dianne Barwick and Henry Reynolds published several articles throughout the 1970s and Ann McGrath published her first. It was into this incipient context, and with generating a widely teachable field of history at the forefront of his mind, that Broome began writing his national synthesis *Aboriginal Australians* in 1979.[7]

This was an important book, laying the groundwork for teaching a national Aboriginal history as a standalone subject for both school and university students. It has been used as a standard text for teaching since then and has been a longstanding success, having been reprinted nine times before a second edition was published in 1994 and a third in 2002, and then rewritten completely as a fourth edition in 2010. In the preface to the first edition, Broome wrote that as a consequence of national inattention to Aboriginal history Australians lacked a full sense of the forces that have shaped our experience. This was a problem he sought to rectify:

> We must know ourselves. The study of Aboriginal history is an important part of that self-knowledge. Through it we can hope to understand not only the actions and attitudes of Aboriginal Australians but something of the nature of European Australians as well. Australia's history since 1788 has been a story of black and white, acting upon and interacting with each other in a great human drama. Yet until recently the Aborigines rarely appeared in our history, so that we have been presented with half a history – half an Australian experience.[8]

His writing of history was then, and has been since, an attempt to help provide this other half of history, the other half of Australian experience. It acknowledges that both Europeans and Aboriginal people have been changed and distorted by their interactions and entanglements, and that careful historical study is a way to peel away colonial misrepresentations and truly know the self and other of Australian history. This was an argument, more extensively articulated in a 2005 article, that 'Aboriginal History and Australian History...while seemingly separate, are at the same time one – bound together in a colonial dance that needs to be understood in a conjoined way'.[9]

And understanding 'the Aboriginal Other' was a central element of this work. Working within a tentative historiographical move towards recognising Aboriginal agency, Broome 'tried to write an Aboriginal perspective into our history', sharing what he felt to be the richness and nobility of Aboriginal cultures.[10]

Voyaging subjects

Written on the cusp of a shift from a first phase of writing in Aboriginal history that sought to record Indigenous presence to a second phase that positioned Aboriginal people as historical actors, Broome's first edition of *Aboriginal Australians* was significant in its emphasis on resistance: the subtitle to that work was *Black Responses to White Dominance, 1788–1980*. Moving away from catastrophic accounts represented by works like Rowley's *Destruction*, Broome instead emphasised spaces of meaningful survival, places where Aboriginal people had struggled and fought to create for themselves the capacity to live in a manner they were able, at least in part, to determine. And as his work developed, he turned to focus on ever more complicated figures. From boxers to farmers, activists to miners, warriors to barbers, it has been these subjects that Broome has emphasised throughout his career, normalising the presence of Aboriginal people in Australian history.

In a 1994 article, also discussed in Lyndall Ryan's chapter in this collection, he wrote that his insistent interest in the diversity of Aboriginal experience was provoked when reading the exhibition catalogue for *Koorie*, then displayed at the Museum of Victoria. Presented in conjunction with the Koorie Heritage Trust, *Koorie* had opened in December 1988 and told a story of the Victorian Aboriginal community from some 40,000 years ago through to the present day. Broome was struck by the presence, in a double-page spread in the catalogue and in a position of prominence in the exhibition itself, of a 'Massacre Map' of Victoria. He was sharply critical of the historiographical trend — even then somewhat passé — of representing the frontier as little more than a 'field of killing'. This focus worked, he wrote, to simplify the 'human realities and competing realities' at play on the frontier. He preferred to understand the frontier as a complex field of shifting interests and relationships; of violence perpetrated by a range of people and directed towards a range of other subjects; of changing terms of engagement, understanding, and misunderstanding. In place of this nuance, exhibitions like *Koorie* instated a one-dimensional account in which 'frontiers were violent places where whites slaughtered Aborigines indiscriminately'. It is true that frontiers were violent places, sites of massacres, but they were so much more. And focusing solely on this specifically directed violence had the effect of 'diminish[ing] Aboriginal people of the past'.[12]

Against a story of the frontier in *Koorie* that could only countenance representations of 'Aborigines as victims and frontier whites as killers', Broome sought to establish a more complicated set of subjects at the heart of Australian history. Some Aboriginal people on the frontiers were victims, but all were 'culturally alive and complex humans', people who were 'active not passive and able to make choices'. It was this capacity to make choices, to act 'from their own cultural imperatives and individual desires' that enabled Aboriginal people to exercise 'active control over their lives'. Making choices, here, was the basis of agency.[13] In articulating this conception of Aboriginal subjectivity, Broome found value in Stanner's anthropological articulation of modern Aboriginal people as 'voyagers', people who made their way in a new world. Stanner wrote of Aboriginal desires to engage with change, arguing that Aboriginal people had 'claimed, coaxed and fought an opening into an incomprehensible new world'. This was a world they had chosen to enter, in which they made their own way as people with rational intellects who had ideas about how life should be and acted accordingly.[14] These are the kinds of subjects Broome has sought out and tried to understand, telling stories of those who fought for openings to live in new ways in a new world.

He has imagined the possibility of this voyaging subject through the use of analogy, constituting the Aboriginal voyager as different to the non-Indigenous historian's self, but nonetheless fundamentally knowable in terms of an abstract humanity. Analogy as a methodological and epistemological device is threaded through Broome's oeuvre. To take but one example, we read that when white settlers established farms the mobilisation and provision of Aboriginal labour emerged as a problem. This labour could be understood, Broome argued, in religious terms: labour 'reflected the deepest meanings of life and one's place in it'. It was 'religiously and personally significant', fulfilling Aboriginal people '"long time ago" as it did those pious Christians who honoured their God through work'.[15] Likening the work of Aboriginal custom to that motivated by a Protestant work ethic rendered Aboriginal labourers knowable in historically intelligible terms. As settlers, warriors, or workers, such analogies established the terms of possible subjectivity, the nature of those Aboriginal people who voyaged and who Broome has written into history. One such 'voyager' was a man known in his adult life as Charles Never. Murrumwiller, from the Murray, was one of the first students at the Merri Creek School established in Melbourne in 1845 as an institution designed to transform Aboriginal children into manual labourers. But Charley, as he was renamed when he began school, wanted more: he sought a place in the upper ranks of the new, white-dominated society. He improved his spoken English and comported himself as a gentleman. Taking a surname, he looked for a white wife and, in 1850, apprenticed himself to a tailor in the city. Soon, Charles Never was to be seen parading around Melbourne in a three-piece suit, complete with boots and gloves, a whip and a hat. But his transformation was incomplete. Lucy Edgar, the schoolmaster's daughter, recalled in 1865 that he had also meant 'to write to the Queen and ask her to give me a piece of land...to build a house on; and I mean to ask her for 400 pounds...to build my house'.[16] What Charles Never fought for was a place of equality in a new world. He sought to be respected as a human being, as an articulate and fashionable gentleman, a member of society, a property owner, an individual in possession. This was not a life forced upon him; it was the life he chose. And it is recognisable to us today as a life of betterment and aspiration.

Presenting figures like Charles Never as voyagers establishes and normalises Aboriginal lives and Aboriginal agency at the heart of Australian history. This is a project that rejects the limitations of a permanent Aboriginal position of marginality or victimhood in favour of one that occupies the space at the centre, even if it is a centre not wholly of their making. But, as a methodological move, it does present some danger. Representing the Aboriginal other as a self within the discipline of history, in Gayatri Chakravorty Spivak's terms, refracts 'what might have been an incommensurable and discontinuous Other into a domesticated Other' and, in this sense, risks representing the world from an imperialist perspective.[17] In political terms, domesticating the Aboriginal subject as historically knowable and understanding Aboriginal action as that of rational choice can reduce that subject to an abstract individuality. Cleaving the Indigenous subject from a political collective can assume, rather than challenge, the colonial dispensation by bracketing the question of sovereignty. Freedom, in other words, can appear not as a future goal to be striven for, but rather as a characteristic of the already free and rational choosing subject — less a state of emancipation than the ability to desire, to calculate, and to act.[18] Where, one might wonder, does this leave us in relation to a project of decolonisation? Nonetheless these may well be risks worth taking, for the payoff — recognising Aboriginal people as historical subjects — is substantial.

As discussed above, Broome's historical method is one that establishes the basic terms of self and other and asserts that knowledge of one must come from knowledge of the other. It is based on a recognition of the other as fundamentally akin to and equal to the self, of the fact that we cannot exist apart. In order to be able to make this claim, it necessarily presumes a coexistence, foregrounds a togetherness, a 'we'. There is no wishing away the fundamental fact that we are bound to one another, receptive to each other in ways we cannot always control. Or, in Clendinnen's words, 'the Other begins not at the skin...but within'.[19] In placing this kind of relationality at the heart of Australian history Broome's work recalls Marcia Langton's account of the production of Aboriginalities through intersubjectivity, a relation that relies on representing both Aboriginal and non-Aboriginal people as active subjects, not mere objects, of history.[20] If freedom, as Michel Foucault suggests, is 'the ontological condition of ethics', then this representation creates the conditions for a genuine and viable intersubjectivity and, moreover, establishes a basis for ethical relations.[21]

Radical hope

The longing for these ethical relations can be seen most clearly in Broome's work on Coranderrk, the station near Healesville on Woiwurrung country where Kooris struggled for and claimed a piece of land on which they could live in a manner they chose. In 1863 a group of Kulin leaders led some 40 of their countrymen and women to claim this land, later requesting and receiving its gazettal, in the name of Queen Victoria, as a reserve. As Broome discusses in his chapter in this collection, Coranderrk is the archetypal effect and generator of 'radical hope': a term developed by the philosopher Jonathan Lear and taken up by Broome to signify 'a hope based on tradition for a future in a new world'.[22] At Coranderrk the Kulin dressed in new ways, lived in new forms of accommodation, worked according to new rhythms and with new incentives and values and, in many cases, converted to Christianity. These changes, for Broome, reflected their adaptation to a transforming colony but did not connote their abandonment of traditional values. These were material changes that maintained the essence of their culture.

At Coranderrk, the Kulin successfully farmed hops and demanded wages while at the same time hunting and collecting bush foods, maintaining an attachment to the land and its governing stories. They were Christians while simultaneously practising traditional rituals and worrying about the effects of sorcery. They lived in huts that housed family units while practising kinship ties and obligations. This, for Broome, 'suggests that by a radical hope, many were trying to survive and retain the best of both worlds — to forge an Aboriginal existence within a European economic mode: farming with an Aboriginal idiom'.[23] And it was successful. Through their work the people of Coranderrk were able, for a time, to create a place in a new world, a place where they could forge a new way of being Aboriginal within and as a part of a transformed Australia.

Exceptional though it may have been, Coranderrk was not an isolated instance of such a struggle. For Broome, there are important twentieth-century movements that reproduce the same logic, manifesting the same kind of radical hope in a changing world. In the aftermath of the Pilbara strike of 1946 to 1949, for example, the strikers formed the Pindan Mining Company, the basis for an independent cooperative community that would be linked to the wider Australian community but would not be at its whim. The Pindan Mob fused elements of traditional law and the settler common law, adapting a range of regulations to ensure continuity in a form that facilitated a new dispensation. Pindan stood as evidence that Aboriginal people could organise their own lives and demonstrated, for Broome, 'their willingness to modify tradition to make it strong'.[24]

The Victorian Aborigines Advancement League of Melbourne was similarly a body that insisted on the maintenance of culture as essential to a strong, modern community in a new world.[25] In calling for white people to support their movement by working under, and in support of, black control and management, the League can be seen as demanding what Broome described in a 2006 article on Coranderrk as 'right behaviour'. Ideas of right behaviour, he argues, reflect the ritualised social relations of Aboriginal cultures, governing and ordering obligations and conduct in ways that could be adapted to the changed world of a post-frontier Australia. Particularly at Coranderrk, Aboriginal expectations of right behaviour could be imposed on non-Aboriginal others, complementing and transforming British paternalism. When respected, they could re-articulate relationships as constituted by reciprocity rather than domination, demanding connectedness rather than abstract authoritarianism.[26] For Broome, a call for right behaviour was legible to men like John Green, the manager at Coranderrk, because of its commensurability with a practice of paternalism, enabling the translation of Aboriginal concepts into newly hegemonic idioms of British manliness.

Calls for right behaviour resonate with calls for an ethical basis for relationships between people, establishing these as part of a repertoire of anti-colonialism. And in suggesting that the effect of Aboriginal practices of radical hope — combining Aboriginal traditional practice with ways of being at home in a new, settler-dominated world — was to make a claim for the reorganisation of relationships between peoples, Broome's work has established the Aboriginal subject as one who not only consciously adapts to the changing world but as one who is thereby capable of contributing to and demanding its transformation. His work to imagine Aboriginal people as legible subjects of history restores the possibility of particular ethical relations: describing ways of being in the world that are suffused with both vulnerability to the other and hope that that vulnerability will be rewarded. He has celebrated those people who have tied their own being to that of others, suturing together two worlds with a place for all. Most importantly, focusing on such historical characters foregrounds the Aboriginal agency that constitutes Aboriginal history as a field of study. And it makes possible the writing of Aboriginal history as a practice of ethics.

This allows us to make normative claims about Aboriginal history, to deplore the thwarting of so many Aboriginal attempts at finding a place in this new world. Broome describes the moments of common humanity that could be seen in early encounters at Sydney Cove in 1788 but soon disappeared as tensions arose. These were the tensions of colonialism, experienced, for instance, by Aboriginal aspirants to colonial respectability like John Bungaree who found, in Sydney in the 1840s, that 'the offer to join white society was a poor one. Europeans would only accept them as the lowest class at the bottom of the new colonial society, confined there by their Aboriginality'. And they can be seen in the frustration experienced by Charles Never, whose gentility was mercilessly ridiculed by white Melbournians and who was refused entry into their middle-class homes. Others 'mocked' Never's 'attempt', Broome writes, 'but we should not'. Our histories should be compassionate; they should chafe against those colonial and racial ideas that limited what men like Charles Never could be, instead opening up new worlds that recognise and celebrate their struggles to make themselves anew.[27]

The fourth and most recent edition of Broome's landmark *Aboriginal Australians* begins with the story of Malcolm Smith. In 1965, aged eleven, Malcolm and his brother Robert took two pushbikes they found leaning against a bus shelter and went joy-riding. This brought the family to the attention of police, welfare officers, and the courts, who judged Malcolm's widowed father to be an unfit parent and placed the boys in a series of homes and foster care arrangements where their Aboriginality was regularly denigrated. Malcolm found himself in and out of jail, a place where he came to be part of a Koori community that both affirmed him and led him to Christianity. In Long Bay Gaol he became delusional and in 1982, having read Matthew 18:9 ('And if thine right eye offend thee, pluck it out, and cast it from thee'), he stabbed a paintbrush so deep into his left eye that he collapsed and died. His life, and death, was one of the 99 cases investigated by the Royal Commission into Aboriginal Deaths in Custody in 1990.[28]

'How', in Broome's words, 'did a joy-ride unleash such a terrible chain of events? The short answer is that Smith was a colonial subject'. While he and his family made their own history, his behaviour can, at least in part, be explained by reference to the colonial situation in which they found themselves. This is the counterpoint to the recognition of humanity exemplified in exchanges like that between Milius and the Boonwurrung men in 1802. Where colonialism generates 'practices that refashioned Aboriginal people into the colonised and oppressed and other Australians into coloniser oppressors', Broome has sought more complicated stories of unpredictable encounters, of interactions between people seeking out truth and the best in each other.[29] In his desire to uncover these possibilities, he has practised a history in which Australia emerges as a nation within which Aboriginal lives could flourish, where Malcolm Smith's tragic death is not, and should not be, an inevitability.[30]

CHAPTER 2

Aboriginal agents, victims and voyagers
Richard Broome's contribution to the debate about the frontier wars in Victoria

Lyndall Ryan

Introduction

When Richard Broome's *Aboriginal Australians* appeared in 1982, it was like a new beginning for Australian history.[1] As the first coherent narrative of race relations between Aborigines and Europeans in Australia from 1788 to 1980, it overturned the long held view that Aborigines were a 'weak and passive race' who simply 'gave way' before the white settlers and then 'faded away'.[2] Rather, it contended that Aborigines not only resisted the European invaders in a long and bloody frontier war for possession of Australia but that, in the aftermath, they retained their identity in resisting incarceration and assimilation and were now reclaiming their rights including the return of their stolen lands. Three decades later, when *Aboriginal Australians* appeared in its fourth completely revised edition, Broome's reputation as one of Australia's most significant historians of the Australian frontier wars was unsurpassed.[3]

From the outset, debates about the frontier wars in colonial Victoria (then known as the Port Phillip District) were central to his work. This is not surprising, for Victoria was the only state where a new generation of historians had already produced coherent accounts of aspects of the war and estimated the casualties.[4] From his location at La Trobe University in Melbourne where he pioneered an Aboriginal history course which became the basis of *Aboriginal Australians*, Broome used their work as a starting point for what would become longstanding and often highly contentious debates about evidence of Aboriginal and settler agency and the statistics of frontier conflict.

This chapter assesses Broome's contribution to the debates from the first edition of *Aboriginal Australians* in 1982 to the fourth edition in 2010. To explore and understand their significance to the discipline of Aboriginal history, the chapter is divided into three sections. The first, from 1982 to 1988, shows how Broome established the concept of Aboriginal agency within a race relations framework pioneered by WEH Stanner, Diane Barwick, KR McConnochie and Henry Reynolds as a counter to Michael Christie's focus on settler activism. The second section, 1994 to 1995, shows how he reconceptualised Aboriginal resistance and agency within Albert Memmi's framework of colonialism in response to Aboriginal claims of widespread massacre on the Victorian frontier. The final section, 2003 to 2010, shows how he devised his own model of settler colonialism based on the work of Patrick Wolfe, Albert Memmi and David Day to foreground the historical experiences of Aboriginal people on the colonial frontier as agents, victims and voyagers.

1982 to 1988: Establishing Aboriginal agency

When *Aboriginal Australians* appeared in 1982, Broome was joining a debate about the colonial frontier wars initiated by Michael Christie three years earlier in his groundbreaking study, *Aborigines in Colonial Victoria 1835–86*. Christie deployed a Marxist model of colonialism to argue that Aborigines 'did not give up their land easily, that they fought a sustained war of resistance and that the eventual decimation of their numbers was not due only to introduced disease, but also to a deliberate attempt on the part of the pastoralists to exterminate them.'[5]

Christie estimated that there were 'between 11,000 and 15,000' Aborigines living in Victoria before 1835, divided among 'thirty-eight tribes, which varied in size according to the richness of the environment'.[6] He considered that 'the coming of white man was disastrous for Aborigines. The colonizers sought land, large tracts of land, the same land that was the basis of Aboriginal culture and society. The brutality with which the pastoralists took and held the land was exacerbated by their derogatory image of the Aborigine and his way of life.[7] In some parts of Victoria, where the terrain and the cohesiveness of certain tribal groupings were of advantage, Aboriginal guerrilla attacks against the settlers were highly successful, with hundreds of Aborigines led by powerful chiefs attacking squatters' runs and maiming or removing their sheep and cattle. In other areas, however, 'the influx of Europeans tipped the numbers overwhelmingly in favour of the intruder and reduced the possibility of Aboriginal offensives'.[8] As evidence he cited several massacres in the Western District in 1841 and 1842 and asserted that a 'common feature of the frontier' was the practice by lonely shepherds and stockmen of regularly abducting Aboriginal women for sexual purposes and then killing them.[9] By 1850, when Aboriginal resistance was finally broken, it was clear that 'Aboriginal spears were no match for the settlers' guns'. Even so, 'the Aborigines still managed to slow down pastoral encroachment on their land.'[10] He then made the first attempt to estimate the statistics of the frontier wars:

> If we accept that there were at least 11,500 Aborigines in Victoria when the white man arrived, then the loss of Aboriginal life during the frontier period numbered 8,000 or more. Introduced diseases, alcohol, changes in diet, and inter-tribal strife accounted for a large proportion of the deaths, but it is realistic to accept E. M. Curr's assessment that between fifteen and twenty-five per cent, or 2,000 Aborigines if we take the higher percentage, died 'by the rifle'.[11]

With this paragraph, Christie set the parameters of the statistics debate that Broome would grapple with over the next three decades.

In *Aboriginal Australians: Black Response to White Dominance 1788–1980*, Broome departed from Christie's Marxist approach in favour of a more inclusive race relations model, devised by anthropologists WEH Stanner and Diane Barwick, sociologist KR McConnochie and historian Henry Reynolds as a way of foregrounding Aboriginal agency and resistance.[12] With this approach Broome could argue that at the outset of British colonisation in 1788, an equal power relationship prevailed between Aborigines and Europeans: Aborigines held the land and Europeans held sheep and cattle. At the onset of the pastoral age in the 1820s, however, during which more than 200,000 British immigrants arrived over the next 30 years, with several million sheep and several hundred thousand cattle to occupy the Aboriginal grasslands, the settlers faced Aboriginal resistance and a frontier war for possession of south eastern Australia broke out.[13]

To examine the frontier wars, he drew on a range of published sources in the period before 1850 and identified three important characteristics of Aboriginal response to European invaders. First was that when settlers arrived in 'new country', the Aborigines in the area initially enjoyed superiority in numbers, knowledge of terrain, weapons and tactics that placed them at an advantage. From this position they usually started the conflict by harassing the settlers, sometimes by taking sheep and cattle for food, at others by herding them into stockyards of their own to learn the art of stock management, and at others by stealing settlers' food rations such as flour, tea and sugar. Then they deployed the tactics they used in hunting kangaroo, such as fire and spears and clubs to stalk and intimidate their prey, to attack the settlers often with lethal effect. For example, they would suddenly appear out of the bush, attack shepherds and stockmen and/or their cattle and sheep with spears and then kill them, burn down their huts and then just as swiftly disappear into the bush with their booty. In some cases the Aborigines would wait in the hills for days or even weeks watching isolated homesteads, waiting for the right moment to attack. Broome provided several examples of settlers in fear of their lives and being too afraid to leave their homesteads.[14]

However, in contrast to Christie's analysis of the Victorian frontier, Broome argued that the Aborigines' tactics and fighting abilities were not matched by organisational skills. Indeed their apparent lack of intertribal military links meant that each Aboriginal tribe conducted its own resistance:

> Thus each battle was really the Milmenrura versus the British, or the Gunditjmara versus the British and not the Aborigines versus the British. However, there is scattered evidence, which may be consolidated in the future, which

suggests that the Aborigines were beginning to adapt their traditions to the needs of the military struggle with the Europeans before they were overwhelmed.[15]

He acknowledged that certain Aboriginal military leaders were known at the time, such as Jupiter, Cocknose and Bradbury, but they were from outside their traditional tribal areas and their prowess and skills were more likely an outcome of the social disruption of European invasion than typical examples of Aboriginal leadership.[16]

How then did the Europeans fight the Aborigines? According to Broome some settlers were under no illusion that they were intruders taking Aboriginal land, but most considered that they had every right to occupy it. When Aborigines took sheep and cattle and in some cases maimed them, the settlers responded with fury. He quoted one settler, John Cox: 'It was the first time I had ever levelled a gun on my fellow man. I did so without hesitation in this instance...I distinctly remember knocking over three blacks, two men and a boy, with one discharge of my double barrel.'[17]

Contrary to Christie's assessment, Broome considered that until the 1850s European firearms were often unreliable under Aboriginal attack, leading many 'over-anxious Europeans' to shoot first and ask questions later. He acknowledged, nonetheless, that shepherds often carried rifles and pistols as protection against Aboriginal attack, abducted Aboriginal women for sexual purposes and built their huts with slit windows to help repulse Aboriginal attacks. Thus they 'hit back, not only in attacking Aboriginal warriors, but by the slaughter and massacre of Aboriginal women, children and the aged' and distributing poisoned flour.[18]

In summing up the frontier wars in south-eastern Australia to 1850, Broome reached the contradictory conclusion that the Aborigines were defeated, not by their alleged inferior tactics, but by the deployment of military and native police forces whose formation, he considered, 'marked the absolute rock bottom of government Aboriginal policy' and the rapid increase in the overall number of Europeans.[19] Against these overwhelming odds he contended that: '[i]t is now beyond doubt that the Aborigines strongly resisted the invasion of their lands, and that Australia's frontier history is a bloody one.' In Victoria alone, he estimated that 64 Europeans lost their lives in the violent conflict but was reluctant to make an estimate of Aboriginal casualties. Across Australia, however, he estimated that the frontier wars caused between 1000 and 1500 European deaths and that more than 10 Aborigines fell for every European, indicating Aboriginal casualties at about 20,000 from a pre-1788 population of 300,000.[20]

The startling statistics brought home to readers that Aborigines had indeed fought for their country, but they also raised a new set of questions about the conduct of the frontier war. Was it a war in the European understanding of the term? How many frontier wars were there? What kinds of weapons were used? How can we estimate the casualties on both sides? Broome would boldly address these questions in the bicentennial year, 1988, when he completed a groundbreaking chapter on Aboriginal agency for the Australian War Memorial.[21]

He began his chapter, 'The Struggle for Australia: Aboriginal European warfare, 1770-1930', by listing the complex ways that Aborigines initially responded to European invaders and how these ways became the pre-conditions for war. They included 'avoidance and distant observation; then fear and flight; defence of their land and families when the Europeans attempted to make friends; a bewildered greeting of the Europeans as relatives returned from the dead; or attempts to establish reciprocal relations in the traditional manner'.[22] However, when they discovered that the intruders were not sojourners but invaders bent on conquest, they generally attempted to drive them away. Once again Broome represented the invaders as initially largely peaceful and the Aborigines as the agents of violent conflict.

He then posed the question: 'Was this a fighting war?' How was it defined? He readily acknowledged that when Aborigines resisted the invaders they were defined by the British governor as criminals or outlaws on the understanding that they were British subjects, because the colonial authorities could not accord them the status of sovereign peoples. Yet, in reality – as Broome points out – they were not British subjects.

> The local authorities often winked at punitive raids against them and on several occasions martial law was declared against them. The Aborigines of course, saw themselves as

independent groups and undisputed owners of the land. No doubt current international law would have upheld their view if proper investigations into Aboriginal land use had been made. Thus in reality Aboriginal-European conflict was hostility between Britain and the various Aboriginal 'nations'. In the particular sense there was much 'armed fighting' making the conflicts truly wars.[23]

He considered that the frontier war to 1850 was certainly 'a classic colonial war', in that it was never openly declared and was guerrilla in style, 'limited for the invader but total for the invaded who had nowhere else to go'.[24] But rather than comparing it to other colonial frontier wars in other parts of the British Empire in the same period, he deferred to anthropological studies of warfare in pre-industrial societies by citing Margaret Mead's definition: 'warfare exists if the conflict is organized and socially sanctioned, and the killing is not regarded as murder'.[25] In relying on this definition, however, he inadvertently constructed Aboriginal resistance as ahistorical and the tactics they used against the Europeans as unstructured, thus creating an unresolved tension in his overall argument of Aboriginal agency against the European invader.

The tension was clearly revealed in his overview of the wars on several colonial frontiers across colonial Australia to 1850: the Hawkesbury River in the 1790s; Appin in 1816; Tasmania in the 1820s; the Swan River colony in the 1830s; the Gwydir, New England, Manning and Clarence River Pastoral Districts of New South Wales in the 1830s and 1840s, the Port Phillip District, and the Darling Downs and Moreton Bay Districts in what is now Southern Queensland. In each case he showed how they were part of a broader pattern of Indigenous response to colonial invasion: Aboriginal resistance, colonial defence and then Aboriginal surrender. He noted that major Aboriginal attacks on settlers, such as the massacre of eight overlanders at Benalla in April 1838 were largely in revenge for shooting Aboriginal men and failing to pay for the sexual services of Aboriginal women. Such attacks, however, were usually the catalyst for the settlers to carry out major punitive expeditions, often resulting in massacre.[26]

In his analysis of Aboriginal tactics he adopted Henry Reynolds' view that they were largely derived from traditional practices, such as 'surprise and ambush, the use of spies and decoys, sorcery, the burning of pastures and huts, and even open fights and pitched battles' in which a crescent formation or tight groups of men were used'.[27] He offered an interesting example of open fighting between an Aboriginal warrior and a European combatant, when a mounted policeman 'cornered an Aborigine he was pursuing' at Port Fairy around 1840. Once spears were

> expended and the officer's powder wet, it became a duel of horse and sword against shield. For some minutes the Aborigine fended off the sword and doubled himself up in a ball under it when the horse charged, forcing the animal to jump him. Eventually the Aborigine wounded the horse in the nose, and the policeman was forced to withdraw, full of admiration for his opponent.[28]

He considered that traditional Aboriginal tactics were very successful in accessing European food sources when their own supplies dwindled, and in the crippling economic war against the Europeans where they consistently maimed sheep and cattle. Contrary to Christie's view, however, he did not believe that intertribal coalitions were formed when traditional tribal enmities broke down, although he did acknowledge that new forms of leadership emerged. Nevertheless, he considered that some of the new style leaders such as Cocknose, Jupiter and Bradbury behaved more like outlaws than resistance leaders.[29]

Nor could he find evidence of Aboriginal warriors adopting European guns or horses in their war with the Europeans, although they knew how to use them. This was evidence, he believed, of the ritual nature of Aboriginal warfare and that this particular style of frontier warfare represented a 'greater break with tradition for the Europeans' who were used to fighting in 'slow-moving regular armies'.[30] It was not surprising then, that in recognition of traditional Aboriginal enmities, from the 1840s the colonial authorities deployed native police as 'quasi-military units' to 'neutralise' Aboriginal resistance. He considered that there was little doubt that 'Aboriginal troopers and their European officers killed several thousand Aborigines on the eastern mainland, making the European victory easier than it might have been.'[31]

In considering European tactics, however, apart from noting evidence of poisoning and the deployment of the native police forces, he tended to focus more on the legal and military resources available in forcing Aboriginal surrender. They included declaring martial law, forbidding Aboriginal men to carry guns or congregate in towns in groups of six or more, despatching large numbers of troops into the field and authorising brutal massacres.[32] He also noted that the Aborigines were considered as British subjects when the 'sovereignty of Australia' was being contested and 'belligerents when control or revenge was desired'.[33]

All these instances reinforced his earlier view that the frontier wars to 1850 represented a match between equals in which the contest between the Aboriginal spear and the European gun 'was not uneven'. The most common firearm of the period, the muzzle-loading Brown Bess flintlock musket, used by soldiers and settlers alike, was slow to load and often inaccurate beyond 50 metres. Yet it was deadly if large numbers of muskets were trained on trapped Aborigines. The Baker muzzle-loading flintlock rifles carried by the 80th Regiment in the Swan River colony in the 1830s was accurate at 200 metres and at Pinjarra in 1834 enabled the killing of 30 Aboriginal warriors in one operation. Shortened muskets and carbines used by settlers on horseback were deadly against the Aborigines on open ground. At the same time he noted several examples of settlers resorting to double-barrelled shotguns to kill numbers of Aboriginal people while others mounted 'small swivel cannons at their doors' to fend off Aboriginal attack. By comparison, the Aborigines' spears rarely killed at a distance of more than 60 metres, hence the lower settler death rate. Nonetheless, Aborigines held the element of surprise, a key tactic in guerrilla warfare whereby settlers and stockmen lived in constant fear of Aboriginal attack. He did admit, however, that once Europeans had access to horses on the frontier, the Aborigines lost their advantage.[34]

Broome's focus on the alleged unreliability of British weapons before 1850 indicated how little Australian historians knew about the conduct of frontier wars in other parts of the British Empire in the early nineteenth century. In the Cape Colony for example, British soldiers used the same kinds of weapons to successfully contend with large groups of Xhosa warriors on the eastern frontier in the period to 1850, and had no difficulty in killing large numbers of them at close range and in guerrilla-style engagements.[35] Even so, Broome demonstrated beyond doubt that the frontier wars in Australia were the only full-scale conflict ever fought on Australian soil and that the colonial administrators used every legal and military resource at their disposal to force the Aborigines to surrender.

In the discussion of casualties from the frontier wars, he retained the estimate of 20,000 Aboriginal deaths and 2000 European deaths that he made in 1982 and reconsidered Christie's estimates for Victoria. While he accepted the 80 per cent drop in the Aboriginal population between 1834 and 1851, he could not countenance the possibility that 25 per cent might have lost their lives as war casualties, for he now contended that in comparison with other colonial frontiers in Australia, where settler casualties were much higher, the statistics of settler casualties on the Victorian colonial frontier indicated that Aboriginal casualties were probably lower.[36] On this point, however, he was vulnerable to criticism from the Victorian Aboriginal community.

1994 to 1995: Aboriginal victims and voyagers

In 1994, the catalogue prepared by the Koorie Heritage Trust for the *Koorie* exhibition in the Museum of Victoria featured a map which identified 68 massacre sites of Victorian Aborigines between 1833 and 1851. The stark representation of the sites appeared clear evidence that settler massacre was a key strategy in the destruction of Victorian Aboriginal people in the period before the gold rushes.[37]

Broome was clearly annoyed by what he considered as the exhibition's one dimensional view of the Victorian frontier and prepared a riposte that clarified his own views about the subject.[38] He considered that, in overlooking the importance of Aboriginal resistance to the invaders, the exhibition 'diminished' their agency. In his view in representing Aborigines as victims of settler violence the massacre map overlooked more recent scholarship which repositioned the frontier 'as the site of encounters between two cultures'.[39]

While he readily acknowledged that the frontier in Victoria was indeed 'a violent place' he also contended that it was the site of 'a desperate struggle' between 'two peoples attempting to occupy the same space'. Aboriginal people, he pointed out, 'resisted in reaction to whites' as well as being killed by them and also 'acted in other ways, made other choices, and not simply in response to whites but from their own cultural imperatives and individual desires'.[40] In this context, he considered that the exhibition not only ignored Aboriginal cultural actions towards whites, but also the social and economic exchanges between the two cultural groups, the impact of disease, and the modicum of cross-cultural tolerance and friendship that existed. The Victorian frontier, he declared, was about much more than just massacres. Some of them were more like 'protracted battles'.[41]

The incident at Benalla in 1838, for example, was initiated by Aborigines against settler George Faithfull and should be considered as a battle in which they 'fought boldly' even though in the end most of them were killed. Moreover, the allegation that 'hundreds' of Aborigines were killed in the Bruthen Creek 'massacre' of 1842 in Gippsland precluded any understanding of the limitations of 'pre-1850 muzzle-loading flintlocks rifles...Flintlocks took 30 seconds to load, were accurate to only 50 metres, and misfired once in every six shots.'[42] Thus, the Bruthen Creek death toll was virtually impossible: 25 to 50 deaths in this incident would have been more realistic.

He then turned to the findings of Beverley Nance, to argue that the exhibition failed to acknowledge that 300 Aborigines were also killed by other Aborigines on the frontier, including 125 killed by native police forces, far greater than the 59 Europeans known to have been killed by Aborigines.[43] These statistics, he considered, were clear evidence of a more complex set of relations on the pastoral frontier than the map represented. Even so, he estimated there were 1500 Aboriginal deaths from white violence over 15 years throughout Victoria, comprising one-tenth of the estimated pre-contact Aboriginal population, a percentage that was considerably lower than 25 per cent of a higher population estimated by Christie.[44]

Above all, he was concerned that the exhibition did not consider the historical experiences of the 2000 survivors of the frontier wars. Rather, it created a 'disjointed story of frontier victims and post-frontier survivors, when in fact both processes operated within the Aboriginal community from day-one of contact'. From the first, he argued, 'Aboriginal people made culturally determined and perhaps individual choices, and exercised some active control over their lives'. Initially, some performed casual work for squatters on the frontier and then, after their traditional economy was disrupted and the gold rushes created a labour shortage, the men were employed as shepherds and mounted stockmen, sometimes by employers who occupied their homelands. Others worked for settlers in the towns and still others traded lyrebird feathers or animal skins. Another group of young men kept their clan identities as members of the native police force.[45] They never lost their sense of who they were as Aboriginal people, preferring their own mode of living to that of the Europeans. As observers or 'readers' of white society, they chose to remain as outsiders, and only a very few of them actively sought to become part of it. In 1859 they persuaded the Victorian government to grant them land at Healesville where they established a successful farm and converted to Christianity. It was only after 1886, when the Victorian government sought to assimilate Aboriginal people of mixed descent into the Victorian community by forcing them off the reserves, that they experienced what he called 'cultural genocide': a 'cold-blooded effort' by bureaucrats to destroy them as a people.[46] The fact that they have survived to the present, 'pursuing Mabo-style claims in European courts' stands as testimony to their cultural tenacity.[47]

In promoting Aboriginal resistance and agency over the entire period of European occupation of Victoria, Broome appeared unable to recognise that, having regained their rights as Aborigines, which he had warmly applauded in the Introduction to *Aboriginal Australians* in 1982, the contemporary community was now seeking restitution for past wrongs. This included acknowledgement by the victors that their forebears had killed large numbers of Aborigines in a bloody frontier war for possession of their homelands. In this tableau, massacre was central to the story.

The *Koorie* catalogue clearly made an impact on Broome, for in his next foray into the frontier wars, in the chapter 'Victoria' which was part of a national project that explored the historical experiences of Aborigines under the British Crown, he repositioned Aboriginal agency and resistance within the paradigm of colonialism, as articulated by Tunisian scholar, Albert Memmi.[48] In this paradigm, colonialism is constructed as a violent and rapacious process in dispossessing Indigenous peoples from their land and destroying their autonomy. As a process, however, colonialism is never entirely victorious, for where there is power, 'there is always resistance to that power'.[49] In applying Memmi's paradigm to colonial Victoria, Broome contended that the 'forces of colonialism reshaped Aboriginal Victorians into victims and voyagers' and thus were more open to 'negotiation and accommodation between coloniser and colonised.[50] To this end, he revisited the highly controversial Batman Treaty of 1835, and concluded that the Kulin chiefs who signed the treaty document probably had a more complex understanding of its possibilities than historians like Christie believed.[51] For Christie never considered that the Kulin signatories could have held any understanding of the treaty or that the members of the Port Phillip Association who promoted the treaty document held genuine concerns for Aboriginal welfare for their leader, John Batman was widely known as the assassin of Aboriginal people in Tasmania.[52]

Broome then revisited the colonial frontier and although he cited no examples of accommodation and negotiation, Memmi's paradigm appeared to give him new authority to once again question as 'too simplistic' Christie's Marxist model of 'white violence and Aboriginal resistance' in that it was based on a number of 'questionable interpretations'.[53] They included Christie's assumption that Aborigines operated from only one motive in resisting 'European intruders', when other factors could have been in play; that 'Aboriginal spears were no match for settlers' guns' whereas the 'facts of pre-1850 weaponry suggest a more even contest'; and that 2000 Victorian Aborigines were killed by the colonists.[54] The estimate, he contended, was not derived from careful 'grassroots calculations' but based on a 'guesstimate' made in 1885, that '15-25 per cent of Aborigines died by the rifle' with only 59 Europeans killed, 'giving Victoria by far the highest black/white death ratio of any Australian frontier, whereas much evidence suggests it was one of the least violent frontiers'.[55]

Yet two paragraphs later he acknowledged that European pastoralism so completely engulfed Aboriginal Victorians between 1836 and 1850 that the outcome could only be described as genocide! 'This is not to excuse the many killings' he hastened to add, 'but to recognise the process for what it was'.[56] The statistics were again repeated: his lower estimate of

10,000 Aborigines in 1836 who were reduced to 1907 in 1853, a decline of 80 per cent in less than a generation and he argued that 'violence caused about 10 per cent of the losses', with disease, malnutrition and infertility accounting for most of the rest.[57] In this catastrophic environment, with so few Aborigines surviving the onslaught, it could be argued that Memmi's paradigm of colonialism was perhaps not entirely appropriate to understand what happened on the Victorian frontier. This could partly be explained by Memmi's focus on the interiority of the 'colonised' and Broome was not, at that particular point in his career, able to give an account of Aboriginal interiority. Meanwhile, his account of post-frontier survival would focus very valuably on forms of employment to which Aboriginal people showed themselves adaptive.

2003 to 2010: Agents, victims and voyagers

In 2003, Broome made a critical intervention in the debate about frontier violence which lay at the heart of the Aboriginal history wars then engulfing public discourse. Keith Windschuttle had initiated this controversy three years earlier, claiming that Reynolds and I had promoted 'widespread frontier massacre' without providing persuasive evidence.[58] Broome was puzzled by Windschuttle's assertions, for our use of the race relations model suggested that settler massacre was not typical of frontier conflict and that Aborigines were more likely to have been killed in ones and twos.[59] At the time Broome was analysing the data on Aboriginal killings in Ian D Clark's register of massacre sites in Western Victoria and his findings represented the single most important intervention in the conflict.[60]

He found that a total of 450 Aborigines were killed in 107 fatal attacks in Western Victoria between 1803 and 1859; that, in 55 of these incidents, one to three victims were killed, totalling 88 people; that in each of 20 or more cases, four people were killed (80 victims); and that in a further 32 incidents, five or more Aborigines were killed (262 victims).[61] Although he could not quite admit it, it was clear that more Victorian Aborigines were killed in 32 mass killings than in the 55 small-scale incidents. The astonishing finding had the potential to completely reframe our understanding of the frontier wars. No longer were they simply fought as a series of small-scale incidents where Aborigines and settlers were killed in ones and twos. Rather, the findings suggested that Aborigines were just as likely to have been the victims of mass killings. His findings not only rendered the race relations model ineffective in understanding the frontier wars, it also killed off the history wars.

Broome, however, was not yet ready to come to terms with the important shift in understanding the frontier wars. When he reviewed Clark's data two years later in *Aboriginal Victorians*, he was not convinced that every one of the 32 incidents in which five or more Aborigines were killed constituted a massacre:

> Such killings are often termed 'massacres' – the killing of defenceless or beaten people...the word is overused and portrays Aboriginal people as passive victims. Some incidents were not 'massacres' but battles in which one side suffered severe losses. The details of the action are too vague in many incidents to confidently label them 'massacres' rather than 'defeats'.[62]

Broome appeared to regard the two labels as mutually exclusive.

In reassessing the historical experiences of Aboriginal Victorians, however, he made some important revisions to his earlier accounts. For example, he acknowledged that, contrary to his earlier belief, Aboriginal Victorian clans were led by chiefs, or men of high degree, and that many of them played very important roles in negotiations with the settlers in the 1830s and 1840s. He also considered that the experiences of Aborigines and colonists on the Victorian frontier were shaped by a particular form of colonialism, the 'structure of pastoralism – the newest child of nineteenth century capitalism, linking the sheep walks of [Victoria] to the woollen mills of England – occupied vast tracts of land, and quickly displaced large numbers of Aboriginal clans'.[63] In taking this approach, he reframed the characteristics of frontier violence. He now considered that the protagonists usually knew each other and that violence usually began when agreements between them broke down. Rather than Aborigines breaking agreements and initiating violence, he now considered that shepherds and stock-keepers were the initiators by their abduction of Aboriginal women for sex. When Aborigines retaliated by killing the white men and plundering their huts for food, the latter would initiate further violence, such as massacre, as a way of gaining control of the frontier. Broome also considered that Aborigines waged economic warfare against the settlers by dismembering sheep and cattle or driving them away.[64]

Finally, he revisited the statistics of frontier conflict. He revised upwards the number of settler deaths from 59 to 80, and although he remained firm in his earlier estimate of 1000 Aboriginal deaths, that is, approximately 10 per cent of the population in 1836, he offered a fresh analysis of the statistics of Aboriginal deaths drawn from Clark's data and made another extraordinary finding: 'Given possibly 80 white deaths and 1,000 black deaths on the Victorian frontier, Aborigines died at a rate 12 times that of whites. Europeans also killed Aborigines with a greater intensity, for while most European deaths occurred in small-scale killings of one to three people, the majority of Aboriginal fatalities occurred in larger-scale incidents.'[65] However, he did not pursue the implications of this astonishing finding. Rather, he seemed more relieved by his other finding that the number of Europeans killed by Aborigines had increased from 59 to 80 which in turn decreased the Aboriginal/European death ratio from 17:1 to 12:1 and much closer to the Australia-wide estimated ratio of 10:1. Even so, his earlier claim that Victoria was one of the mildest frontiers could no longer be sustained.

Broome would address this important issue in his next book, the completely revised fourth edition of *Aboriginal Australians*, subtitled *A history since 1788*.[66] He replaced the race relations model of the earlier editions, in which Aborigines and Europeans were considered as equal partners in the early colonial years, with his own model of settler colonialism that consisted of three components. The first was Patrick Wolfe's settler 'logic of elimination' which drove the confrontation between the Aborigine and settler. The second component was Albert Memmi's 'usurper complex', the false ideology by which those who take power unlawfully have to justify such acts – to themselves and others, which Broome considered explained how the 'practices of colonialism narrowed and shaped the options of both Indigenous and settler Australians'.[67] The final component drew on the historian David Day's three-stage model of Indigenous dispossession: a legal claim, a practical assertion of ownership, and a moral assertion of ownership. According to Broome, Captain Cook and Governor Phillip represented the first stage, while the second took place over the following century through naming the country and reshaping its use and increasing the number of invaders to the point that the invading population swamped that of the Aborigines. The third stage, again drawing on Memmi's 'usurper complex', was initially an ethnocentrism, albeit one based on environment and education rather than race, that was then replaced by a 'civilising mission' to make the Aborigines just like Europeans.[68]

The anthropological term 'European' was also replaced with the more historically appropriate 'British', 'settler' and 'colonist'. The new edition also reinforced the new insights about the frontier wars that he set out in *Aboriginal Victorians* in 2005, including the view that it was the British rather than the Aborigines who initiated the encounter. In finally dispensing with the static anthropological model of race relations in favour of more dynamic historical models, he was drawing closer to Christie's Marxist model of settler activism. Even so, Broome's analysis of the frontier wars to 1850 was remarkably similar to his assessment in the first edition in 1982 and the chapter on Aboriginal forms of warfare he prepared in 1988. The only major changes were that he now considered that the British initiated the frontier war for possession of Australia and that the Aborigines were usually led by warrior chiefs, although he still believed that the best known chiefs were 'outsiders' from other clans. He could not really accept Clark's data from the Western District of Victoria, where one-third of Aborigines killed before 1850 were more likely to have lost their lives in multiple killings of five or more. Indeed, he still considered that until 1850

> most guns had unreliable flintlock firing systems, which had a time delay between the flash and the discharge of the bullet, which gave the Aborigines time to duck. Misfires were common and even in dry weather on average only one in six shots was actually fired. However at close quarters they fired a nineteen millimetre lead ball which travelled at high speed, which could shatter flesh and bones on impact, making recovery difficult.[69]

It was as if the failings of the flintlock rifle on the Victorian frontier kept the settlers' reputation intact.

Once again he considered that the skills of Aboriginal warriors were honed by a lifetime of hunting and their spear throwing almost equalled the speed and accuracy of the legendary English bowmen. Aboriginal spears flew 50 metres a second, but could be evaded. Skilled Indigenous warriors initially outnumbered early settlers and with their superior tactics in intertribal skirmishes their tactics and military skills were superior to the settlers, given that most of the settlers had no weapons or military experience.[70] Yet, as Christie pointed out in 1979, a remarkable number of settlers and stockmen whether bond or free were former soldiers and sailors and most of them certainly knew how to fire an array of weaponry.[71] Aboriginal warriors also used the traditional methods of fire and the element of fear and surprise to suddenly emerge from the bush to destroy property and drive shepherds out like game and then withdraw to celebrate their victory with a corroboree. They rarely used guns which they considered as cowardly. In this tableau he considered that settlers did not outmatch Aboriginal warriors until the 1860s, when the advent of breech-loading repeating rifles and more widespread use of horses made them invincible, vanquishing the Aboriginal resisters. Yet, in comparison with Tasmania where horses were rarely used, the use of horses on the Victorian frontier appears to have been widespread from the outset of settlement in 1835.

He also acknowledged once again that the colonists 'hit back' by perpetrating massacres, but cautioned that the 'word massacre should not be used too freely, for its overuse labels Aboriginal people as passive victims awaiting slaughter'.[72] Yet he admitted that many of them took place in secret, 'as vigilante groups rode hard, bent on subduing all Aboriginal resistance' and were 'normalised by...stories about them' and that the

> listing of particular slaughters from sites across southern and eastern Australia could go on – if one could stomach it. People of both races were being brutalised by a ruthless battle for the land, begun by European encroachment, but settlers were more efficient at massacring simply because of the combined power of guns, horses and government troopers.[73]

He concluded that Australian frontier history was 'a bloody one. Just how bloody is difficult to determine, as many Aboriginal killings went unrecorded or were covered up, and not all European deaths were tallied'. He then returned to the statistics of frontier conflict across Australia as set out in his 1988 chapter. He estimated about 1700 violent European deaths occurred by Aboriginal hands across Australia with more than 10 Aboriginal people being killed for every European, with a death toll of 17,000 and up to 20,000. Despite Clark's data from Western Victoria, he was unwilling to revise the statistic that he first used in 1982.

Conclusion

In assessing Broome's contributions to the debate about Aboriginal agency and the frontier wars in Victoria over the last three decades, several important findings emerge. First is that the race relations model which dominated his approach in the 1980s enabled him to explore the parameters of Aboriginal agency in considerable detail and that the settler colonialism model that he began to adopt in the first decade of the twenty-first century enabled him to investigate settler activism more closely. He found that the settlers were the more likely initiators of frontier conflict and that the wars were bloodier and more complex than he first believed. This is an important finding.

Second is that, despite the changes in approach, his account of the frontier wars in 2010 reveals a remarkable consistency with the original accounts in the 1980s. They include the claim that the firearms the settlers used before 1850 were often inadequate in the contest with Aboriginal spears and in the face of Aboriginal attacks more generally. Yet he does not seriously address the fact that the Aboriginal/settler death ratio of 12:1 for Victoria remains higher than the Australia-wide average of 10:1.

Finally, the absence of a comprehensive account of the frontier wars in Victoria, in which each region is carefully considered within the same conceptual framework, has precluded Broome from making more significant findings. For example, his reluctance to assess more deeply the statistics he gleaned from Clark's investigation of the frontier wars in Western Victoria and apply the methods across colonial Victoria suggests an unwillingness to come to terms with the brutal reality of frontier violence and in particular frontier massacres and their long-term impact on the Aboriginal community in Victoria today. In view of his ongoing commitment to the contemporary community, the oversight is puzzling.

Nonetheless, Broome's accounts of the frontier wars in Victoria over the last three decades have placed them firmly in the mainstream of Australian history. His great strengths lie in his crisp prose, his evident compassion and commitment to the Aboriginal people of Victoria today and his determination not to stray too far from the published sources. Readers can be assured that in his accounts of the frontier wars Broome has always erred on the side of caution and not 'taken them for a ride'.

In this context, it is useful to recall the important point he made in the Preface to the first edition of *Aboriginal Australians*. Broome said he was writing the book for his father and for a sceptical conservative historian, neither of whom it appears had ever considered that bloody frontier wars for the possession of Australia could have taken place. For Broome the audience has never really changed. In presenting the story of Aboriginal agency and resistance on the frontier in the face of settler activism he laid the groundwork for recognition of their rights today. This fact alone renders his work on the frontier wars over the last three decades a mighty achievement.

CHAPTER 3

On Paternalisms and Aboriginal Agency
From missions to neoliberal policy in the work of Richard Broome and Noel Pearson

Claire McLisky and Ben Silverstein

In 2006, paternalism emerged as a keyword in discussions of the Howard Government's Indigenous Affairs policy, but, though cited frequently, it was an unstable signifier. Was 'paternalism' a slur, condemning an antiquated approach to Indigenous Affairs and distancing an enlightened present from the outdated past? Or was it a valid policy setting, as relevant today as it had been in the 1950s? Though this divergence was largely uninterrogated at the time, at least two prominent public intellectuals had begun to reconsider the term. That same year, 2006, Richard Broome published a powerful exploration of what he termed the 'two-way dynamic' of paternalism on Coranderrk station, an approach that fundamentally rethought the way that paternalism took form in the mission era. And the previous year the Cape York Indigenous leader Noel Pearson had meditated on the difficulties surrounding the term while at the same time advocating an explicitly paternalist social policy. This set the two of them apart from the many other public commentators and historians who, in the context of the history wars, deployed the term either to endorse or condemn past relationships between white authorities and Indigenous Australians. Many framed it in a negative light, as a system of domination and control. Others understood it as signifying 'fatherly' authority exercised benevolently in a family-like situation, with the non-Indigenous missionary, employer, policeman, bureaucrat or politician occupying the paternal role. In both of these accounts, paternalism was cast as a system crafted by an all-determining paternal figure, the only serious actor to whom one need pay attention. However, for both Pearson and Broome (in subtly different ways), Aboriginal people past and present have actively shaped the development of paternalist relationships, rendering these relationships dynamic syntheses of Indigenous and settler traditions.

These profound definitional disagreements have serious consequences both for our understanding of historical relationships between Indigenous and non-Indigenous people and for the terrain of contemporary Australian politics. Nonetheless, despite the prominence of the term in popular debate a decade ago and its continued currency today, these consequences have provoked surprisingly little scholarly reflection.[1] In this chapter we argue that placing the historiographical debate alongside the contemporary popular one offers new insights into both fields of inquiry. The work of Richard Broome and Noel Pearson is our focus, and because both Broome and Pearson developed their theories of paternalism primarily (though not exclusively) through their work on Christian missions, we emphasise this context. In particular, we propose that Broome's definition of paternalism could be usefully taken up by both mission historians and contemporary critics seeking to understand the backgrounds and motivations of those who invoke it.

Paternalism has been central to Broome's understanding of mission history since the publication of his 1982 book, *Aboriginal Australians: Black Response to White Dominance*. His theorisation of the concept has since evolved significantly, culminating in a 2006 article where he proposed that the operation of paternalism on Christian missions could not be understood without studying it as a site of engagement between missionary practice and Aboriginal people and cultural systems (such as kinship obligation).[2] This mode of analysis embedded Aboriginal agency in a concept that had previously often been understood in terms of domination and control. While his work on Christian missions has generally been influential, this particular definition of missionary paternalism has not yet received the attention it deserves.

Broome's work on Aboriginal Australia is not without its critics. Lawrence Bamblett describes reading *Aboriginal Australians* as 'a still-developing discovery of how a non-Indigenous Australian views the colonization of Aboriginal Australians'. Bamblett has argued that scholars need to be much more cautious about generalising about past Aboriginal people's hopes, feelings or perspectives, an observation which concerns all works of scholarship and commentary on missions, including this one. However, for us as for Bamblett, the role of the critic is to move beyond affirming or rejecting past practices and scholarship we find troubling and instead to explore the ways the scholarly ideas that are their legacy influence us today.[3]

In this chapter we start, therefore, by exploring the origins and subsequent history of paternalism as an analytical category in the academic field of Aboriginal mission history, and an assessment of Broome's continuing and possible future influence on it. Next, we comment on the current state of *popular* debate on paternalism as it relates to Aboriginal governance in Australia, particularly focusing on Pearson's work in relation to welfare reform. In both sections we are especially interested in the ways different commentators posit the relationship between paternalism and Aboriginal agency, and the implications that this may have for their understandings of historical 'problems' and contemporary 'solutions'.

The search for Aboriginal agency has animated a great deal of scholarly work but this work has often rested upon a theory of subjectivity that reflects nineteenth-century liberal thought, imagining the free subject as both self-authoring and self-authorising, unbound by external strictures and free to exercise will independently. It is no surprise, then, that historical analyses of paternalism have tended to describe it as a system which constrained this agency by introducing commands and obligations to the otherwise self-contained individual subject, curtailing Aboriginal people's capacity to determine their own selves, their circumstances, and their histories. In his powerful critique of historical projects that seek to return agency to enslaved people, a critique to which we are indebted, Walter Johnson argues that after some 40 years of such work the injunction 'to give slaves back their agency' no longer reveals new and important historical truths. In fact, it now obscures investigations into resistance, the conditions of enslaved humanity, the processes of forming social solidarities, and into subaltern analyses of the *system* that exploited them.[4]

Broome and Pearson have approached this problem differently, formulating models of paternalism that do not preclude Aboriginal agency but instead re-frame it, imagining agency at both an individual and a collective level as lawful and constraining and wilful and self-determining. For Broome, Aboriginal efforts to incorporate missionaries and protectors into systems of kinship – transforming British paternalism into a syncretic system – evidence the agency of Aboriginal actors, both individual and collective. Likewise, for Pearson it was a similar system of paternalism that provided the grounds on which Aboriginal people could exercise their individual agency. Its apparent destruction in favour of self-determination had enabled rights-bearing Aboriginal subjects who lived in poverty and dysfunction; its re-instatement might instead guarantee what he terms the 'right to take responsibility'. Paternalism emerges as both the effect, and the guarantor, of Aboriginal agency.[5]

Pearson's writing is of particular importance both for his prominent public embrace of paternalism and because he explicitly situates his calls for paternalism today within an historical analysis of Christian missions. In his historical writing Pearson, like Broome, associates Aboriginal agency with what he sees as the success of the paternalist era; in his policy Pearson takes this association one step further to argue that paternalist structures are a crucial part of enabling future Aboriginal agency. In reading his work, many white politicians, for whom the crucial agents of history are invariably white, have recognised his celebration of the possibilities of paternalism as a call for white authority, for their exercise of paternal power over Aboriginal subjects. We suggest here that both these options are historically reductive: paternalism was not a just system in which Aboriginal people could take full responsibility for themselves, and nor do the shortcomings of the past 45 years of policy reflect Aboriginal incapacity and beseech a renewed paternalist authority. Such oversimplifications of the notion of paternalism not only elide complexity, they also obscure what is at stake in the ways various commentators define paternalism, both historically and in contemporary politics. We call here for a return to the historical argument that Broome (and indeed Pearson in his early historical work) has proposed, understanding paternalism as a system of relationality that need not annihilate the possibility of Aboriginal difference and its capacity to determine meaning.

Part I: Paternalism and Agency in Mission Historiography

Early formulations of paternalism and agency in Australian Aboriginal mission history

As the work of Richard Broome and many others have shown, Christian missionaries in Australia and beyond often conceived of their relationships to Aboriginal people in familial terms. From the early nineteenth century onwards missionaries in Australia wrote of their 'paternal' or 'parental' relationships to Aboriginal people, their fatherly or motherly love and the gratification that they felt when they considered that this was returned by 'their' Aboriginal 'children'. They invoked familial metaphors in the contexts of education, religious instruction and discipline. However, when nineteenth-century missionaries discussed their approaches to Aboriginal management they generally did not use the term 'paternalism', which was at the time most commonly used to describe relationships between workers and their employers, governments and their citizens, or imperial powers and their colonies. When in the late nineteenth century the term did begin to be used across the English-speaking world to describe the approach of missionaries, it was mostly deployed as a criticism of their work. Missionary paternalism, it was held, led to ongoing dependence on missionaries, weakened native churches, and resulted in 'much damage to the true fraternal spirit of the Gospel'.[6] By 1901, the *Hartford Seminary Record* was calling paternalism 'the curse of modern Protestant missions'.[7]

This conceptualisation of paternalism was reflected in the work of historians writing on Australian missions in the 1960s and 1970s. In her 1969 book *The Road to Mowanjum*, Maisie McKenzie cast paternalism as a negative force that stifled Indigenous initiative, defining it as white people 'making decisions for (Aboriginal) people and meeting their immediate material needs'. But the missionaries of Mowanjum, near Derby in Western Australia, she claimed, were different. They practised 'an enlightened policy of non-paternalism', encouraging the Worora to 'make their own decisions, to be self-reliant, to maintain their dignity as human beings'.[8] Charles Rowley's *The Destruction of Aboriginal Society*, published the following year, understood 'paternalism' similarly, as did Michael Christie in his 1979 *Aborigines in Colonial Victoria*, who described a general 'air of racial superiority and paternalism' which subjugated Aboriginal people living on missions.[9] In these works, paternalism was defined by what its critics perceived as its effects *on* Aboriginal people — dependence, passivity, loss of dignity — rather than their engagement *with* it. Little effort was made to define paternalism in any detail, to explain its origins or how it had become so prevalent on missions in Australia.

Broome and others develop the concept of paternalism, 1982–2006

It was in this climate that Richard Broome's *Aboriginal Australians* was published in 1982. Seeking to comprehend the ways Aboriginal people and missionaries understood mission life, Broome devoted greater attention to the dynamics of personal relationships than most previous historians. He identified paternalism as a key element and made a first stab at explaining its origins, writing that:

> Christian thought is permeated by images of fathers and sons, of shepherds and sheep, of teachers and listeners, and hierarchies. Every minister (called fathers in some churches) heads his own flock of parishioners which he cares for and guides into the Christian way of life. It was little wonder that when these Christians went among 'their' black 'heathen children' to show them the truth and the light that they 'alone' possessed, their sense of fatherhood, protectiveness and paternalism was dramatically increased.[10]

Thinking with Christian theology in this way was unusual for a historian writing Aboriginal history in the early 1980s, and was perhaps a product of Broome's previous work on early twentieth-century Protestantism in New South Wales.[11] By linking missionaries' notions of themselves as patriarchal figures to their religious backgrounds, Broome pushed previous analyses one step further to provide a glimpse into the worlds of the missionaries themselves. He was sensitive to the missionaries' ideals but also realistic about how they functioned in practice. While writing that missionaries understood paternalism as a natural system of protective care, he emphasised the deeply contingent ways they applied it, making life for Aboriginal people a 'lottery' in which they could end up living under a beneficent patron or a tyrant. Ultimately, however, his conclusion that paternalism 'became the blot on the humanitarianism of the missionaries' was not so different from that of his predecessors.[12]

At the same time, new developments in Australian Aboriginal history were underway, with a growing emphasis on agency, adaptation, accommodation, and synthesis.[13] Ann McGrath was the first to use the concept of paternalism in a way that emphasised its potential for agency. In her 1987 monograph *Born in the Cattle* she built on Eugene Genovese's analysis of master–slave relationships in the U.S. to argue that paternalism on cattle stations in Australia's north had operated as a two-way system which had at least some benefits for all parties. For Aboriginal people who accepted class relations of patronage and dependence it provided 'a promise of protection for themselves and their community, allowing them to stay on their traditional lands'.[14]

Two years later Bain Attwood applied this approach to the history of Aboriginal missions in *The Making of the Aborigines*. Drawing on David Roberts' work on paternalism in early Victorian England, he framed missionary paternalism as a system with a broader social resonance and an established logic. Under paternalism everyone had a particular role to play and duties to perform, producing a mission world of reciprocity which 'bound missionary and Aborigine together in a most personal way'. On many missions 'the missionaries were regarded warmly by Aborigines, and their deference and loyalty to missionary rule cannot be doubted'.[15]

This was the first time that a post-1960s historian had suggested that Aboriginal people themselves had a stake in paternalistic relationships with missionaries. Attwood noted the unpopularity of such an idea amongst 'later generations' of Aboriginal people who denounced 'the dependency and subordination it entailed'. However, he wrote: 'One cannot ignore the fact that the paternalistic order gave dispossessed Aborigines a refuge and reinforced their sense of community; nor should one overlook the ways in which Aborigines were able to assert themselves within this order.'[16] In bringing these aspects to the fore Attwood married two themes — paternalism and Aboriginal agency — which had hitherto seemed mutually exclusive in the context of mission history, while continuing to recognise the hierarchy and structural inequalities of mission life.

This new brand of interpretation was not without its critics. While the concept of agency, according to Jan Kociumbas, 'drew attention to the importance of individual "consciousness" in determining "being", and of individual actions and choices in determining destiny', an over-emphasis on agency led to a distorted view of the Aboriginal experience of colonisation.[17] Patrick Wolfe, meanwhile, argued that far from providing Aboriginal people with opportunities for agency, missionary paternalism was better understood as an instance of missionaries practising elimination through a form of incorporation.[18] For the historian to assume the success of that incorporation (and represent that success as at least in part the result of Aboriginal agency) was to render Aboriginal people part of a settler collective by 'analytic fiat'; in so doing, the historian lost the ability to analyse paternalism as a strategy deployed against Aboriginal people.[19]

These writers to some extent foreshadowed Johnson's later, more systematic, critique of the concept of agency in descriptions of oppressed peoples' lives. Reviewing the use of the term in histories of the transatlantic slave trade in 2003, he argued that historians' keenness to locate enslaved peoples' humanity in their agency had led to the specific political and cultural contexts of their actions being overlooked. The concept of agency, he argued, was itself 'saturated with the categories of nineteenth-century liberalism' which assumed the universality of selfhood, even as it denied that selfhood to enslaved and oppressed peoples. By applying 'the jargon of self-determination and choice to the historical condition of civil objectification and choicelessness', historians had 'shoved to the side...a consideration of human-ness lived outside the conventions of liberal agency'.[20] While not addressed specifically to the Australian Aboriginal context, Johnson's arguments about agency were representative of a broader move towards complicating the concept, which was to have important implications for the writing of Aboriginal mission histories.

In 2005 Richard Broome published *Aboriginal Victorians*, in which he offered his first thoroughgoing definition of paternalism. Here, he departed from his earlier characterisation of paternalism as a Christian tendency and instead framed it as a social force, drawing, like Attwood, on David Roberts' work. Paternalism was now cast as 'an intimate, face-to-face, two-way power relationship based on the view that all had an ordained place in the world: masters were to rule and underlings to serve, but with obligations on both sides'.[21] Like Attwood, Broome argued that 'many Aboriginal people acquiesced in this paternal relationship in the hard post-frontier colonial world, where protection and help was needed'. But he also contended that 'such a reciprocal hierarchical relationship came naturally to people who traditionally had elders to mentor, guide and protect them through the rigours of gaining knowledge, becoming initiated, and living within a group surrounded by *mainmet* – dangerous strangers'. Paternalism, that is, could be incorporated into Koori practices of kinship as they were articulated with nineteenth-century settler colonialism or, in Johnson's terms, their specific political and cultural contexts. Indeed, Broome argued, Attwood had 'underestimated the degree with which some Aboriginal people voluntarily embraced cultural enlargement and enrichment'.[22] He observed, rather, that through the ebb and flow of paternalism's reciprocal relationships, the 'reserves were not "concentration camps"...but places of refashioned community and identity: places that became "home", complete with oppressions and opportunities like any home'.[23] While this last point certainly overstated the degree of Aboriginal autonomy on nineteenth-century missions,[24] Broome's emphasis on Aboriginal political and cultural priorities shifted the terms of discussion. Rather than limiting his definition of agency to Aboriginal people's ability to assert themselves within settler power structures, Broome acknowledged the significance of Aboriginal as well as settler systems of meaning.

Some of these claims were further developed in a 2006 article on the Coranderrk Aboriginal Station, in which Broome showed how seeming Aboriginal 'acquiescence' to missionary paternalism could in fact be interpreted as the assertion of their own notion of 'right behaviour'.[25] The convergence of these values, he argued, allowed Aboriginal people to gain leverage by imposing their moral expectations on missionaries and reserve managers.[26] The breakdown of mutually beneficial paternalistic relationships, he argued, was 'not a result of paternalism itself, but rather the *devolution* of reciprocal agreements over generations from "proper maintenance and protection" into a welfare dependency'. At this point, what he called 'patron-client relationships...lost paternal closeness, became coercive, and shifted in the patron's favour'.[27]

From 'the blot on the humanitarianism of the missionaries', paternalism had for Broome become a concept with much more positive potential. He now understood it as a system that could facilitate as much cross-cultural understanding as misunderstanding, framing relationships between missionaries and Indigenous peoples as complex and ever-changing and, perhaps most importantly, allowing for intention and agency on both sides. Paternalism, for Broome, was an instance of incorporation but one that was characterised less by elimination than by mutual transformation, as peoples came together in new relationships that changed each of them, as well as potentially changing the very nature of paternalism into something closer to 'right behaviour'. Paternalism was less a strategy directed against Aboriginal people than it was as a site of negotiation.

Defining paternalism post-Broome

Despite the fact that Broome's work has been highly influential, his formulation of the idea of paternalism has not been fully taken up by the next generation of mission historians. Some historians have continued to draw from Rowley's and Christie's model, emphasising missionaries' need for control, their moralism, and the arbitrariness of their exercise of power. Marguerita Stephens, for example, has examined the history of the Coranderrk Reserve and characterised the missionary's interactions with Aboriginal peoples as moving from an openness to a 'negotiated balance' with residents to a determination to 'impose his will on the Kulin...to ensure their conformity and subservience to the colonial order of things'.[28] Similarly, in his 2007 *White Christ, Black Cross*, Noel Loos described the Anglican Church's approach towards Aboriginal people from the mid-nineteenth to the mid-twentieth century as a 'one-hundred-year-old policy of paternalistic domination'.[29] Despite significant differences between their analyses of mission histories, both these authors used the concept of paternalism to signify a blunt exercise of power, which they contrasted with approaches and individuals who they considered to have been more inclined towards dialogic relationships with Aboriginal people.[30]

In a 2009 article considering space and surveillance at Ebenezer Mission, Jane Lydon moved closer towards Broome's initial definition of paternalism as a potentially benign system of power relations with a long history in Christian tradition, drawing on the work of Anne McClintock to argue that paternalism positioned missionaries as 'watchful guardians whose benign discipline was sanctioned by God in the apparently natural and nonviolent affiliation between father and children'.[31] Yet Lydon still portrayed paternalism as a vehicle for missionary domination rather than a two-way dynamic. Jessie Mitchell's 2011 book *In Good Faith?* was one of the few to take up Broome's notion of missionary paternalism as a two-way power relationship in an academic history. Here, Mitchell presented a view of power relations on Christian missions that supported Broome's argument that 'European dynamics of paternalism could be incorporated into Indigenous understandings of asymmetrical mentoring and kinship'.[32] She also sought to complicate the picture of mission power dynamics beyond the notion of paternalism, arguing that early nineteenth-century missionaries' statements about Indigenous dispossession and entitlements showed 'an interplay of ideas about paternalism, imperial obligations, and deserving poverty, as well as Indigenous people's own beliefs about entitlement, exchange and personal connections to philanthropists'.[33]

In incorporating Indigenous perspectives in an attempt to elaborate the ways in which Aboriginal people were actively involved in negotiating relationships, living conditions and their status in the colonial world, Mitchell's work represents the major emerging trend in Australian mission history. (Aboriginal historians have, of course, long been interested in Aboriginal perspectives but have not usually, until recently, had the institutional backing to write and publish these histories in an academic forum.[34]) Yet, as we have seen, few contemporary historians have explored the inner workings of paternalism in the ways described by Broome, or have even taken the time to define it in detail. The absence of an ongoing academic discussion of paternalism has implications for the public sphere, where there is often precious little agreement as to its meaning or its perceived value.

Part II: Paternalism and Contemporary Aboriginal Governance

Paternalisms past

In 2006-7, a number of public figures debated calls for a 'new paternalism' in Aboriginal affairs. At a time when the formal institutions of 'self-determination', built over the previous three decades, were being dismantled in favour of 'mutual obligation' and 'intervention', the term 'paternalism' evoked a sense of return to the protection era which provoked either hope or dread, depending on one's political stance. As Elizabeth Povinelli has argued, in rejecting representations of Aboriginal incapacity and vulnerability, anticolonial and new social movements of the decolonisation or self-determination era had 'refigured the arts of paternalistic, civilisational care into acts of colonial domination'.[35] Witnessing the return of the idea — held by many in the Commonwealth Government — that Aboriginal culture, rather than settler colonialism, was culpable for Aboriginal disadvantage, the heirs of these movements once again criticised such moves as recapitulating paternalism, by which they meant domination.

However, this presentation of the past as anathema was not shared by all. For some, the time before self-determination was an object of nostalgia. White reactionaries like then Minister for Health and Ageing Tony Abbott or Prime Minister John Howard considered it a time of social order where everyone knew their place and white leaders could act as guardians, or fathers, of Aboriginal communities. For Noel Pearson, that nostalgia was tinged with a recognition of the trauma of racism and discrimination, of exclusion and deprivation.

Since 1993, Pearson has risen to a position of great prominence in national politics. He has been the Aboriginal adviser of choice for several prime ministers, transforming his prescriptions for redressing Indigenous disadvantage in his Cape York stronghold into national policy. Scholarly accounts of his intellectual trajectory have often placed him in the context of third-way politics, a philosophical approach to government that emphasises the role of the state in creating incentives for subjects to take responsibility for themselves and contribute more to society.[36] While the growing dominance of neoliberal styles of governance are important in accounting for Pearson's ideas and their influence, we argue that he might also usefully be situated historically: that his political philosophy arises from his reading of Aboriginal pasts. Tim Rowse has similarly suggested that Pearson's diagnosis of the Indigenous predicament, and his proposed solution, rest heavily on his historical imagination.[37] We suggest it is Pearson's transposition of history into a nostalgic idiom that has been both more compelling to the Australian political elite, and more effective in leading to specific policy propositions. The stories Pearson tells about the past present a morality tale that leads him to a broadly tolerant – albeit nuanced – position in relation to state paternalism.

Pearson is rarely understood as a mission historian, but his 1986 History Honours thesis, published in an edited collection in 1998, provides an illuminating glimpse into his understanding of the paternalism of the mission era. Hope Vale Mission, Pearson's home and the subject of his study, was formed at Cape Bedford in North Queensland in 1886, and became a home for many Guugu Yimidhirr people dispossessed of their land by the influx of settlers sparked by a gold rush from 1873. From 1887 to 1942 the mission was ruled by Muni, Father George Schwarz, who Pearson cast as a 'legendary' figure, a 'paternalist' whose legacy is both substantial and complex. Pearson described Muni as 'a devoted and insistent missionary who endured immense hardships and obstacles in his work, which he carried out with a determination and care for his vocation'. But at the same time, he was also 'an often callous, ethnocentric authoritarian who often failed to accord *bama* [Aboriginal people] respect as equals', who 'discriminated racially and perhaps instilled and definitely perpetuated some of the worst attitudes among the *Guugu Yimidhirr* people, attitudes that still survive today'.[38]

Schwartz, in Pearson's telling, demanded obedience and acquiescence, seeking to regulate every aspect of Guugu Yimidhirr people's lives and to remake them in his Lutheran image. Mission residents responded to him with ambivalence, with 'love and hate, sorrow and anger, happiness and disappointment, loyalty and frustration, respect and criticism'.[39] The mission worked, Pearson argued, because the authoritarianism was not total; Guugu Yimidhirr were able to live overlapping public mission and private village lives, generating a Christian Guugu

Yimidhirr culture. Describing this effort, Pearson relied upon oral histories to emphasise Aboriginal action, to argue that the success of the mission 'was based on the people taking it on and making it their own'. The Guugu Yimidhirr 'were *active creators* of the mission culture that was very strong as long as it remained meaningful for them. It is a misinterpretation to view this mission as merely a history of missionary activity over Aboriginal passivity.'[40] This formulation anticipated Broome's later emphasis on Aboriginal agency in fabricating relationships on the mission, proposing an interplay between 'mission' and 'village' in which an imbalance of power did not connote Aboriginal people's inability to determine their lives.[41]

Noel Pearson's 'Native Nostalgia'

In Pearson's writing since 1999, his account of the past has been expressed in a different idiom, that of nostalgia. Etymologically, nostalgia refers to a painful longing (algia) for a return to home (nostos), a home that Svetlana Boym argues no longer exists or has never existed. Nostalgia, then, is 'a sentiment of loss and displacement, but it is also a romance with one's own fantasy'.[42] Pearson's is a complicated nostalgia; it resembles that which the South African scholar Jacob Dlamini has described as 'native nostalgia'. Nostalgia, Dlamini suggests, is essentially a response to feeling adrift in a world that is out of control, searching the past for a time of order. For Dlamini, 'native nostalgia' is a native response to the disorderly experience of decolonisation, a yearning for the certainties of life before.[43] In Pearson's writing, an historical emphasis on the relatively settled accommodations of the mission in which Aboriginal residents were, at least in part, responsible for the nature of relationships, enable its articulation as the object of nostalgia. The effect of this attachment is to produce a story of the past in which social problems of the present can be traced to the breakdown of that mission order, the loss of the stable home.

In this nostalgic idiom, Aboriginal passivity and victimhood appear as consequences of the post-1967 decline of missions and their social order. The advent of Aboriginal citizenship in this era led to a range of developments that Pearson identified as apparently positive but whose 'unintended consequences' were ultimately negative. In 2007 he suggested 'three factors as decisive contributors to the descent into hell three decades later': the introduction of equal wages and the consequent exodus of Aboriginal people from the pastoral industry, the replacement of pastoral work with access to welfare payments, and the right to drink. To these he added the availability of Legal Aid as a means of subjecting Aboriginal communities to the law, undermining the previous 'workable system of social order based on moral and cultural authority...which had provided structure to life' on missions and settlements.[44] Aboriginal decline, he thus argued, was a result of the break with paternalism, the overly celebrated rejection of the mission dispensation of social order. The 'awful truth', Pearson wrote, 'is that we threw the baby out with the bathwater'. Aboriginal people 'should have found a way to move beyond the paternalism of the past without destroying the moral and cultural order which had been such a strong quality of our community'.[45]

Pearson's preference for the time before the self-determination era was emphasised in his fond memories of home on the mission. In a speech delivered in 2000, he described that home as a site of material poverty but in other respects a source of 'great wealth'. On the mission, people 'had families and a community. They had golden things and I think they often knew it.'[46] Against this he counterposed an image of Hope Vale today, which Pearson has described as a 'Hobbesian' dystopia of drinking, sexual assault and abuse, death and despair, all funded and enabled by Centrelink. Young children emerge from houses 'as if from a war zone'. There they are easy prey for the molesters their inebriated parents invite in; sometimes the only action they can take is to spend the night outside, 'scared to go back home'.[47] The paternalism of the mission may have been oppressive but it created opportunities. Its removal transformed home into a space of terror.

Seven years earlier, Pearson had discussed paternalism at Hope Vale in more negative terms. In describing a communal political awakening, he wrote:

> The increasing awareness that the Queensland government's policies concerning Aboriginal people breached fundamental human rights, and that our mission friend [Schwartz] was a leading and vehement opponent of

Aboriginal rights, brought on a significant identity crisis for the community. This crisis led to a realisation that paternalism within the family might be a natural, affectionate relationship, but when it involved adults of different races it was undeniably racist, and arose from a fundamental assumption of inferiority and superiority. The government and the church had assumed our innate inferiority and their own superiority. Like many paternal relationships put asunder, the bitterness of this realisation was painful.[48]

This was not, it should be clear, a rejection of paternalism itself, but rather a complaint as to its articulation. Pearson differentiated between a natural (familial) paternalism and a racist (external) paternalism, creating a legitimate space for a paternal practice that could be articulated within the home.[49] The nurturing home on the mission and the destructive home of the town today are archetypal elements of what we suggest can be productively understood as Pearson's nostalgic imagination.

In the context of Pearson's historical account, this home stands in for the way things were, the social order of the period roughly spanning from the beginning of the twentieth century until the replacement of assimilation policy with self-determination in 1972, an era McGrath has termed that of the 'state as father'.[50] Nonetheless, while his is a nostalgia for a time of paternalism it is not the paternalism of progressive critique, where missionaries were empowered to command every aspect of Indigenous people's lives. Rather, it is paternalism in the sense Broome explored, where Aboriginal people were able to adapt their traditions to a new context, creating unified communities and meaningful lives. Dismantling paternalist regulation in favour of self-determination had, Pearson argued, 'seen the decline, not of what the missionaries had achieved among the people, but rather the decline of what the people had themselves achieved in the face of dispossession and colonisation'.[51] This was a paternalist system compromised by racism and authoritarianism, but it was a social order in which productive and functional Aboriginal subjectivities were possible. The self-determination era, Pearson argued, had rendered such success impossible.

Welfare reform and mutual obligation

Rowse has argued that Pearson's policy question, grounded in his historical imagination, became: 'What is to replace "paternalism" as the authority on which "community" – for a time – rested?'[52] This question reflects, we suggest, a nostalgia that seeks to restore the remembered orderly home, an attachment that circumscribes the search for policy futures. Nostalgia stages negotiating a disorderly future not as an embrace of the uncertainty of a contingent world – as we see the Guugu Yimithirr of Hope Vale Mission do in Pearson's history – but as the work of reconstructing an idealised past. Seemingly unable to fathom a future he hasn't already experienced, Pearson has confined his policy reforms to searching for ways of replacing the paternalist figure in Aboriginal communities rather than seeking a wholesale reform of settler colonialism. He has argued for the need to 'build responsibility and reciprocity into all of the economic relationships and transactions in our society'. And he has instrumentalised welfare, already a technology of state intervention into individual and communal life, as a privileged means of achieving this, arguing for welfare reforms that incorporate relationships of paternalism between members of Aboriginal communities and the institutions of community leadership.[53] As he was to suggest later, the 'nub of the problem in remote communities' was that 'government funds dysfunctional behaviour'. In place of this funding, which Pearson has compellingly dubbed 'passive welfare', he has suggested transforming welfare into a conditional entitlement that is less a right than a reward for good behaviour.[54] Only by doing so, he argued, could Aboriginal people be made functional subjects.

When framed in a nostalgic idiom, Pearson's reforms were susceptible to being read as calling for a return to mission paternalism. His early articulations of these reforms had been lauded in *The Australian* in 2003 as representing a 'new politics...that is about community, devolution of power and responsibility, mutual obligation and reciprocity, and the rejection of outmoded ideological grandstandings'. But as his ideas developed they were also frequently criticised, especially by Indigenous commentators and activists, as 'paternalist' and a 'return to the policies of yesteryear'.[55] In 2004, the Howard Government announced a new approach to providing services to Indigenous communities, including the advent of 'shared responsibility agreements'. Though initially sceptical, by 2005 Pearson had aligned himself with the Howard Government's policies of 'mutual obligation', which made Indigenous welfare payments dependent on recipients meeting conditions not required of non-Indigenous claimants.[56]

Pearson defended this position by arguing that 'Indigenous support for mutual obligation has nothing to do with the paternalism of the past'. However, he attributed social ills to a failure of self-determination symbolised by inadequate or negligent parenting. Children starved, he argued, because 'their parents malnourish and neglect both themselves and their children'. Pearson further argued that

> in left-liberal and progressive discourse the words 'patronising' and 'paternalistic' have become hot buttons that stifle thought. Once a policy has been branded patronising and paternalistic, debaters...feel no need to examine facts or try to understand the rationale and the intentions of the policy so branded.[57]

While Indigenous sensitivity about paternalism was 'understandable', he argued that policy should be weighed on its merits rather than its similarity to previous paternalistic policies or practices.[58] Pearson had no problem with the label of paternalism. However, it is important to note, his proposals for the institution of a kind of paternalism were crucially different to those of the Howard Government. Both instrumentalised the provision of welfare as a lever to encourage good behaviour, but they differed in implementation and the relations thus produced. For Pearson, community involvement in welfare regulation was essential. For the Howard Government, by contrast, policy rested on the idea that community control was the problem: in place of a self-managing community, the state must step in and take control.

'Colonial Nostalgia'

Pearson's arguments helped create a space for the articulation of the merits of paternalism, a space into which Tony Abbott jumped when in 2006 he called for a 'new paternalism' in Indigenous policy. In a speech ostensibly about Aboriginal health, Abbott attributed poor Indigenous health statistics to a 'culture of directionlessness in which so many Aboriginal people live'. Aboriginal self-management had failed, and, under a policy of self-determination, government had fostered this failure. A 'form of paternalism – based on competence rather than race – is really unavoidable if these places are to be well run'.[59] Notably, Abbott strongly defended the work of missionaries, who 'took solidarity with Aboriginal people to be their personal responsibility' and whose 'sense of calling...motivated them to commit their lives to Aboriginal people in ways that can seldom now be matched'.[60] Though he admitted missionary imperfection, Abbott found in their lives a sense of whiteness as virtuous service for unfortunate others. His was a nostalgia for this imagined time of self-sacrifice, of white lives lived through an ultimate devotion. It was a form of what Patricia Lorcin has described as 'colonial nostalgia', representing the lived experience of the past not as that of contestation but as ordered, mannered, and good.[61]

Reflecting the public sense that paternalism rather denoted a relation of domination and subordination, Mal Brough, then Minister for Families, Community Services and Indigenous Affairs, declared he was troubled by Abbott's use of the word.[62] Aboriginal leaders were more strident. Mick Dodson described paternalism as a 'horribly discredited approach' and called for solutions shaped around 'indigenous success' rather than the 'view that Aboriginal people are hopeless and incapable'. Similarly, former ATSIC Chairperson Lowitja O'Donoghue observed that Australia had 'tried paternalism' but 'the problem is they have not given Aboriginal people the capacity to run their own affairs'.[63] For Tom Calma, Aboriginal and Torres Strait Islander Social Justice Commissioner, the problem with Abbott's paternalism was that 'it doesn't allow individuals to learn to develop responsibility, and it's always somebody doing something for you, and what we've seen is that's been a failure in a lot of communities'.[64] Pearson was critical too, warning of the dangers of a return to this form of paternalism: 'When it comes to government and when it comes to people of another race presuming to carry out a paternal role...I think we're returning to an old institution that became extremely problematic for Aboriginal people.'[65] Here, Pearson distinguished between state paternalism and the community-led brand of paternalism he had defended earlier, a paternalism that would make self-determination, the right to take responsibility, possible.

However, at the same time, as noted above, many Indigenous leaders were levelling similar accusations at Pearson. His welfare reforms, which created paternalistic relationships between welfare recipients and community leaders, slipped in Abbott's reading into a paternalist relation between the Aboriginal communities as a whole and the state. In 2007, Pearson's Cape York Institute recommended that four obligations must be attached to the receipt of welfare payments: a 100 per cent school attendance record for any children in the care of the recipient; no neglect or abuse of children; no drug, alcohol, gambling, or family violence offences; and those in public housing must abide by tenancy conditions. Welfare recipients would be assessed by a Family Responsibilities Commission, with local panels chaired by a retired magistrate and including two senior elders from that community.[66]

When Calma suggested in a radio conversation that this was a kind of paternalism that would breach the *Racial Discrimination Act*, Pearson exploded:

> Ask the terrified kid huddling in the corner, when there's a binge drinking party going on down the hall, ask them if they want a bit of paternalism...Ask them if they want a bit of intervention, because these people who continue to bleat without looking at the facts, without facing up to the terrible things that are going on in our remote communities, these people are prescribing no intervention, they are prescribing a perpetual hell for our children.[67]

Paternalism, Pearson believed, could step in to replace incapable Aboriginal parents, rescuing children from their families. This was a story that resonated with conservatives across Australia.

One week prior to Pearson's castigation of Calma, the report of the Northern Territory Board of Inquiry into the Protection of Aboriginal Children from Sexual Abuse had been released. It identified widespread child abuse and located it as a reflection of lasting social problems in the north, making 97 separate recommendations for addressing these problems.[68] Inspired by Pearson's call for paternalism, a group of white men — Howard, Brough, and two senior bureaucrats — developed a Commonwealth response, declaring an emergency and announcing a series of coercive measures that would apply to all people living in remote Northern Territory Aboriginal communities.[69] These included alcohol restrictions and a ban on pornography, welfare reforms, compulsory health checks for Aboriginal children, the acquisition of Aboriginal townships, increased policing, and many more.

There is no space here for a full discussion of the ramifications of the design and implementation in 73 remote communities, initially by military force, of what became known as the Northern Territory Intervention. What is important to note, though, is that the Intervention as a whole was designed to 'bring to an end to the recognition of, and support for, Aboriginal people living in remote communities pursuing culturally distinctive ways of life'.[70] It was intended, in other words, to mark an end to what Howard named as 'separate development' policies and what was generally understood as the self-determination era — and it did so in the name of the child. For Brough, the Intervention placed the 'vulnerable children of our nation...front and centre of the national stage'. The stakes were high: anyone who criticised the intervention, Brough declared, was 'either not a parent or doesn't have a soul'.[71] Valuing self-determination, valuing Aboriginal rights in general, was cast as a discourse of sacrifice: rights could only come at the expense of children. Instead, the strong paternal power of the state was the only way to rescue Aboriginal children.

Conservative commentators celebrated this 'new paternalism' of intervention in instances of 'bad [Aboriginal] parenting',[72] but others were more critical, casting the paternalism of the Intervention as a 'return' to a failed and anachronistic policy, one that 'reinforces dependency' and carried 'an aggressive subliminal message that lays all blame at the feet of indigenous people and legitimises the view of indigenous dependency'. Paternalism, in other words, was applied to Indigenous people, circumscribing their capacity for action to make their own world.[73] To this Pearson responded by arguing that the accusation of paternalism was overly simplistic and dismissive. He asserted that the 'sum total' of critics' objections to the Intervention — based, among other things, on a condemnation of a return to 'missionary paternalism' — was 'inaction and procrastination while children's lives continue to be ruined'. It was not, he wrote, 'that the points made by the critics are wrong – they are often correct – but their criticism does not translate and often cannot be translated into action.' For him the question was always of the suffering child: 'what do you do when a child is being subjected to abuse this very day? What do you do when a child is likely to be abused next week?'[74] Though the Intervention was not precisely the program he would have designed himself, it was one he was more than happy to support.

Paternalisms today

The Howard era came to be known as one of paternalism in Indigenous Affairs.[75] This was a time in which Pearson's work had great political purchase. However, he was frequently and sharply criticised both by commentators on the Left and by Indigenous people across Australia. Aboriginal activist and Director of the Carpentaria Land Council Murandoo Yanner said of Pearson in 2012 that one could:

> Pick up a newspaper from the 1950s or the 1960s, and it's word for word, white people saying the same thing as he's saying now. He's a paternalist. The reason our people take drugs, bash each other, is dispossession and the racism inherent in white society. We don't need the Great White Man to come in and manage things for us.[76]

This was an accusation Pearson would not reject outright:

> I've wrestled with this, and I'm unapologetic. Every successful society depends on a degree of paternalism. What I'm trying to grapple with here is, how do we solve poverty? How do you activate that fire in the belly that's necessary to lift people from their circumstances?[77]

For Yanner, Aboriginal disadvantage or dysfunction was attributable to dispossession and racism, to the forces that structure Australian society. He saw Aboriginal emancipation as a goal that was only achievable through dismantling structures of oppression. Pearson, by contrast, told a story in which paternalist structures could, in fact, enable Aboriginal agency. He considered it possible to 'solve poverty' by buttressing such structures in ways that would activate Aboriginal people as agents of their own lives, people who would take responsibility for their circumstances.

Though he shared, in his policy articulations, a liberal conception of self-authoring and self-authorising subjectivity, Pearson's notion of paternalism differed importantly from that of Abbott and his fellow travellers. While for Pearson the active agents in his stories of the paternalist era — those who crafted paternalism as a system of meaning, reciprocity, and relationality — were almost always Aboriginal, for Abbott the active agents were white men in authority. For Pearson, Aboriginal people actively created mission culture; for all its racist authoritarianism, paternalism did not prevent Aboriginal people from making their world, making history. It was, rather, the end of paternalism and the replacement of its coercions with a system of passive welfare, entitlements irrespective of the actions of the recipient, which generated disorder. A right to welfare produced Aboriginal subjects as passive victims, as people whose actions held no personal consequence, and who accordingly became dysfunctional.[78]

Advocates of 'mutual obligation' policies, such as Pearson and Abbott, saw paternalism as enabling Aboriginal people's agency by creating the conditions in which they could exercise their right to take responsibility. The aim of this new, twenty-first century paternalism was a neoliberal one: to generate individuals who worked in the 'real economy'. This project was enabled by Pearson's nostalgic reading of mission-era paternalism, and by his subscription to what Johnson has called 'the conventions of liberal agency' — the belief that historical actors, and especially oppressed peoples, have the power to act freely and of their own volition. While Pearson's earlier historical work acknowledged the importance of Aboriginal actions both on the 'mission' and in the 'village', and the myriad ways in which Schwartz's paternalism limited the choices available to mission residents, his policy formulations now invested sole value in the economic and social successes of mainstream Australia and were predicated on the idea that agency, in the form of 'personal responsibility', was available untrammelled to all. This work displaced the rich complexities of his earlier accounts, eliding the decolonising possibilities of Aboriginal communal practice that he had previously imagined.

Paternalism emerged, for Pearson, as a system of obligation and opportunity, a way of producing Aboriginal people as subjects of consequence, people who could play a part in their world, who could self-determine, taking responsibility for their destiny. As he wrote in 2005 in advocating for welfare reform based on reciprocity, the 'state should play the *junior* role in the definition of reciprocity.'[79] It should be up to Aboriginal society, and its leaders, to set the terms of reciprocity'. For Abbott, the former trainee Jesuit priest, on the other hand, white authority figures (including missionaries) were not compromised figures who pursued racist policy; they were people to be celebrated. They set the just terms on which relationships were based. Aboriginal people were not necessarily agents in the stories Abbott told, in fact they barely figured. His call for a return to paternalism rested on a theory of Indigenous incapacity, an inability to self-determine. The difference between understandings of agency in paternalism was marked. It registers the distinction between Pearson's mobilisation of Indigenous community and those Marcia Langton described as 'neo-conservatives [who] steal Pearson's ideas and impose punitive measures on entire populations trapped in alcohol and substance dependency, deprive them of economic capability and subject them to a miserable, violence-ridden existence on the margins'.[80]

As Raymond Williams has written of nostalgia, 'what seemed a single escalator, a perpetual recession into history, turns out, on reflection, to be a more complicated movement'.[81] The paternalism to which the Howard Government sought to return expressed a desire to reinstantiate white government over black incapacity. But for Pearson the paternalist era was one in which Aboriginal people could be active agents making their world. Correspondingly, his vision of the Aboriginal agency made possible by his proposed policies was a fuller one, incorporating the arena of Indigenous culture and life embodied in the 'village' of his historical work. This resonates with the paternalism of Broome's historical analysis. The paternalism that Pearson proposed resembled that of the missions but with a twist; it would be a new home where paternalist relationships were articulated not between non-Indigenous and Indigenous people, but between responsible community elders and irresponsible community degenerates. The slippage between these two nostalgic objects, each signified by paternalism, is crucial.

Conclusion

It is perhaps unnecessary to observe that the problems facing historians attempting to describe life on nineteenth-century Aboriginal missions are in many ways different to those facing the community leader or politician attempting to formulate policy for twenty-first century Aboriginal communities. Yet Broome the historian and Pearson the community leader have for some time shared a professed desire to return 'agency' to past or present Aboriginal people. In pursuing this project Broome and Pearson share a conception of agency as not (necessarily) circumscribed by, or in conflict with, paternalism. This is an idiosyncratic view. Most public commentators counterpose paternalism and agency, describing as 'paternalist' the policy they oppose.[82]

In exploring these ideas we aim to reckon with the legacies left by both missionary paternalism and historical scholarship. The debris of paternalism appears today in different and complicated forms, generating tensions in both Broome's and Pearson's writing. Their complex and dialogical interpretations of paternalism suggest the radical potential of an account which portrays missionary paternalism as cross-cultural rather than assimilating, in which there remains space for Aboriginal meaning and relations to flourish. And, in productive ways, they leave unresolved the question of the relationship between Aboriginal incorporation into the larger settler polity and independence from it. They also provide a warning that subtle historical analysis can be instrumentalised by public figures committed to rehabilitating pernicious tendencies of the past, illustrating the underlying settler colonial continuity of which paternalism is a symptom. Nonetheless, as is so productively foregrounded in Broome's account, such policies are subject to the corresponding and continuing force of Aboriginal action, action that bends the world.

This research was supported by a grant from the Australian Research Council (FL110100243).

CHAPTER 4

The philosophy, opinions and inspiration of Jack Johnson

John Maynard

> The rites of boxing 'simplify everything. Good and evil, the winner and the loser'. More than anything else, the boxing match has served as a metaphor for opposition — the struggle between two bodies before an audience, usually for money, representing struggles between opposing qualities, ideas and values...those struggles involve nationality, class, race, ethnicity, religion, politics and different versions of masculinity.[1]

Introduction

For black, Indigenous and oppressed peoples across the globe during the early decades of the twentieth century there was no greater example of being an agent of one's own destiny than the heavyweight champion of the world, Jack Johnson. Johnson ignited courage, pride and self-belief for Aboriginal and other oppressed groups around the world. Demonstrating that he was master of his own destiny, Johnson trod a path that many wanted to emulate. In this chapter I will focus on boxing and the influence of Jack Johnson on later Aboriginal exploits in the ring.

Richard Broome's focus on boxing has included his initial study 'Professional Aboriginal Boxers in Eastern Australia 1930–1979' in the journal *Aboriginal History*, another study in the same journal titled

'Theatres of Power: Tent Boxing circa 1910-1970', his book *Sideshow Alley* (written with Alick Jackomos) that also included the travelling boxing tent shows, and his study 'The Australian Reaction to Jack Johnson, Black Pugilist, 1907-1909'.[2] Broome was one of the young historians heavily influenced by the global, social and political changes of the 1960s that challenged the drum-beating nationalistic myths of past Australian history. These biased histories had conveniently erased, forgotten and missed an Aboriginal presence in Australia's past except as a people belonging to the Stone Age or as a dying race. Broome's work on boxing in particular provides detailed analysis of the constructed sporting and racist barriers that were a part of the everyday lived Australian Aboriginal experience across the greater part of the twentieth century. In an early article, published in 1980, he stated that many Aboriginal men hoped that this sport would provide a way out of the race barrier and poverty. Yet he argued, through interviews and research, that, overall, boxing was not a help, and most Aboriginal fighters ended their days in poverty.[3]

Some 16 years later Richard Broome rethought his earlier statement and had 'developed a stronger sense of power from below and the agency held by Aboriginal historical actors'.[4] This greater awareness of agency, developed over a longer time period of reflection, offered a much deeper understanding of the complex experiences and relationships that Aboriginal people experienced. In 1996 Richard Broome argued 'that Aboriginal tent fighters were part of a multi-layered theatre of power, in which they were not only victims of white power and racial discourse, but also agents and manipulators of that power and discourse'.[5] These individuals were intent on shaping their own futures and providing for their families.

Until recent decades, with the opening of the AFL and NRL dressing-room doors to Aboriginal football involvement, boxing had been the sport in which Aboriginal people have had more success than in any other — in the 1980s it was calculated that 15 per cent of Australian boxing champions have been Aboriginal.[6] Boxing has always held a great fascination for me personally. It is important to understand that like both the NRL and AFL today, with so many great Indigenous players acting as beacons of pride for the Aboriginal community, in the past boxing was the main accessible sporting arena that provided such inspiration.

Boxing: The sweet science — A personal reflection

My own interest in boxing was fostered from an early age. I must have been around six or seven when an uncle used to come around with boxing gloves for me and a bigger cousin and other kids to go at it throwing leather. It was also at this time that I first became aware of Muhammad Ali, or Cassius Clay as he was known then, through reading newspapers (I was from an early age addicted to reading the news) and listening to adult conversation. Ali won the gold medal in the Rome 1960 Olympics, beating Australian Tony Madigan on the way to the Olympic final. In 1964 Ali was bigger news when he announced to the world at just 22 that he was indeed the 'greatest' in stopping Sonny Liston in Miami to become heavyweight champion of the world. Throughout the turbulent 1960s and 1970s Ali was a constant source of inspiration through his exploits in the ring and his political rhetoric out of it. I remember vividly when he was stripped of his world title and prevented from fighting for more than three years for his refusal to be drafted into the American army and his often quoted 'I ain't got nothing against them Vietcong' and the often misquoted addition 'they never called me nigger'.[7]

Aboriginal involvement with boxing through those years was also inspiring to a young boy. I can remember seeing Lionel Rose beat Rocky Gattellari on a grainy black and white TV set. Early the next year, in 1968, Lionel went to Tokyo and won the World Bantamweight Championship from the legendary Fighting Harada. I sat by a radio listening to the live broadcast of that fight and saw all of his later title defences against Takao Sakurai, Chucho Castillo, Alan Rudkin and eventual defeat by Ruben Olivares on TV. After winning the title in Tokyo and returning to Australia, Lionel was greeted by a crowd of more than 100,000 in Melbourne — more people than had greeted the Beatles on their visit to Australia. I kept a large scrapbook of newspaper cuttings of Lionel's fights and would pore over this book, devouring every tiny detail of the fights in the blow-by-blow accounts as delivered in the press. In 1968 Lionel Rose visited Newcastle to promote his new biography *Lionel Rose: Australian*, and at that particular moment in time he was unquestionably the most famous and popular Australian in the country. At the age of twelve I stood in a long queue that spilled out of a Newcastle department store and down the street, waiting for the chance to speak to Lionel and get him to sign my book, which he duly did. I can't even remember the words he said to me or if I even managed a reply. I was completely star-struck.

Newcastle, my hometown, was famous for Aboriginal boxers. The legendary Sands brothers had trained at Tom Macguire's gymnasium in close walking distance from my home and did their roadwork (boxers run on the road to build up stamina) on Broadmeadow racecourse where there was a community of Aboriginal jockeys, including my father Merv Maynard. Sadly Dave Sands was killed in a trucking accident before he had the chance to win a world title. His was one of the biggest funerals ever witnessed in Newcastle. In the late 1960s and 1970s I watched TV Ringside and followed the exploits of Tony Mundine and, no disrespect to 'Choc', but his father was a much better boxer. Hector Thompson from Kempsey was the best Australian fighter I ever saw, a beautiful boxer, with power-laden body punching – Hector fought unsuccessfully for two World titles including going up against the legendary 'Hands of Stone' Roberto Duran. However, Hector had killed two fighters in the ring and understandably was not the same fighter afterwards. I remember in the early 1970s a mob of us following Hector Thompson down Beaumont Street in Hamilton (the Newcastle suburb where Hector lived at the time), heading to the Newcastle show. We pulled palings off the showground fence and entered by climbing through under the trotters' horse stalls. We followed along behind Hector to Jimmy Sharman's Boxing Tent and we got in under the back of the tent to watch Hector flog the Sharman boxers.

I only had one fight in a boxing ring and I derive a great deal of pleasure from its memory. In school I had to cop the usual playground taunts of 'Abo' that carry the same connotation as 'nigger' in the USA. When I now look back I don't blame the kids. Children are not born racist; they are taught it. I blame the parents: they all knew who my father was and that he was married to my mother, a white woman. During the later days of primary school and early high school there was one particular kid, a dead-set bully, who taunted me constantly with the racist tag at every opportunity. He was apparently a 'Golden Gloves' boxing prodigy at the local police boys and RSL clubs. One particular day I was walking past the front of the local RSL club's Youth Centre that had its big doors open, and you could look in and see a large group of people, kids and the boxing ring. With my boxing interest my eyes went straight to the boxing ring and there, standing in the corner wearing a pair of gloves and staring out to the street, was this kid. He had spotted me walking past and now yelled out, 'Hey "Abo", why don't you come in and have a go?' I stopped, looked, and then began to walk on. He called out again, 'What, you too scared?' I stopped again, turned and walked in, and said, 'Yeah, I'll fight you'. One of the men helped me up into the ring and some old bloke sat me down in the corner and put the gloves on me before asking 'Can you fight mate'? I just said, 'I'll go alright'. The bell clanged, and I came out like Jimmy Carruthers against Vic Toweel, the South African world champion. I don't know how many punches I threw in a blistering onrush, but 90 per cent of them connected and a lot of pent up anger was unleashed onto the so-called 'big thing' of local kid boxing. Eventually he fell to the floor under a hail of blows, and the referee had to haul me off as I continued to bombard him on the ground in the corner. He was just sitting there on his backside howling in a torrent of tears and I had this incredible sense of satisfaction. I was surrounded by a number of the older white guys saying they wanted me to join their boxing club. I just said, 'No. Not interested'. I climbed down out of the ring and walked out the door without a backward glance. Not many can say they have a 100 per cent ring record and knocked out a 'Golden Gloves' champ in the process.

I guess boxing was always something of a passion because we had so many great fighters. Boxing has always been a magnet to Aboriginal men hoping to make an impact and improve their families' living conditions.

The inspiration of Jack Johnson

It is now more than 100 years since Jack Johnson first visited Australia. Johnson was not just a boxing-ring sensation but an articulate, charismatic, politically outspoken and inspiring individual. Johnson's boxing invincibility, and his defiant determination to be master of his own destiny in the ring and out, shook the white world's perceptions of racial superiority to the very foundations. Johnson began his working life on the docks of Galveston, Texas, and it was his intersection with Aboriginal dockworkers (including my grandfather, Fred Maynard) in Sydney that would influence long-term Aboriginal political voice and dissent. Jack Johnson would leave a lasting impression and provide the forerunner of long-term international Black influence upon Aboriginal people across the twentieth century. The influence of many notables including Marcus Garvey, Martin Luther King, Malcolm X, Muhammad Ali and the Black Panthers would follow.

Jack Johnson first visited Australia in 1907, and I've previously written about my grandfather Fred Maynard who attended a farewell to Johnson in Sydney that year, organised by the Coloured Progressive Association.[8] Both Richard Broome and I wrote of the impact of the Tommy Burns and Jack Johnson heavyweight title fight held in Sydney during Johnson's second visit in 1908. Johnson's victory unsettled white Australia and rattled the white world outside of the ring as well. During the late nineteenth and early twentieth centuries, as Broome writes:

> most Australians were deeply influenced by the prevailing ideas about race and human development. The most popular notion was that there was a hierarchy of races based upon their material development, which placed the Anglo-Saxon race at the top and the dark skinned peoples at the bottom, nearest the primates. Social Darwinist thought heightened this belief in unequal and competing racial types, which were involved in the struggle for existence. These ideas existed against the backdrop of Aboriginal–European conflict; the long struggle to establish immigration restriction legislation to keep Australia white; and the increasing fear after 1900 of an invasion of the wide open Australian spaces by the Asian 'hordes'. It was in 1908 that this race struggle pressure forced the *Bulletin* to abandon its parochial banner of 'Australia for Australians' and proclaim, 'Australia for the white man'.[9]

Jack Johnson would not only challenge these misinformed inaccuracies and terrify the white world with a sharp reality check, but make an inspirational impact on black, oppressed and Indigenous communities across the globe. Richard Broome described Jack Johnson as much more than just a magnificent boxer: 'He apparently sang well and played the double bass at every chance. He was a great talker, quite a wit, and an extrovert of the first order – altogether a man of considerable intelligence for those who cared to see it.'[10] Certainly the coming of Johnson to Australia gave Aboriginal people an identifiable black icon of great celebrity to cheer, and to emulate. In the wake of Johnson's victory over Tommy Burns in Sydney, journalist Randolph Bedford bemoaned the fact that: 'Already the insolent black's victory causes skin troubles in Woolloomooloo', further lamenting that, an 'hour after, I heard a lascar [Indian sailor] laying down the law of Queensberry to two whites, and they listened humbly. It is a bad day for Australia'. Another writer in the *Bulletin* complained: 'Johnson's behaviour in the ring was objectionable, so much so that if it had happened in America, someone would have shot him dead to the cheers of the crowd and given the film as defence evidence and got a verdict of "justifiable homicide"'.[11]

The global black population's adulation was clearly evident in the words of a Solomon Islander who was at the fight. He later stated it was simply 'the greatest day of my life'.[12] Johnson himself would recall looking out through the crowd during round breaks and spotting a black man in the crowd:

> As my gaze wandered out into the surrounding territory, I saw a coloured man sitting on a fence watching the fight with open mouth and bulging eyes. My glance returned to him again and again. He was one of the very few coloured people present, and he became a sort of landmark for me.[13]

On Jack Johnson's return voyage to the northern hemisphere, the RMS *Makura* stopped in Fiji. On its departure Johnson 'was greatly honoured by the natives, who assembled in hundreds to bid him farewell'.[14] There had been a similar response on his return voyage back to the United States from Australia in 1907, on board the *Somona*:

> The manner in which Johnson conducted himself in the centre of Auckland's lionising crowd, if not over modest, was at least reasonable...At Pago Pago, the United States possession in the Samoan group, Johnson was followed by crowds of admiring natives, who are themselves no mean specimens as regards size and build.[15]

A report of an Aboriginal sports day held at Tilba Tilba on the South Coast of NSW in 1909 noted that Jack Johnson's victory over Tommy Burns 'was evidently uppermost in the minds of the [A]borigines, as most of the day was devoted to boxing contests.'[16]

The joy Aboriginal people had taken in Johnson's victory over Burns in Sydney had not abated and evidence reveals that they had continued to follow his exploits around the globe: 'Johnson's notoriety while in Australia and the high degree of racial hostility associated with his fights here and in the USA meant that many people were eagerly following the fight with Jim Jeffries in 1910'.[17] Heather Goodall unearthed a wonderful story of a farmer on the north coast of NSW, Cunningham Henderson, who had recorded his memories of the Johnson–Jeffries fight:

> It was the day of the Johnson–Jeffries fight in America. Because of Johnson's colour the black boys took a keen interest in the fight and were discussing it. Just then a blasting shot went off in a stone quarry a few miles away, which we heard plainly. Yabsley turned quickly to Alfie (an Aboriginal labourer) and said – 'Did you hear that?' 'Yes Boss, What that feller?' 'That was Jeffries hitting Johnson!' Alfie quickly cupped his hand, held it to his ear, and striking a listening attitude, said – 'No Boss, I never heard the people shout!' (meaning there was no applause) The laugh was against the boss.[18]

Goodall writes that the fact that Henderson remembered the Aboriginal men's discussion and banter suggests that 'its significance ran deeply for them all'.[19]

Even in Pentridge Prison black pride was running high, after Jack Johnson's demolition of the 'Great White Hope' Jim Jeffries in Reno. A commentator noted that 'bright and early on Tuesday last, and not long after midday every prisoner in the stockade knew the result':

> The proudest man among all the shady characters confined in the big prison was the shadiest of them all, the [N]egro King. He puffed up with racial pride, assumed a most arrogant demeanour towards the white trash, as he termed his

fellow prisoners, and made no bones about letting all and sundry know his views concerning the undoubted superiority of his race, as proved by the victory of Jack Johnson.[20]

Aboriginal people longed for inspiration to break the chains of oppression and, writes Broome, 'boxing provided needed heroes for a people attempting the difficult task of resisting cultural domination'.[21] It is little wonder that Aboriginal people found Jack Johnson just such a hero. He was his own man, had cars, money and adulation. Even the most forbidden fruit for a black man of that time period – a white woman – was not taboo to Jack Johnson. He made it quite clear: 'I am not a slave and...I have the right to choose who my mate shall be without the dictation of any man'.[22] His preference for white wives, girlfriends and consorts shocked, scandalised and challenged the white world and in particular disturbed the perceived dominant position of white manhood. In Australia, 'very few dark men marry white women, as there is tremendous feeling against such matches on the part of the white community. The only way in which Aboriginal men could hope to cross the caste barrier was, they and others believed, through sport.'[23] Successful Aboriginal boxers seemed to prove that point, as Ron Richards, Dave Sands and Lionel Rose all married white women.

The first Aboriginal Australian boxing champion, Jerry Jerome had no hesitation in stating that it was Jack Johnson who inspired him to take up boxing. Jerome also followed Johnson's stance of demanding his place of equality on all counts. Jerome led a strike at Taroom Aboriginal settlement in 1916. He refused to work and incited 'all others to refuse work unless paid'. The government administrator regarded him as 'a pernicious and retarding influence, his position as a moneyed gentleman gives him privileges which he abuses and takes a mean advantage of to obstruct discipline and defy authority'.[24]

Years later, Johnson's inspiration still continued in Aboriginal communities. In Broome in the Kimberley in 1923 a newspaper report revealed that three Aboriginal 'vegetable garden robbers' of watermelons had been apprehended. All three, the article attested were of the 'half-caste menace breed'. Two were cautioned and one told to be out of Broome within 24 hours. One of the men, Christopher Taylor, stated boldly that he would go to Perth and become a boxing champion. The white men present in the courtroom burst into laughter and said, 'You would get killed in the ring'. Taylor retorted defiantly, 'They couldn't kill Jack Johnson,' silencing the court.[25]

Jack Johnson would hold the world title for seven years, but eventually fled the United States because of trumped-up charges of trafficking white women (the white woman was actually Johnson's girlfriend at the time and the White-Slave Traffic Act, known at the Mann Act, had been enacted just for Jack Johnson).[26] In 1915 Johnson lost the title in Havana to Jess Willard, although controversy over the decision, and over the aftermath of the fight, rages to this day. Johnson claimed that he was made an offer that, if he lost the fight, the charges against him would be dropped and he could return to the United States. He did return but was jailed for nine months, and though he returned to boxing was never given the chance to regain the lost title. Johnson at age 68 was killed in a motor accident on 10 June 1946.[27] Apparently he was 'speeding at more than seventy miles an hour. The reason for Johnson's speeding is said to have been indignation that, at a dinner, he'd been told he could only eat out the back'.[28] Eventually Johnson would be regarded along with Joe Louis, Sugar Ray Robinson and Muhammad Ali as one of the greatest fighters of all time. He is an inspiration to future generations of black athletes and was a trailblazer of black inspiration, self-belief and triumph.

The philosophy and opinions of Jack Johnson: Archaeology, science, art, music and literature

Nonetheless, through all of the commentary and reporting of the fight with Burns in Sydney and Jeffries in Reno, the vast majority of accounts were written from a white perspective. What did Johnson himself have to say about Australia and race relations? What were his interests? What did he think of boxing? Today, through the aid of Trove we have access to thousands of newspaper accounts of Johnson's visits to Australia, including a couple of revealing letters by and interviews with the man himself.

Jack Johnson had displayed interest, knowledge and appreciation of traditional Aboriginal life during his visits to Australia. 'I spend most of my spare time in the art galleries and the museum,' he stated:

My principle hobby is archaeology. When I visit your museum and see the numerous specimens of prehistoric man's art, your boomerangs of many varieties, your stone axes from various States and the many examples of Palaeolithic and Neolithic man's skill – simply I envy you. We in America have our rude stone flint quartz implements but they do not show anything like the same forethought or skill as yours. Your central Australian natives must have been men of genius to have turned out such artistic and ideal weapons.[29]

In analysing Jack Johnson's statements, interviews and observations it is evident that he was genuinely interested in and knowledgeable about the arts and science. He was well read and a competent and keen musician. In writing to a Sydney friend, William Phillips, he enquired:

How are all the boys in your part of the world? Do you know whether David (Professor David, of the University of Sydney. – Ed.) made a success of that little theory he was engaged upon when I was last there? I refer to those fossilised specimens, which he got at 100deg from the Pole. I fancy he must come to agree with me that they belong to the quaternery [sic], and not the tertiary period. I saw Shackleton when in New York. We had him down for a couple of days on wildfowl sport.[30]

Professor Edgeworth David was in his own lifetime a very famous name as a geologist with the University of Sydney, and an Antarctic explorer (he led the first expedition to the South Magnetic Pole). He was awarded the Distinguished Service Order and promoted to Lieutenant Colonel in WWI, and was responsible for discovering the Hunter Valley coalfields.[31]

In another letter to Phillips, Johnson further revealed his scientific interest and insistence on meticulous questioning: 'We scientists Phillips are curious fellows. We all quibble over what to the uninitiated would appear trivial, but in all my researches I make a point of working my theories in a methodical manner.'[32] The interests of Jack Johnson and his thirst for knowledge and in developing his own self-motivated education and ideas were truly amazing. Boxing itself he felt at the time was but a means to an end:

> I live for art and science and music alone. The fistic business is but my recreation. I do it to keep my mind pure and simple. I would sooner give up my studies in chemistry, archaeology, and astronomy than lose art...England, France, Rome and Germany are the places we professional and cultured artists ought to live in.[33]

Clearly, for Jack Johnson it was not just about beating white opponents in the ring but also demonstrating that he was the intellectual equal or superior to anyone. He would leave no stone unturned in that pursuit. He revealed that in the lead-up to the Jim Jeffries heavyweight fight he relaxed after breakfast reading his 'favourite authors — Shakespeare, Tennyson, Milton, Tacitus, Juvenal, and Pliny'. He was clearly well read and unpacked the deep meaning of texts in relation to his own experiences. In another letter that found its way to the newspapers, Johnson wrote:

> I was reading 'Paradise Lost.' You know this passage:— 'Darkened so, yet shone above them all the Archangel, but his face deep scars of thunder had entrenched, and care sat on his faded cheek, but under brows of doubtless courage and considerate pride, waiting revenge.' Tis the same with me.[34]

He would then after lunch 'betake myself to our large drawing-room, and rattle, first of all, a few rhapsodies or extravaganzas from Beethoven, Brahms or weird Wagner on our grand piano'.[35]

The issue of Australia: Race, religion and boxing

Jack Johnson saw and promoted himself as the first wave of an inevitable global challenge to the white world's perception of its lofty place at the head of the racial table. He openly challenged the colonial concepts of power as held by Australia, England, France and the United States:

> Read the reports of the increase of the coloured peoples of India, Japan, and China. Read the increase of the people of my own race in their own country. Do you think it is to

go on forever, this domination of the millions of people of colour by a handful of white folks. I think it is not. It may not come in my time nor in yours, but the time will come when the black and yellow man will hold the earth, and the white man will be regarded just as the coloured man is now.[36]

In a personal letter to a Mr Hicks Hardy of the Sydney Motoring School, Jack Johnson revealed the inherent racism of his own country, the United States:

I need not tell you, Hicks, that in America the racial question is very rampant just now. Our country [Africa], taken from us, is ruled by whites, and any sign of superiority on our part is regarded as a crime. They regard people of my colour as little better than dogs. Education does not count, and neither does refinement or high breeding. Colour with them is everything. Now fancy, Hardy, Could you believe such things possible? Here I am a cultured man, fit to converse on any topic – from astronomy right down to ancient classics – tabooed by white individuals whom I regard, both as regards race and education, as my inferiors.[37]

Johnson's political position is complex to say the least. Nonetheless, he was a very proud black man and his achievements were recognised by some of the most influential black leaders of the time. WEB DuBois was adamant that Jack Johnson was hated by the white world not because he was a champion boxer, but simply because of his 'unforgivable blackness'.[38] Marcus Garvey, founder of the biggest black movement ever established in the United States, the Universal Negro Improvement Association, was an ardent follower of Jack Johnson. Despite Johnson having lost his world title in 1915, Garvey gave him consistent coverage in his paper *The Negro World*, even running a serialised comic strip on his life.[39] Johnson's comments that Africa had been stolen 'from us' to be ruled by whites echoes Garvey's thinking. Garvey realised that Johnson challenged the racial doctrine of the time, and clearly proved that blacks were not just the equal of whites but could be their betters.

Jack Johnson firmly believed that it was not just his magnificent physique that enabled him to become such a formidable boxing champion. He outsmarted other boxers and was a great strategist and tactician in the ring and out of it. Even more importantly, it is evident Johnson was using boxing as a vehicle to demonstrate that his race was not inferior – either physically or intelligently – to anyone. As early as 1912 the FBI (or BI, as it was known then) was formulating plans to target and undermine both Johnson and 'the hard-hitting New Negroes who followed Jack Johnson' with such pride.[40] There was a growing, genuine fear on the part of the authorities over the inspirational uplift that Johnson was having upon the oppressed masses.

Jack Johnson delivered a lecture at the Coloured Branch of the New York YMCA in 1910 where he outlined his own personal insight into boxing: 'To approach intelligently or to apprehend the psychology of pugilism, it is essential that the student grasp the distinction between the venal side and that side that makes for the up-building of manliness with all that, in the common acceptation of the terms it implies.' Adding further: 'Learn to use your hands, and not to fall over your own feet. Your social success will follow as the dawn the dark'.[41] Certainly in his early career Jack Johnson was meticulous in his preparation for a fight and this continued right through to his match-up with Jim Jeffries in Reno in 1910. He did frequently divulge rumours that he was not training and was drinking far too much champagne before bouts so as to get a better price to gamble on his own victory. In the aftermath of the Jeffries bout he clearly did not train to the same high standards he had previously set himself. Nevertheless, he still had no trouble in beating his opponents in the ring. Johnson was able to draw his strength and self-belief from multiple and often surprising influences including religion.

Throughout his life Jack Johnson was a devout Methodist. Broome has speculated that the raw political edge to Johnson was honed back in Texas by being 'a leading member of his local (black) Methodist Church, and also involved in municipal politics in Galveston, at a time when black civil rights were coming under renewed attack in the south'.[42] He attended church in Australia but could not hide his contempt for the Australian clergy and its ministers stating that the 'leading members of the Church simply drew the colour line, and consequently did not turn up at the fight'.[43] He was extremely critical of the hypocrisy of religion in the hands of some, and the bias that the white world used to manipulate their sense of position, entitlement and power:

> These people – these Christians – attend church, pray regularly, and yet pick out of the New and Old Testaments only those things, which are agreeable to themselves. Worse than this, the very clergymen recognise that unless they pander to the popular taste they might as well shut up shop.[44]

Johnson did convey best wishes to the Reverend WG Taylor of the Central Methodist Mission in Pitt Street, Sydney 'whose sermons Sunday after Sunday gave me great comfort...Like myself he is fighting the good fight – far ahead of pugilistic encounters'.[45] Back in Australia, there was a public backlash labelling Jack Johnson's statements of attending church as 'humbug', but Reverend Taylor came out in the press and confirmed that 'while in Sydney, Johnson was a regular attendant, with his wife, at the Methodist Church, and that he was a most devout worshipper'.[46] Johnson also passed on his regards to 'all my old comrades in Methodism whom I met there'.[47] It is another point of possible connection with my grandfather Fred Maynard, who also was a Methodist.

On Australians Jack Johnson had some sobering news:

> You Australians, Hardy, are not what I should call an altogether bad lot. You have your faults, of course. Every young nation is bound to have a lot of what is termed 'rotters,' and in this respect I sincerely sympathise with you, for certainly you have more than your share.[48]

During the fight with Tommy Burns in Sydney, Jack Johnson had continuously provoked the crowd by grinning and smiling widely to those at ringside. This was later immortalised by writer Jack London, who wrote of one irate spectator screaming: 'He'll knock the smile off you directly, you flash nigger'. Johnson, ever the consummate showman and in complete control of his space, 'turned as cool as ice. "Well! He's jes' doin' his little best," he yelled back: "but I can't help smilin'. He's a ticklin' me to death!"[49] As Joyce Carol Oates reveals, Jack Johnson had 'perfected the precarious art of playing with and to a hostile audience, like a bullfighter who seduces his clumsy opponent (including the collective 'opponent' of the audience) into participating in, in fact heightening, the opponent's own defeat. To step into the ring with a Trickster is to risk not only losing your fight but your dignity'.[50]

Johnson, like Muhammad Ali all those years later, had his own 'shuffle' in the Burns' fight in Sydney: 'Johnson opened round 8 with a jig step as he rose from his corner'.[51] Ali would infuriate the establishment with his refusal to be drafted to fight in Vietnam, and in a similar fashion in an interview in London Jack Johnson stated: 'Fight for America? Well I should say not. What has America ever done for me or my race?'[52] During World War I he further fuelled racist antagonism stating 'Oh, to hell with them, [the USA] I would not believe any promises they would have made me. The Germans treat me as a man, and my wife as a lady'.[53]

Conclusion

In conclusion, and on a personal note, I express my admiration and respect for Richard Broome who, like me, has seen the importance of an Aboriginal presence in the history of this continent. We have written to overcome the missing, forgotten, obscure, overlooked and erased Indigenous aspects of Australian history. I have as part of this chapter displayed the main drivers of my own historical practice that includes restoration history combined with personal experience, observation and narrative in delivering an Aboriginal perspective of our experiences. Both Richard and I have had an avid interest in boxing as it pertains to Aboriginal fighters and in this essay I particularly focused on research of Jack Johnson and his impact in Australia and upon Aboriginal people. Johnson was an incredibly courageous individual who was the master of his own direction through life and provides insight to the concept of agency by oppressed individuals and groups in history. The racism Jack Johnson experienced in Australia in the early decade of the twentieth century opens a window for judgement and appraisal on how far Australia has actually progressed. Many would state that it is all a distant chapter of our past – but today we continue to witness the vilification and opposition to boat people and Muslims and the continuing appalling statistics of disadvantage suffered by Aboriginal Australia. In a modern day re-enactment of the racist hostility hurled at Jack Johnson we recently witnessed the shocking white crowd behaviour directed at Aboriginal AFL star Adam Goodes and the subsequent media-fuelled circus that followed.[54] Stan Grant, in an inspiring recent talk, spoke of the sad reality of the Australian Dream and concluded that on reflection that dream is someone else's nightmare.[55]

> I leave the final word on Jack Johnson to Muhammad Ali:
>
> Throughout his life, people said 'no' to Jack Johnson. But Johnson believed he had a right to succeed and that no one, not strangers, not even friends had the right to set limits on his ambition. Jack Johnson did not lead an easy life. But he trusted his own judgement; he believed in his abilities and he was willing to work to achieve the goals he set himself. Jack Johnson became Heavyweight Champion of the World and one of the most famous fighters of all time because he knew it doesn't matter how many people say 'you can't', so long as you believe you can.[56]

Postscript

Since writing this article the world has lost the 'Greatest', Muhammad Ali. I never met Ali but he was an inspiring influence upon me. It was not just his exploits as a boxer but as a man prepared to stand by his principles and add his voice for the wronged, disadvantaged and impoverished. He was a champion in every sense of the word. Vale Muhammad Ali.

CHAPTER 5

Nyungar domains
Reading Gyalliput's geography and mobility in the colonial archive

Tiffany Shellam

I was privileged to have Richard Broome as a lecturer during my undergraduate degree in History at La Trobe University. I enrolled in all of his units: Australian History 101, his Aboriginal History units and History, Heritage and Landscapes, which was Richard's first foray into teaching environmental history. Richard was an enthusiastic and engaging lecturer, and his passion for history and Aboriginal rights was infectious. With Marilyn Lake, Richard also supervised my honours thesis, during which time he offered generous mentorship, guiding me through the sometimes tricky maze of Aboriginal history and the political nature of museums, areas in which he has solid expertise.

One of Richard's Aboriginal history lectures was particularly influential for me. It was a lecture on Aboriginal land management and Richard had collected a range of sources that were recorded by settlers who were living close to Aboriginal groups on the threshold of colonisation. The lecture highlighted Aboriginal people's deep connection to their country and the social maps and stories that are inscribed on the landscape itself. The lecture created a rich discussion amongst the students about how historians might search for such connections to country in traditional colonial archives. One of Richard's overhead slides projected 'Mokare's Domain' onto the wall. It was a European map of Mokare's country, delineating his estate with exact borderlands and campsites within it. This map revealed deep history. Richard added to this map by telling us some of the names for Mokare's campsites and placenames for aspects of his country; he described how Mokare's kin networks allowed him to travel over particular tracts of country and explained the management involved in caring for his country. I remember suddenly recognising Mokare's domain, realising that I knew it well, but not as intimately as the way Richard could describe it with this map and other sources.[1] Mokare was a Mineng Nyungar man from King George's Sound, near the site of the present-day town of Albany, in the south west of Western Australia. I grew up in Perth and my family would escape the city's summer heat and move to the south coast for a month each year. I had walked through Mokare's domain many times but had only understood it in a superficial way: through the shops and beaches and forest walks around the seaside town.

Richard's lecture was powerful because it revealed to me the interdisciplinarity of historical sources — archaeology, geography, botany, ethnography — and the possibilities they offered for understanding past Aboriginal landscapes and geographies. 'Mokare's Domain' eventually led me to my PhD research where I would use Mokare's geography and environmental knowledge as an important backdrop to explore intimate relationships between the Mineng Nyungar and the garrison soldiers of the 39th Regiment who had been directed by the Colonial Office in London to set up a depot on the fringes of Mokare's country in December 1826.[2] Some of the soldiers, such as Captain Collet Barker, Commandant of the settlement between 1829 and 1831, and Alexander Collie, Government Resident at the settlement between 1831 and 1833, understood that they were *visitors* and Mokare and his family were *hosting* them on their country. Collie expressed his presence on Mineng country in the following way: 'we certainly had come into their country and set [ourselves] down at, if not in, their homes and upon their territories'.[3]

During my PhD research in the National Archives in Kew, UK, I came across a sketch of another Nyungar campsite, scratched onto paper with a quill and ink in 1833 by a man named Gyalliput. This map describes Gyalliput's geographical and social domain. Unlike Mokare's domain which was a map constructed by a historian utilising a variety of source material,

Gyalliput's map was expressed and drawn by Gyalliput himself. Aboriginal maps of country are necessarily specific to a locale. However, the genesis of Gyalliput's map – the encounter during which it was constructed – is also a reminder of Aboriginal mobility. Gyalliput was not on his country when he drew this map, but on a political embassy in the Swan River settlement where he had come to connect with Nyungar people who were engaged in violent conflict with the settlers. This embassy was heralded as a success throughout the colony. Georgiana Molloy, with whom Gyalliput stayed at the nascent settlement at Augusta during a stopover on a subsequent voyage, wrote that Gyalliput's diplomacy at Swan River had effected 'a treaty'.[4] Gyalliput's map and story, therefore, represent the grounded geography of a mobile networker. This paper explores the context of the encounter which led Gyalliput to inscribe his country onto paper with a quill and ink, exploring further the idea of Gyalliput's mobility as *grounded*. By drawing on other archival records denoting Aboriginal geographies, this paper also seeks out possible motivations for Aboriginal people in this era to have their maps and statements about their country recorded.

Mineng Nyungar *boodjar*/country

Gyalliput was a Nyungar man from the south west of Western Australia. It was not easy to identify him with one specific place as he was a revered traveller and, therefore, appears in the colonial records across many districts during the early 1830s. He was most likely a Mineng Nyungar man as he frequently lived around the settlement at King George's Sound, and, after travelling, this is where he always returned. Therefore his country was somewhere in the vicinity of Mokare's domain, but he had kinship networks which extended to the north and west, near Augusta, a place where he also spent much time.[5]

The garrison settlement that was established at King George's Sound in 1826 was set up as a small holding-station or depot to deter threats of French possession, taking up a relatively small patch of Mineng land. The settlement was controlled by New South Wales until 4 March 1831 when it came under the jurisdiction of Swan River, which had been established as a private enterprise by Governor James Stirling in 1829. Unlike Swan River, which rapidly dispossessed the Whadjuk Nyungar groups, at King

George's Sound intimate, carefully negotiated relationships developed between garrison soldiers and Mineng people. Richard Broome's research that emphasised nuanced accounts of Aboriginal actions on Australia's frontier helped to inform my framing of this unique frontier relationship; it was a space where genuinely amicable cross-cultural relationships developed, albeit acted out with a fragile and sometimes dangerous diplomacy.[6] Nyungar novelist Kim Scott has suggested that in this era Mineng Nyungar were a community so confident of their place in the world that they welcomed the new: 'they were hospitable and generous landlords at that, curious about new cultural "devices" and cross-culturally competent enough to display the "habits" of the other in the interests of cross-cultural communication'.[7] The soldiers and convicts were single men, or stationed without their wives, and this enabled close friendships to develop with single Nyungar men, some occasionally sleeping in the soldiers' huts. Such relationships came about over time through patient negotiations by soldier and Mineng alike. King George's Sound became a model of a friendly cross-cultural community where the Aboriginal inhabitants were deemed 'peaceful and friendly' by settler-observers and travellers who visited the settlement.[8] Indeed, so peaceful was this little settlement that, during the early 1830s, settlers living in the violent, tumultuous world of the Swan River settlement believed that a visit from the 'friendly natives' at King George's Sound would greatly benefit them in their hostile situation at Swan River.

Embassy to Swan River

While the garrison at King George's Sound was not a colonising, expanding settlement, at Swan River migrants had spread their townships over three different Aboriginal territories: Beeliar, Beeloo and Mooro. Unlike the amicable relationships at King George's Sound, when the settlements at Perth, Guildford and Fremantle began to expand, spearings and shootings followed. Predictable tropes depicting 'violent Aborigines' quickly developed. One warrior from Beeliar country, named Yagan, was detained in 1832 and, with two others, Donmera and Ningina, were held captive on Carnac Island off the coast of Fremantle. Robert Menli Lyon, a humanitarian settler concerned about Nyungar welfare, requested to be included as part of Yagan's detention on Carnac Island. He was eager to instruct these Nyungar men to read and write, and he hoped to learn their language. As he did not yet speak their language he suggested that some of the 'friendly natives' from King George's Sound come to Carnac Island to mediate between Yagan and himself. At this time, settlers did not realise the diversity in language and customs of Aboriginal groups in relatively close proximity. Lyon sailed to King George's Sound to discuss the idea with the Government Resident; however, as Lyon did not have the support of the Colonial Secretary at Swan River the Mineng were not allowed to accompany him to Carnac Island and so he went there without them.[9] After one month on Carnac Island, Yagan, Donmera and Ningina escaped, taking the island's only boat in the middle of the night and rowing back to the mainland.

On hearing Lyon's request for assistance to mediate between the Aboriginal people and settlers at Swan River, and learning about their dire relationship, in early 1833 Gyalliput and his co-traveller, Manyat, also a Mineng Nyungar, urgently 'requested' to travel in the government schooner to Swan River.[10] This request was agreed to by the Colonial Secretary and they arrived in Fremantle on 18 January 1833. These two men stayed at Swan River for one month. They were clothed and housed by prominent settlers such as George Fletcher Moore and George Leake, who were very interested in these enigmatic Aboriginal travellers and who held high hopes of their 'friendly' influence among the Swan River groups. Moore described them as 'good humoured, quiet fellows'.[11] The Acting Governor, Frederick Chidley Irwin, ordered the storekeeper to issue them with flour, salt meat, tea and sugar from the colonial stores.[12] Stories about their tour featured in each edition of the *Perth Gazette* during their stay.[13] The Aboriginal groups around Swan River were equally interested in these southern visitors, and several meetings were set up. They met with the now outlawed Yagan at Monger's Lake on Mooro country. This was not Yagan's country, but the country of Yellagonga. Meeting on Mooro country may have been symbolic of the upheavals rupturing traditional rights to land at this time. At this meeting Yagan and Gyalliput engaged in a spear-throwing competition; they also exchanged their kangaroo skin cloaks which Manyat and Gyalliput had brought with them from King George's Sound, and, as the paper recorded, 'a description of their native District' was also transacted. Yagan adopted his visitors into his own group by exchange of names, a sign of their acceptance into Beeliar country. According to the *Perth Gazette*, Gyalliput and Manyat described their country to Yagan, told him about 'the kind treatment and benefit they had received from the "white people" and an exhortation to Yagan and his followers to conduct themselves in a peaceable and friendly manner towards their white neighbours.'[14] Yagan, in response, described his recent imprisonment on Carnac, and the 'nature of [his] connection with their white associates'.[15]

At a separate encounter they met with senior Mooro man, Yellagonga. The *Perth Gazette* reported that the languages of Yellagonga and Manyat and Gyalliput were so dissimilar that they could only 'interchange of the names of their respective districts, and those of some of the adjoining tribes'.[16] Identifying Aboriginal strangers with their geographic domains was crucial before proper meetings could take place.

At Morgan's table

At Swan River Manyat and Gyalliput were hosted by settlers in their homes. In the second week of their visit they stayed with John Morgan at his residence. Morgan was a complex colonial character who wrote conflicting representations of Aboriginal people at Swan River.[17] As Government Resident in Perth, in 1833 Morgan made it clear to the settlers that firearms were available from him if there was a need for 'prompt and heavy punishment on the natives, should their conduct at any time be considered to deserve it.'[18] He was also a scribe for Gyalliput and later for the 'wild white man', William Buckley, which adds further complexity to his character. Morgan had arrived with the first migrants to Swan River on the *Parmelia* in 1829 to take up the position of colonial storekeeper, residing first on Garden Island off the coast of Fremantle, before moving to Perth when he was made Justice of the Peace and Government Resident. In 1830 he was granted 2000 acres of Nyungar land along the Canning River, south of Perth. During his residence at Swan River he wrote many letters to Colonial Undersecretary Robert

Hay, describing the colony's progress. Hay's influence with British Prime Minister, Viscount Goderich, later assisted Morgan's rise when he was offered the role of police magistracy at Richmond, Van Diemen's Land, which he took up in 1834. In Van Diemen's Land he became foundation editor of the *Hobart Town Advertiser*. It was in this role of editor and journalist that he met Buckley, a convict who absconded in 1803 from the settlement camp at Sullivan Bay, near present-day Sorrento, and lived amongst the Aboriginal people of Port Phillip for 32 years. Morgan scripted and published Buckley's narrative in 1852 – 17 years after Buckley had walked into John Batman's camp at Indented Head near Geelong.[19] The published narrative was a jointly-authored product, constructed for financial reasons that would help both Morgan and Buckley. Buckley was on a government pension and Morgan had recently retired as editor of the *Hobart Town Advertiser*. The publication would give them both an income. The Victorian government added 40 pounds to Buckley's yearly pension and Morgan profited from the sales.[20]

Morgan acted as scribe for the semi-literate Buckley, and in the process embellished Buckley's experiences to suit their readership. Morgan reflected on his choice of language and style: 'In giving the history of a life in the first person, and under such peculiar circumstances, I have endeavoured to express the thoughts of a humble, unlearned man, in the language of simplicity and truth which, in my mind, is best suited to the subject, and to the circumstances as they passed in review before me.'[21] Writing Buckley's narrative, Morgan transformed Buckley's vignettes into a distilled story by selecting action, choosing adjectives carefully, particularly when describing the behaviour of the Aboriginal people that Buckley encountered. Morgan's narrative of Buckley's story is a negotiated telling.

Sitting at his table at his Swan River residence with Gyalliput on 28 January 1833, Morgan also acted as a scribe. While they sat together at Morgan's table, Morgan began to write a letter to Colonial Secretary Hay in London. It is not clear whether Gyalliput asked for a quill and ink, but Morgan gave them to him with a piece of paper. In this letter Morgan wrote a description of Swan River, describing daily life in the colony, shortages of labour and food, a recent exploration he had been involved in, and the tense and hostile situation that then existed between Aboriginal people and settlers. Morgan's letter is 15 pages long. At the end of the letter, Morgan wrote that Gyalliput was with him at the table and, 'has been with me the greater part of the time I have been writing this letter.' And, 'after amusing himself with a pen, at my table, which he now holds tolerably well, – he has just now drawn for me, a sketch of his native encampment.' Morgan thought this sketch was 'the first...certainly drawn by any Aborigine of this country'.[22] He was very impressed with Gyalliput's drawing skills. Gyalliput had, of course, been inscribing pictures, stories and maps in the sand and earth with a stick for many years.

Gyalliput's father, Maragnan was also a revered traveller throughout the Nyungar world. Aboriginal travellers had geographic knowledge far beyond their own domains or estates. In 1831 at King George's Sound Captain Barker quizzed Maragnan about the whereabouts of some escaped crown prisoners. Maragnan described campsites on a route from King George's Sound to north of the new settlement of Augusta, a distance of over 300 kilometres. He described all the major harbours, lakes and river mouths that existed along the Nyungar *bidi* or trackways.[23] At the same time he was describing the country verbally he also drew distances and shapes of harbours on the floor of Barker's sandy hut. He described distances in reference to landmarks in Mineng country: 'Nornalup is as far away from Quaranup as King George's Sound is from Green Island'.[24] Maragnan's evanescent map was made tangible and portable by Barker who committed his dirt map to paper in 1831.[25] This travel map is not represented as thin black lines on a blank page like a coloniser's map. Rather it is similar to the way that Paul Carter has described Inuit maps: 'fat, palpable and regional'.[26] It includes the number of moons travelled to indicate markers of distance and time and references Nyungar seasonal calendars to express times of the year: *Mondianong* for example.[27] Aboriginal maps are topographically structured and emphasise spatiality and connectivity. As David Turnbull suggests, both European and Aboriginal maps can only be read through the myths and stories that both groups tell about their relationship to the land.[28]

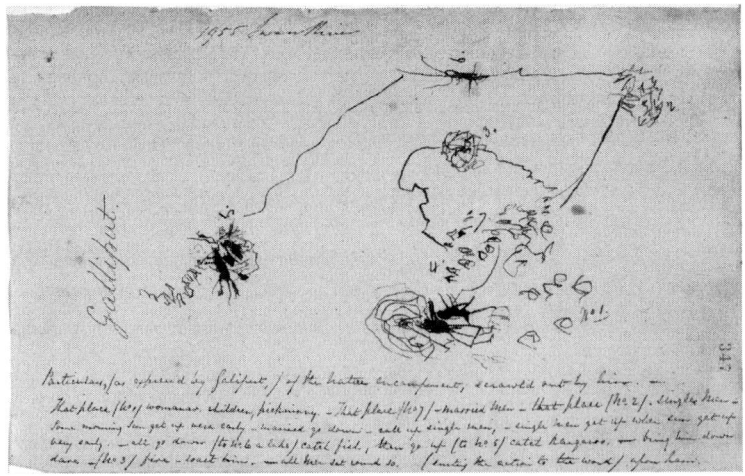

'Gyalliput's sketch', with permission of National Archives UK (CO 18, 13, f347, 1833, National Archives, UK).

Gyalliput's sketch is an aerial view of his campsite. Gyalliput and Morgan must have discussed the sketch, sitting side by side at Morgan's table while Gyalliput further explained his scratchy drawing. As Clint Bracknell has recently shown, Nyungar people often spoke in a recitative style, part spoken, part song, and Gyalliput chanted (and possibly acted out) the story of the sketch to Morgan as he transcribed it at the bottom of the map, adding a corresponding numbered reference to the pictures.[29] Morgan wrote: 'Particulars (as expressed by Galliput), of the native encampment, scrawled out by him.' It reads like this:

> That place no. 1 womanar, children, pickaninny. — That place (no. 7) — married men — that place (no. 2) single men — some morning sun get up very early — married go down — wake up the single men, — single men get up when sun get up very early. — all go down (to no. 6 a lake) catch fish, then go up (to no. 5) catch kangaroo — bring him down dare (no. 3) fire — roast him. — all men sit around so (entering the action to the word) upon ham.[30]

The last line of Gyalliput's story, 'all men sit around so...upon ham' can be understood as the men sitting on their backsides, as the term 'ham' was commonly used to describe a buttock with its associated thigh.[31] Morgan also suggests that Gyalliput's chant was accompanied by his actions and movements, for example, he showed Morgan exactly how the men sat on their 'hams', as Morgan wrote: 'entering the action to the word'. Morgan appears to have recorded Gyalliput's speech verbatim, reproducing his pronunciation and the rendition of his speech phonetically. While this story of Gyalliput's could be considered a co-production between Gyalliput and Morgan, it appears less entangled than Buckley's story, or for example, Eora man Bennelong's letter of 1791 for which Bennelong also had the assistance of a scribe.[32] Morgan wrote what Gyalliput dictated, evident in the sentence 'as expressed by Gyalliput'. As Penny Van Toorn has suggested, this style of recorded Aboriginal speech has Gyalliput's 'authorial authority'.[33]

As viewers we hover above the campsite, looking down onto it. We see that this map is more than a sketch of a campsite. It is a Mineng Nyungar geography that includes a lake where fish are caught and a kangaroo hunting ground. Gyalliput connected the different elements of place with people and daily routines, linking them with lines on the page. Morgan numbered these as Gyalliput recited his story.

It is telling that the fire (no. 3) is in the centre of the camp in Gyalliput's sketch. At King George's Sound, Captain Barker recorded that 'the Blacks...do not talk of such a one's hut but, to express his home or resting place, they say such a one's fire.'[34] This map reveals that 'Country' was inseparable from social spaces and stories about daily life that were so frequently recounted by Mineng people. Bill Gammage has noted the depth of Aboriginal geographies in his acclaimed book *The Biggest Estate on Earth: How Aborigines Made Australia*:

> In their country a family saw an environment shaped in the Dreaming and thronged with sites and stories, witnessed the familiarity plants, creatures and elements had with particular localities, and thought itself part of these intimacies. Not only obvious features which Europeans name, but every pebble and ripple disclosed both the ecological logic of its existence and the Dreaming's presence.[35]

Mokare, whose domain Richard had revealed to us in his lecture, shared Captain Barker's hut at King George's Sound. Without intention, he reinforced Gyalliput's story-map when he recounted similar daily rituals of the community to Barker: 'Now, now (about 9pm), the married men are all gone to sleep but the single men will talk and laugh till 12 o'clock. Tomorrow morning single men "sleep plenty" married men obliged to call them to make them get up.'[36] Similar elements appear in these two stories by Gyalliput and Mokare, which tell of ritualised social order. When they were recounted they were a reinstating of these men's understanding of their social space, in compliance with their gender, age and status within their community on their country. Mokare's story was given in response to Barker's description to him of his own country, England. Mokare wanted to know what countries were near it, making Barker tell him the names of all the adjacent countries and how they were situated in relation to England.[37]

As talk between Morgan and Gyalliput turned to Hay who lived in England, and the power invested in him as Undersecretary, Gyalliput may have been prompted to sketch his own country while Morgan wrote to this powerful white man. What was the motivation for Gyalliput's map? The space in which he drew it – John Morgan's house – while Morgan was writing a letter to a man of high authority, and sketched during Gyalliput's own political embassy to Swan River where he had heard about hostilities between Nyungar and settlers from Yagan, suggests a more powerful declaration or statement about his place. In Gyalliput's meetings with Yagan and Yellagonga, an exchange of the names of each groups' country took place, and a description of their domains. Did Gyalliput's sketch of his country stand in as a transaction of sorts with Hay – a powerful, distant white man? Gyalliput's map was slipped into the back of Morgan's letter, making its way to Hay in London. It is now housed in the National Archives in Kew, UK.

Pen and paper

The suggestion that Gyalliput's map was a powerful statement about his country may seem contrived, but when read alongside other colonial documents which record Aboriginal people's descriptions of their geographies, such as census records, we might read such a map as a determined recording of an Aboriginal domain.

During Lyon's self-enforced exile with Yagan on Carnac Island, he sat with the prisoners with pen and paper. Yagan told him about his geographic domain and that of other Nyungar groups and Lyon transcribed them onto paper. For example, Lyon wrote that Yagan's Beeliar territory was 'bounded by the Melville water and the Canning, on the north; by the mountains on the east; by the sea on the west; and by a line, due east from Mangles Bay in the south'.[38] Lyon was the first settler to record Whadjuk Nyungar territorial domains onto paper. Statements about Aboriginal boundaries and which individuals were connected to which tract of country were frequently told to newcomers who had a pen and paper in their hands.

Following the government-sanctioned Pinjarra massacre in 1834, Governor Stirling appointed Francis Fraser Armstrong as Interpreter to the Natives. Armstrong had learnt some Nyungar language and was friends with several Nyungar people. In September 1833 he had acted as a mediator when Munday and Miago met with Governor Stirling, speaking 'with a degree of fluency' the *Perth Gazette* reported, 'that we could have scarcely anticipated'.[39] While earlier attempts at enumerating the Aboriginal population had been conducted from a stationary depot in Perth, Armstrong was ordered to 'go amongst' the Aborigines, beyond the settled boundary, and collect statistics. Armstrong was mobile; his travels allowed him to get to know different groups of people away from the settlement, and to lay out their tribal boundaries onto paper through his descriptive statistical lists. Of course, he had the aid of Aboriginal intermediaries, cultural experts who shared their knowledge and brokered between him and the more distant Aboriginal groups, whose language he did not speak. I wonder what benefits they saw in having their knowledge and their placenames recorded by Armstrong. Motivations for collecting geographic knowledge by colonial authorities are easier to gauge. In his discussion on the connections between intimacy and knowledge gathering in Murihiku, a region south of the Waitaki River in New Zealand in the 1840s, Tony Ballantyne shows how colonial official Edward Shortland cultivated a 'strategic intimacy' with local iwi (tribe), Kai Tāhu. He describes how one chief, Te Huruhuru, told Shortland stories about his people, and laid down the geography of the interior of the South Island of New Zealand, 'sketching a map showing great lakes and inland plains, explaining the nature of the terrain, and the location of resources that Kai Tāhu valued'.[40] These intimate relationships, and the indigenous geographic knowledge recorded as a result, are central, Ballantyne argues, 'in understanding the fundamental mechanisms through which colonial authority was extended and consolidated'.[41] How did the colonised view this transaction?

Armstrong's 1837 census consists of seven lists of tribes in which he named the tribes, the individuals and families within them, their geographic location and territorial boundaries. Some of these lists, such as: 'Natives of Kan-eeng Boo-yang Beela or south side of the Murray Tribe', linked individuals to their specific ground and recorded the names of their country in their language as well as settler's geographic terms (south side of the Murray, for instance). Earlier enumerations had expressed Aboriginal geography relative to its proximity to the Perth settlement – first northern tribe for example – and did not include Indigenous names for country. The process of enumerating Aboriginal people at Swan River could be understood as attempts to sedentarise Aboriginal populations, at least in the minds and archives of settlers; however, we might see an alternative Aboriginal perspective of this colonial practice that viewed the recording of their country with pen and paper, to be kept in the colonisers' archive, as a significant gesture towards the acknowledgement of their custodianship of country.[42] Is this the way Nyungar people – who were in the midst of a destructive disequilibrium of their way of life – viewed such knowledge collection processes in the 1830s?

While Gyalliput's interest in the coloniser's pen and paper is unknowable today, Morgan suggested that he took time to learn how to use the pen properly as he sat at his table. While Gyalliput had most likely drawn his country on sand before like his father Maragnan did for Barker, it was at Morgan's table that Gyalliput picked up a quill and ink, and this is evident in his first-timer scratchy sketch. Morgan was so impressed with Gyalliput's sketch that he believed Gyalliput 'would very soon learn to write our language' – suggesting that Morgan wanted to persuade Hay about Aboriginal capabilities. It is interesting that Kim Scott recently highlighted Gyalliput's sketch as an 'example of literacy "readiness"'.[43]

Scott also argues that Gyalliput was 'more than ready to adopt new technologies in the interests of storytelling and communication'.[44]

Inga Clendinnen has described Chief Protector George Augustus Robinson's roam through Port Phillip in a similar way to Armstrong's mobile knowledge collection at Swan River and Lyon's recording at Carnac Island – these men collected the names of individuals, clans and geographies.[45] Fortuitously for historians, as Clendinnen says, the Aboriginal people Robinson met thought he was 'mapping the Aboriginal world of meanings and imagination...That makes him a man worth talking to: He meets an old woman near Mt Cole who responds to his questions after they have lit a fire, and sat down around it'. Robinson sits with his pencil in hand as the woman 'enacts a variety of events connected with the history of her country, and then, in a dejected and altered tone, laments its loss'. Clendinnen argues that 'Robinson interprets all such eagerness to talk with him as naïve tributes to his personal charisma. He does not ask why the magic works best on blacks who have already experienced white depredations.' Robinson, like Armstrong and Morgan at Swan River, presents himself 'as a man of authority, claiming connection with distant white powers'.[46] Armed with his pencil and paper, Clendinnen suspects it is *this* rather than his personal allure which makes Aborigines ready, even desperate, to talk with him.

While colonial maps consistently ignored Aboriginal peoples' territories and land ownership, Armstrong's census was map-like, inscribing Nyungar ownership statistically and descriptively, linking Aboriginal occupation and territorial boundaries with Aboriginal people's names and numbers. In this way, it could be argued that these statistical reports are, as well as an effective tool for dispossession, an example of the state's acknowledgement of Aboriginal ownership, or at least, of Nyungar occupation. Maragnan drew his domain into the very texture of the country he was describing; other place-statements were made in a rapidly changing world – within the thickness of colonial destruction. Gyalliput, who had negotiated a way to successfully survive the strange new world of the garrison at King George's Sound, drew his country in a place where the violence of a new order was apparent, evidenced in Yagan's eviction from his own country. Gyalliput's empathy with Yagan's exile may have strengthened on his voyage home to King George's Sound. The schooner that he and Manyat were travelling in stopped at Carnac Island for one night after leaving the port at Fremantle due to a strong head wind. Gyalliput caught fish off the island beach with the spear that he had exchanged with Yagan a few weeks before.[47]

In concluding I will briefly return to the tension in the idea of Gyalliput's mobility as being *grounded* in place. Like other Nyungar travellers Gyalliput and Manyat's mobility were enabled within their own community constraints, rather than an independent freedom of movement. Several settlers that he met with on his travels noted the 'deal' which had been struck by his countrymen at King George's Sound and the settlers regarding Gyalliput's safe return home after the embassy to Swan River. Before they travelled they had to receive 'full consent from their tribe'.[48] And their safe return, was, according to Lieutenant Governor Irwin, 'hailed by their Tribe with great satisfaction, and increased confidence in our good faith and friendship'.[49] Georgiana Molloy reported from Augusta, that 'having restored peace' at Swan River, Manyat and Gyalliput 'quitted the Swan to fulfil the promise to their tribes of white man transporting them back', and were later 'permitted by their king to take a second voyage'.[50] I am interested in the tensions implied by Gyalliput's grounded mobility. As Alan Lester and Zoë Laidlaw have suggested, historians have found it difficult to strike a balance between highlighting Indigenous mobility on a broad, transnational scale, with looking more locally at specific Indigenous localities in order to produce deeper stories of culture in-situ.[51] In dealing with this tension Lester and Laidlaw take a 'networked approach', which they argue can assist in unearthing Aboriginal mobility as something that reflects the ways in which a mobility such as Gyalliput's could be 'grounded' but not 'static'.[52] Karen Fox has similarly urged historians to focus on 'connections to land and place' as these 'were and remain critical for Indigenous peoples, and hence central to Indigenous histories.' She stresses that: 'We must not ignore these connections or their importance, and nor should we ignore calls to ground our histories in an understanding of Indigenous knowledges and frameworks.' However, at the same time, she argues that 'putting Indigenous cultural knowledge at the centre of historical scholarship need not mean only researching and writing in local frameworks, but rather looking at the national and the transnational from a position grounded in the local'.[53]

While these archival traces of Aboriginal statements of belonging are wispy, to say the least, I am obviously making a big claim for them here. If nothing else they are a reminder of the significance that Aboriginal people attributed to the coloniser's paper and ink.[54] Clendinnen closes her reading of Mr Robinson with an imagining: Mr Robinson is 'riding through a cold rain. A figure runs beside him...He is already a ghost. Perhaps he knows that, because as he runs he names the places of this his country. Measuring his breath to his stride, he sings its names and its beauty. It is possible that someone, some day, will read, and remember.'[55] Mark Dunn has recently revealed a similar scenario between Robert and Helenus Scott, settler-explorers in the Hunter Valley of New South Wales, and their guide Ben Davis. As they travelled through Davis' country in 1823, Davis 'seemed very much pleased, and kept talking all the way he went but we did not understand him but by what we could make out he was telling us about the country'.[56] As Dunn suggests, 'rather than simply giving a physical description of the land, Ben Davis was offering a narration of country, imparting some of the deeper connections and knowledge that helped him navigate physically and spiritually through the Hunter Valley'.[57]

Nyungar people waited nearly two centuries for someone to remember and act on Armstrong's lists and Lyon's observations of Nyungar territory. In 2003 this archive was included as evidence in the historical report which supported the successful Single Nyungar Land Claim.[58] Gyalliput's map, Mokare's domain and Maragnan's travel map could be added to strengthen such evidence of Nyungar geographies.[59] As a historian I am bound in a relationship to honour these past people whose thick connections to country are carried on the coloniser's thin paper. As I reflect on this rich Nyungar archive of country, inter-regional networks and mobility, I am aware of the debt I owe Richard Broome for engaging a novice like me in the process of doing history. Richard urged me to search for historical examples which illuminate moments of an ongoing Aboriginal domain, where we can read fragments of experience and understand claims of Aboriginal authority amidst colonisation.

CHAPTER 6

'Memoirs of an Aboriginal Woman' by Theresa Clements
Reflections on my great grandmother's life
Julie Andrews

I have chosen to write on this topic to pay respect to my great grandmother, Theresa Clements. I had not been born when she was alive but her strength and personality is known to me through family stories told by my grandmother, mother, aunts and uncles. This topic appealed to me because there have not been any papers written by Theresa Clements' immediate family in connection to her memoirs. I am one of the third generation of grandchildren descended from her and considered it was time to add to her memoirs for future generations by including contemporary Aboriginal voices and reflection. Additionally, it is important to point out that her words still live on through her many descendants (see Figure 6.1). In this chapter I have included the stories of my elders about their grandmother; when they speak of her they have such a fierce loyalty to her strength and nurturing as a mother and grandmother. Their memories of their grandmother enrich her writings and help correct some of the inaccuracies or emphasis on white people introduced by what I argue are external influences on the memoirs. Below I discuss the memoir and some of the oral history of Theresa Clements that does not appear in them.

The absence of Aboriginal writing in Australian history is glaringly obvious and has left a void in the community. This has been steadily changing over the past 20 years.[1] Publishers targeting Aboriginal writing

Theresa Clements (née Middleton), 1955, Coburg, Melbourne. (Courtesy AIATSIS, JACKOMOS.A04.BW-N03784_10).

have increased the number of published Aboriginal and Torres Strait Islander autobiographies. Aboriginal writing tells a story entwined with history and sadness as many stories are filled with the memory of being forcibly removed from family and are termed 'resistance literature'.[2] The voice of the writer steers the story to show resistance, social justice and pride, and a need to document the family's place in Aboriginal society and mainstream society alongside non-Aboriginal family dynasties.

Yet writing about family in academic discourse can be quite challenging as one is faced with ties of loyalty and a structured cultural ideology around rearing Aboriginal children in an Aboriginal family, or by living

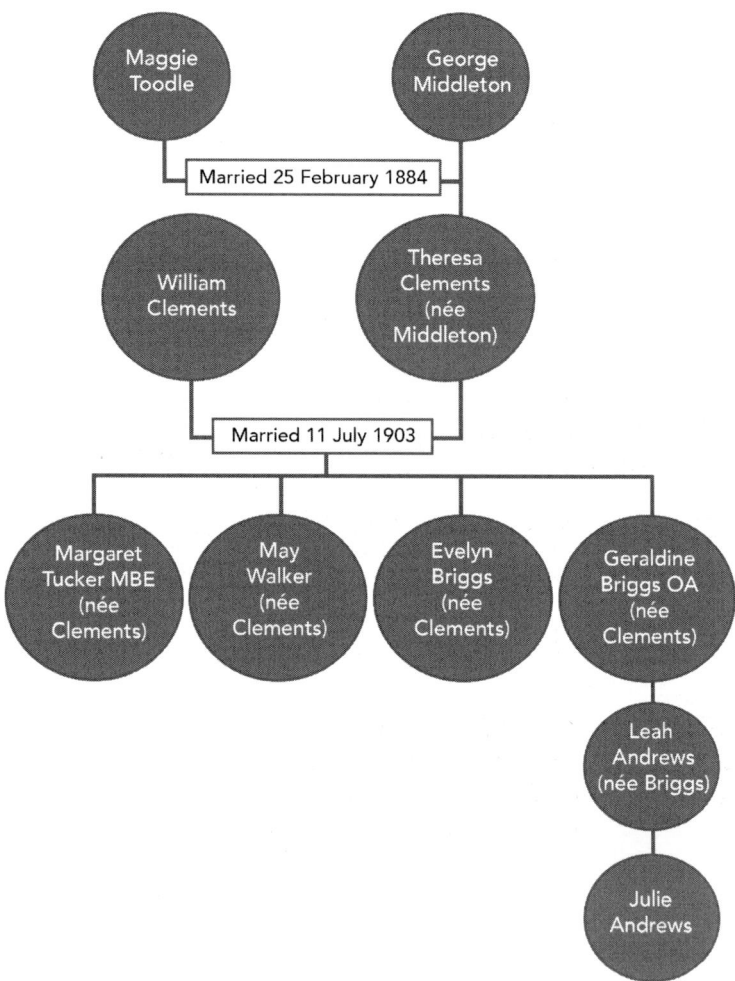

Figure 6.1: Theresa Clements' family tree

and interacting with one's Indigenous community or one's Indigenous family.[3] The term 'ways of Indigenous knowing' is often used today in the Indigenous academic arena when discussing identity and Indigenous interaction.[4] It is based on Indigenous people's shared experience of history, narrative and humour. Indigenous ways of knowing can be identified in the strength of Aboriginal survival because they are the voice of commonality. Maddison acknowledges what I observed while growing up in my Aboriginal community of Victoria, that colonisation continues to affect

Indigenous people today.[5] Here I will reflect upon the life of my great grandmother through her memoirs that record her experiences of living on Aboriginal missions. Although Broome states that Aboriginal missions were safe havens for Aboriginal people from a white population that had little regard for their lives, residency at Aboriginal missions had a high cultural fee.[6] There, the Aboriginal residents were not allowed to speak their language, and were forbidden to practise rituals of initiation, sing Aboriginal songs, corroboree or teach culture. It was forbidden for Elders to practise ceremony or arrange marriages according to kinship structure. The harsh discipline from missionaries for practising culture broke the culture down. However, my great grandmother's memoirs show a strong, intelligent woman full of pride and love for her family, despite the hardships which seem to me to have occurred all of her life.

My Indigenous life has seen a continual Indigenous resistance to white expectations of what an Aboriginal person is and should be. This resistance stems from solidarity among Indigenous people who share the same historical experiences through stories passed down from generations of Indigenous ancestors. The stories have created what we know of the Indigenous Australia of today. The stories tell how, over two centuries, Indigenous people were made to feel inferior by government policy and government surveillance, with many living their lives in fear of racism and intimidation. Close kinship and community interaction helped with coping to live on the fringe of a society that operated on ethnocentric values. Strong connection to community and family maintained Aboriginal identity and society. In a large Aboriginal family, I have grappled with the issue of permission for writing about family members, particularly if we are descended from the same ancestor. This originates from one's positioning in the family lineage and from being taught to be a member of the family group where the elders speak and represent us. My great grandmother's memoirs represent our family and, following her memoirs, a writer from each generation has documented our family story from that era. This is not writing for the academy but so that our brothers and sisters can document their place in history. In contrast, this chapter is written to place my great grandmother's story in the wider community, and to fill in gaps where the memoir is silent whilst reflecting upon her life and bringing her experiences into the present.

My immediate family has been at the heart of Victorian Aboriginal history but our life experiences are not documented enough in academic literature. In my doctoral dissertation I chose to focus upon my mother and her quest to pursue education and employment as an Aboriginal single parent, for these were her life challenges that I observed while growing up.[7] I also observed the close family networks my immediate family had with each other and their political advocacy for Aboriginal rights in Victoria. I have found in my research that the life of my great grandmother, Theresa Clements, from the early 1900s has striking similarities with my mother's life from the 1940s. Both faced extraordinary hardship as single parents, both struggled with racism, and both had to fight for their children to have a favourable outcome in their future. However, there is a difference: my mother, despite her achievements in higher education, has not been acknowledged enough outside the family. At a photo exhibition of Aboriginal and Torres Strait Islander graduates at the Indigenous academic support unit in one of the most prestigious universities in the country, her graduation photo was placed behind a door, and more recently the same exhibition was shown again and her photograph was not placed in a position that indicated her importance and achievements. I felt saddened and embarrassed. I could only fathom that her contribution to the university and community was not being acknowledged, despite her being one of the older students photographed. As a lecturer and social worker my mother's work seemed to have become lost and others were given priority. My mother's contribution to and involvement in the Aboriginal community today is still known and discussed by her family and the wider Aboriginal community, but – unlike Theresa Clements' – not within the academic context.

My great grandmother's memoirs, *From Old Maloga: The Memoirs of an Aboriginal Woman*, are a document of great historical significance. Through them I am able to trace the movement of my ancestors as they began to live on Aboriginal reserves. Recalling her relocation, my great grandmother wrote, for example, 'We didn't want to go, but soon we found that our mother (Maggie Toodle) [my great great grandmother] and grandmother [my great great great grandmother] were coming [to the mission too]'.[8]

In the Yorta Yorta native title case Clements' memoirs were presented as evidence to be considered as proof of our heritage and legacy; our family believed that a written document stating our heritage from our ancestor would be powerful evidence. However, Justice Olney, who presided over the case, ruled there was inconsistency between two documents, namely, the birth certificate of Clements' father, George Middleton, and Clements' memoirs. Middleton's birth certificate stated that both his parents were Aboriginal yet Clements' wrote in her memoirs her father 'was one of the first white half-castes in the area'. This caused Justice Olney to state that Clements' father's 'antecedents were far from clear'.[9] Pitty argued, as had the Yorta Yorta claimants, that this meant white settler accounts and government historical documents — no matter how incomplete — cancelled out their oral history.[10]

I queried my Aunt Beverley about which document we as family should believe and she immediately stated:

> I believe what Nanny Theresa said because she said it! They (bureaucrats) didn't care about our people when they recorded us for birth and marriage — they'd just put anything down but we knew who were related. They didn't even put Grandfather Middleton's birthplace correctly on his birth certificate — no one knows where that place is that they put down for his birthplace. Our people didn't get to see what they wrote down on our records until my generation. I've seen a list that shows groups of Aboriginal people being recorded for birth on the same day from the one office — just recently I've been sent by other Aboriginal people a list of birth records where three babies were registered on 1st January from the same office.[11]

The above quote shows that there is a tension between black and white interpretations of historical records and oral history.[12]

The numbers of Aboriginal people researching history through such records are increasing, and are spurred on by the need to expose the documents that still cast doubt over oral history. These historical documents can have control over Indigenous people's lives today. I observed my family's distress over Olney's interpretation because they believed generations of oral history were not supported by official documents. This is where history can upset Indigenous people and influence others, changing and shaping people's interpretations of themselves. Casting doubt on oral history in this way is an affront to Indigenous identity and is psychological warfare that can impose on Indigenous people's present-day lives if documents are not properly interpreted, or consultations not held with the family. Judgments based entirely on written documents of births and marriages of Aboriginal people are considered as suspect by Aboriginal people. Despite others' interpretations of our family history and genealogy, my family continues to base our beliefs about our heritage as it is represented in Clements' memoirs.

I spoke to a member of my Aboriginal family who stated that: 'The bottom line is – we'll never know every detail in history and there will always be people, black and white, even in our family who will have a different opinion. I just say to them "Well, you've got your opinion and I've got mine – and we'll leave it at that".'[13] Clements' memoir may differ from other historical documents, but it makes a worthy contribution to understanding a timeline of an Indigenous woman's life under the government assimilation policy, spanning a time of great Yorta Yorta activism. Memoirs, as Peter Read argues, can give a different sense of Aboriginal activism.[14]

Scholars have been uncertain about when my great grandmother's memoirs were written and published, dating them either to the 1930s or 1950s.[15] Read, Peters-Little and Haebich date Clements' memoir to 1954 and credit hers as the first Indigenous female autobiography.[16] By linking the marriage, birth and other family information my great grandmother documents in her memoirs, I have now also identified that the memoirs were written in the mid 1950s.[17] There are no written records to show any editing assistance to Clements' memoirs, but I strongly suspect that some outsiders contributed to the finished product. Jones points out that power dynamics emerge in collaborative writing relationships, which no doubt applies to the Clements' writing.[18] The relationship between memoirist and outside contributor can produce selective text and memories to focus on what a wide audience will relate to, rather than on what an Aboriginal family or audience would like to read and share commonality with. I have observed my family and other Aboriginal people eagerly waiting for a book to be published, only to see them disappointed and upset with the accounts written, stating, 'I can't read that — it doesn't sound like him/her. That's not what it was like when we were growing up.'

Outside intervention could account for the large gaps in the timeframe, the lack of detail of Clements' life story and the language used, such as 'half-caste' when referring to her father, and 'dark men'. Additionally, the memoir includes detailed information of the names of white missionaries and government officials and only minor points of reference to Aboriginal issues. It also includes an invitation to Mr Daniel Matthews from the organisers of the 'Back to Cummeragunja' celebrations to attend.[19] Matthews could not attend but sent photographs of his family and photos of the Maloga schoolchildren with Thomas Shadrach James. The photos were included in Clements' memoirs as Clements identifies herself in the group of schoolchildren, adding substance to her life story.

Below is an excerpt from a letter written by Clements in 1955 to Miss Reid, a friend, while Clements was living in Gore Street, Fitzroy, Melbourne. It is not only an example of her style of networking and her friendships, but also introduces her family to others. Clements refers to my mother, Leah, and her siblings and cousins. This piece of writing was given to me by my aunt and it demonstrates change in the Clements family as they progress to adulthood. I read this as proof of how learned she was, skilled and descriptive in her writing, and how it reflected a woman in her senior years, optimistic for her grandchildren and conscious of how important her family is to her:

> My daughter Margaret (Mrs Tucker) also three granddaughters have rooms in this residential. Also a grandson and his wife. We have a kitchen and I cook for them all. They get their own breakfast and give me a cuppa in bed before they go to work so you see I am well cared for. Well now I will come to the point in writing this. I received your letter in reference to the booklets and am sending three to [unclear] address and also a couple to you with some snaps of my granddaughters. The part of your letter which

Theresa Clements (née Middleton), on left, with her sister Christina Patten (née Middleton) holding Patten baby, c.1905, Location unknown. © Patten and Clements families.

wrote of courage to dear old Puckawidgee revived old memories of myself and my dear sister Chrissie. However, I am thankful that God has spared me to see my daughters and granddaughters grow to be an ambitious family for me to be proud of. One granddaughter (Leah Briggs) is a nurse. She is now on holidays in Sydney with her cousin Lilian Nicholls. Another granddaughter boarding here is working in the Melbourne Mint. ...She is 22 years of age (name Geraldine Briggs). Another is engaged to an Indian university student and she will married sometime next month (that's Hyllus Briggs). I am enclosing a cutting out of *The Argus* with Leah's picture – the nurse. I am sending to some friends who are interested in the Aboriginals and also mention your dear mother's name as one who befriended and uplifted two of our race 'myself and Chrissy' – Dear Mrs Reid.

Some of these family members are shown in the following photographs.

In another letter she writes:

> I will be changing my address to Shepparton East C/- Mrs Cedric Briggs. My grandson's wife will be going in Maternity Hospital Shepp. East so I have to go home to look after 3 little ones till everything is over early next month. I suppose I have to stay there through Xmas Holidays. Remember me to Rene and give her my best.

Caring for her family was a priority as a young mother and this caring attitude continued when she was in her senior years. Her grandchildren regarded their grandmother as the family matriarch.

From Ulupna Station to Maloga Mission

My great grandmother was born towards end of the nineteenth century. It is clear that most of her early life was spent living on Aboriginal reserves and stations, but there is not enough information to indicate how happy or complicated my great grandmother's family's life was at 'old Ulupna Station' (see Figure 6.2). Clements' opening statement for her memoirs identifies where her traditional lands are and her cultural background: 'My mother was a full-blooded aboriginal [no capital 'A' used in original text], and my father was one of the first white half-castes in the Tocumwal district....I belonged to the Ulupna tribe...I was born on the old Ulupna Station.'[20] This opening statement immediately situates her Aboriginality and connection to country – Ulupna – which is near Tocumwal, NSW, and that there was white blood present in her family by the late 1800s. Her strong reference to her Aboriginal heritage shows that her identity was strongly aligned to her Aboriginal family, in comparison to her white bloodline which is hardly discussed at all. This is because she had grown up in her Aboriginal family and customs, not the white ones, and her identity had been constructed as such. She was known in our family as Nanny Theresa and her tribal name was Yarmuk.[21] I discussed the name Yarmuk with my mother's sister, Aunty Frances Matthysson (née Briggs), who stated: 'When I was in the company of Nanny and we were with the old people they all called her "Yarmuk" when they spoke to her' suggesting it was either Nanny Theresa's skin name or a kinship reference – her name

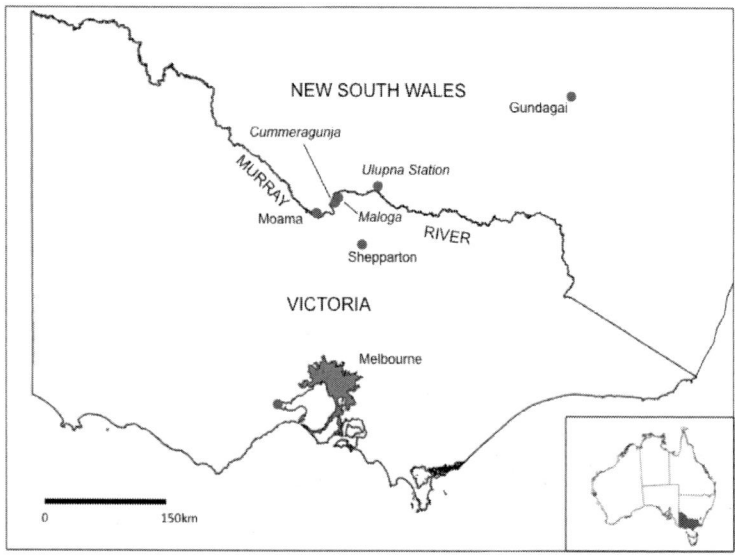

Figure 6.2: Map of Victoria and Southern New South Wales. © Julie Andrews and Andrew Butt, 2017.

has continued within our family over generations to denote our family ownership with our family cultural activities.

Clements writes about the movement of Aboriginal people onto Maloga Mission. She states that she was three years old and terrified of the Presbyterian missionary Daniel Matthews when he arrived to convince her mother to move from Ulupna Station to Maloga. Theresa's mother was a laundress with a good reputation but this work seems to have ceased once she moved to Maloga as there is no mention of her continuing to work in the wider community.[22] Schilling states that many of the squatters in the area were concerned that the relocation of Aboriginal people to Maloga would impact upon their workforce, and 'affect their practice of using Aboriginal people as dummy selectors in order to obtain more land than their 130-hectare limit'.[23]

Though Clements was scared of him at their first meeting, her words are full of excitement and happiness when she recalls the moment Matthews came to collect her family from Ulupna Station to live at Maloga, saying to her 'And you're going to school!'[24] Once Clements had left Ulupna Station, her life at Maloga was structured with learning. The men and women were taught skills of labour and mending. Matthews and his wife were mentioned quite a lot in Clements' memoirs. In all the accounts of Aboriginal people that I have heard most commonly the missionary or the station manager is the centre of most Aboriginal people's memories. The presence of the manager or minister comes first before cultural memories. Not many discuss in detail normal family daily activity and enjoyment. Despite the racism Aboriginal people faced living on reserves, missions and outstations, most Aboriginal autobiographical accounts that reflect on these eras show the happiness in their family lifestyle and living together as a community, enduring the strong assimilation policies and the financial hardship brought about by lack of food, employment and housing.

Despite Matthews' preference for assimilating Aboriginal people to live as whites, Clements made reference to the social organisation of Aboriginal people living on Maloga as 'still very clannish and each had its own separate camp'.[25] This is understandable as they were families living together. Like other missionaries, who made it their purpose to educate Aboriginal children in religion with the promise of school, Matthews did not include Aboriginal cultural teachings already learnt by the children.[26] Clements does not make any reference to her cultural teachings from her family; the emphasis was on the western education. However, discussions with her grandchildren (a generation before me) reveal that Clements taught them songs in the Yorta Yorta language, and they recall her teaching them words and telling them stories about living with her Aboriginal family as a young girl.

Along with other Aboriginal children, once at Maloga Theresa was educated by a young Thomas Shadrach James (she estimated his age to be around 18 years old) and states 'We all liked him very much'.[27] Clements indicates that she enjoyed education and excelled in scholarly work, stating: 'I was quick at school, and I was promoted quickly from class to class. Often I used to get first prize'. Broome also notes that Clements was James' brightest pupil.[28] Clements and James are credited with collaborating together and converting the hymn 'Turn Back Pharaoh's Army' from English to the Yorta Yorta language.[29] The song is also known as 'Burra Ferra' (also spelt 'Bura Fera', or 'Nowwa Bora

Pharoh' by Broome) in our family and I have observed my grandmother sing it to me with a beaming smile many times, particularly when teaching it to the young children. It was made famous by the film *The Sapphires*, which depicts the lives of Clements' granddaughters as a singing group, and is now widely known.[30]

Mr James was liked by many of the Yorta Yorta people. I recall my grandmother, Geraldine Briggs, referring to James as a 'great man' who 'taught our people well'. It is most likely that James' education lessons were instrumental for the Yorta Yorta freedom fighters who later became politically active. Organising themselves as a group, they networked with each other and other Aboriginal communities in Victoria and New South Wales, wrote petitions to the King of England and protested to the Aborigines Protection Board about poor living conditions of Aboriginal people.[31] Their contributions to the advancement of Aboriginal people are still recognised and celebrated today.

Mr and Mrs Matthews taught the Aboriginal people female and male work and trades; the men learnt farming and carpentry while the women learnt domestic duties such as sewing. Theresa indicates that her mother excelled in sewing and bought her own sewing machine. The men began farming in between shearing seasons. Maloga was a semi-self-sufficient mission as Clements recalls the community growing sorghum, tomatoes, pumpkin, and other fruit and vegetables.[32] Yet, all this positive development towards farming and learning skills was at a price – their language and cultural practises such as rituals of initiation, kinship, and marriage were submerged and taught privately within family groups rather than as a socially organised practise. Hagen states in his interpretation of anthropological evidence for the Yorta Yorta case that early writings of Matthews indicated no evidence of continued practices of traditional laws or customs.[33] Bin-Sallik makes the point that educational teachings did not have the same impact on cultural values and identity for many Aboriginal people as religious teachings. Religious teaching and skill training eventually became the dominant daily activities of Maloga people.[34]

Members of my family all stated that Clements was a Christian and that that explains her positive comments about life at Maloga in her memoirs, which after all was a public document for a white readership. Yet there was another side to her storytelling about Maloga to her grandchildren. My aunt Frances tells how Clements would tell them the stories of Matthews' harsh punishment for those practising their culture:

> Nanny [Theresa] used to tell me Matthews would beat them with a horse whip to make them stop talking the language or making artefacts. He'd lock them away in a shed if he caught them practising their culture. But when the kids would come away from the children's dormitory to visit their parents and the old people at Maloga; the old people would speak to them in the language. Nanny kept her language, she was very good at language.[35]

Other Aboriginal residents were favourably disposed to the religious lifestyle of Matthews and his wife.

Claire McLisky states that women were more accepting of religion because they were less mobile than the men who were travelling for seasonal work and therefore more exposed to the missionaries' proselytising.[36] Other than descriptions of attending church, Clements' memoirs do not make specific references to religion, and do not show any resistance to religion. Her contribution to translating hymns into the Yorta Yorta language indicates her ability to combine religion and her culture.[37] Some men, namely Aaron Atkinson, Bagot Morgan and Edgar Atkinson, originally resisted Christianity but then converted because they realised the benefits of religion in relation to securing land rights.[38] McLisky states that these men were also signatories to the 1881 Maloga petition to secure land, a petition expressed in terms of the Christian values of justice that they had been taught. Broome similarly stated that the connection of school and Christianity produced educated Aboriginal people who — believing they were equal to whites in the eyes of God — later petitioned for their rights.[39]

In her memoirs Clements noted the progression of the Aboriginal men from learning to farm to requesting their own houses. Later in her memoirs Clements stated that her father had a farm, something Tucker also mentioned in her autobiography, while my grandmother in the film documentary *Lousy Little Sixpence* (1984) indicated that there were several men who worked on their own farms.[40] My research shows that Maloga residents had close connections to William Barak from Coranderrk Aboriginal Reserve, who often visited and stayed at Maloga.[41] Farming was a large part of the community lifestyle at Coranderrk and there were very good relations between the Coranderrk manager and the Kulin, built on what Broome identifies as 'right behaviour', respectful social relations based on the Kulin protocols and reciprocity. As a consequence, there was bound to be discussions on independent farming.[42]

There were 42 Yorta Yorta men from the 'Moira and Ulupna tribes' residing at Maloga. Broome states that these men signed the petition for several significant reasons. First, the Maloga men were inspired by the stories of the Coranderrk Aboriginal men who fought to have land of their own after progressing from training in agriculture to successful farming.[43] The Maloga men wanted the same and yearned for individual land to do so, however, the petition was rejected. In 1887 William Cooper and several other Aboriginal men petitioned the Governor of the Colony requesting 'farming assistance' in an effort to obtain land.[44] Atkinson states that Matthews lobbied the government and newspapers to support the petition and that two years after the petition 1800 acres was set aside upriver from Maloga which residents fenced, cleared and cared for sheep, working without wages.[45]

This land became known as Cummeragunja: Cummeragunja means 'my home' or, as Broome writes, 'my country', where land was granted on a temporary lease to 'house Aborigines'.[46] Once on Cummeragunja the Maloga people toiled for another 12 years and built the Cummeragunja township and small farms quite successfully without a wage.[47] Yet the government continually gave settlers the land on which Cummeragunja residents toiled; creating a secure future for their families was becoming increasingly hopeless.[48] This is a prime example of forced change and rebuilding on Aboriginal farms all over again, making Aboriginal people refugees on their own traditional land.

One hundred years later their request for land for farming was used against the Yorta Yorta people in their land claim in 1998, adding insult to the hardship they had already endured for wanting to be self-sufficient as a people. Justice Olney, presiding over the case, ruled that asking for farming assistance indicated that native title for the Yorta Yorta land claim had been extinguished. However, Atkinson argues that, instead, the request showed there was a very long push from the people seeking compensation for the loss of their land that was brought about by European arrival.[49] Seidel points out that no Yorta Yorta women had signed the petition and Olney acknowledged that Matthews had written the Maloga petition.[50]

It is with reference to farming that the details in Clements' memoirs become noticeably different from our oral family history. The narration is clearly unbalanced in the number of specific details of white people in comparison to details about Aboriginal people. For example, Clements states:

> Later on a local committee of the Aborigines' Progress Association was formed. Men were called to meetings. Mr. Ardell was at the head of the group. He said to the dark men, 'Whatever you men want, please ask for.' They said, 'We want board houses like yours. We want glass windows and brick chimneys and iron roofs. We want to live like you do'.[51]

Clements states that the Aboriginal men's request was granted and the men were taught to build furniture and the women made blinds in preparation for the houses, but there is no further mention of the houses being finished or of anyone living in the houses.[52] However, there is a discrepancy with this information, particularly in relation to the time sequence. Maloga Mission was established in 1870, the school was established in 1874 and in 1880 the Aborigines Protection Board was established.[53] Towards the end of the Maloga era Aboriginal people were resisting the early-morning worship and strict rules of Matthews and had moved to Cummeragunja.[54] Clements' memoirs read like they aim to record historical events in case they were forgotten in the future. As a result the timeframe within the memoirs can be unclear. For example, the 'Aborigines' Progress Association' mentioned above is known today as the Aborigines' Progressive Association and was established in 1937 by Jack Patten (Clements' nephew) and Bill Ferguson.[55]

Life after Maloga

Schilling states that arguments between Matthews and the government Aborigines Protection Board had been steadily increasing.[56] According to Broome, 'Matthews' paternalism began to grate by the mid 1880s' and the Aboriginal men of Maloga began to leave, never to return.[57] The Board was concerned that government funds were being used to build houses for the Aboriginal community of Maloga on Matthews' private land and it therefore made available, just several kilometres away, government land where the Board established the Aboriginal reserve known as Cummeragunja, in 1888.[58] Like the lack of detail on the cultural loss at Maloga, Clements' memoirs do not detail her move to Cummeragunja Aboriginal Reserve except to state: 'Then for some purpose, a change was made. We were all moved to Cummeragunja — everything and everyone went, farm implements and all'. Matthews was banned by the New South Wales Aboriginal Protection Board from contacting Cummeragunja residents or going on the reserve.[59] Atkinson states that Aboriginal residents who had already moved to Cummeragunja were threatened by the Aborigines Protection Board with having their rations stopped if they visited anyone at Maloga.[60]

Details on Clements' father, George Middleton, are unclear — there is no record of Middleton being on Maloga; however, Clements indicates that he was on Cummeragunja. Middleton's farm was next to Cummeragunja Aboriginal Reserve. Clements states, 'Father came out from Cummeragunja and bought a farm. He became a respected citizen between Barmah and Echuca. People in the district knew George Middleton of Barmah but his only son died so his name has died out'.[61]

Reflecting on Aboriginal history, Aboriginal people buying a farm during these early times must seem unusual to today's world, but my research on oral history in my family indicates that this is what occurred with Clements' father. My family believes Middleton's dual Aboriginal and white ancestry helped him in secure work with white farmers, and that he was skilled in saving money. Sources from my family considered that there were other Aboriginal men who purchased farms as well; the men were supporting each other against the monopolies of non-Aboriginal farmers who manipulated the water supply to force Aboriginal farmers to sell their properties. After selling his farm Middleton bought a saloon at Moama (see Figure 6.2) which he later also sold.

As noted earlier, in Clements' memoirs there is strong evidence of the constant change to Aboriginal lives brought about by early European arrival and settlement. When they moved from Maloga to the Cummeragunja Aboriginal Reserve in 1881, the missionary manager was replaced with white government-employed managers. There were many changes of managers at Cummeragunja, as Clements recalls their names quickly: 'First Mr. Bellings, then Mr. Harris, Mr. Pridham and Mr. Ferguson and I think there were others'.[62] This constant change of managers proved to be unsettling for the Aboriginal residents as many managers had no interest in Aboriginal people. Attwood et al. provide narrative accounts of similar experiences at other missions and reserves, with many Aboriginal people experiencing paternalistic attitudes and constant surveillance from both the managers and their wives.[63] The duties of the managers and their wives were to administer the Aborigines Protection Board's regulations that included everyday life, and did not leave much for the Aboriginal residents to control themselves. There are many stories of strict regimes, such as the ringing a bells to control people's activities, 6 a.m. starts to working days, no pay, limited education, cruelty, and being made to feel ashamed of their race.[64] One narrative on missionary life details how blankets had two red stripes with 'NSW Aborigines' printed on them, while the clothing that the Aboriginal residents were given was made with little regard for their dignity or comfort, with the material 'crackly and hard' with either an open crutch or no crutch at all. One Aboriginal mission resident imagined the white people managing the missions saying while making the clothes: '"These blacks are know-nothings. They won't know how to take down [their] pants and do a turd and do a wet". That's the reason why they sewed them the way they did, I reckon.'[65]

Clements does not elaborate in her memoirs about the living conditions on Cummeragunja. However, her daughter Geraldine Briggs (my grandmother), spoke in the film documentary *Lousy Little Sixpence*, and similarly stated to the historian Bain Attwood that: 'The Manager's wife was supposed to visit the people. She visited us right enough! She would walk into everyone's room and walk around as if she was the only one who knew how to clean anything. The women copped that every week.'[66] Increasingly, Cummeragunja residents were unhappy about their living conditions.[67] Aboriginal residents were forced to subsist on government rations and Aboriginal people had no authority over their lives, their homes or their families. All decisions were made by the government managers. Employment was scarce and Aboriginal men needed to seek permission to leave and re-enter the reserve when seeking work. By the time Aboriginal people walked off the Cummeragunja Reserve in 1939 the station manager at the time, Mr McQuiggan, had effectively run it at a loss, using threats and violence against the people and enforcing his rule through the police. Additionally, it was becoming a place of despair, with Aboriginal children being forcibly removed from families, overcrowding in substandard housing, the farming water supply in need of repair, farming equipment given to other reserves, and racism from other farmers and locals impacting on employment opportunities.[68]

Although there are limited records of Aboriginal practices at Maloga and Cummeragunja, what is clear from my research is that knowledge of kinship connections played a major part of Aboriginal people's interaction; their family connection had remained strong. Despite the hardship of living on Cummeragunja, a place they regarded with affection as their home, Aboriginal kinship was strong and helped them cope with hardship and poverty. It also brought a sense of solidarity and optimism. As Atkinson pointed out, residents developed a coping mechanism based on kinship and a common situation that ensured they helped each other.[69]

When Clements and her family relocated to Cummeragunja the one important element that did not change was Mr James, the teacher. He moved to Cummeragunja too. Clements states: 'Mr. James still taught the school. I think he must have taught our people for about 50 years. He married an aboriginal woman. I liked him. He did a lot for our people'. It is clear that Mr James had provided a comfortable education experience for Clements who used this education extremely well throughout her adult life and more so when later advocating for her family.

Theresa Clements and her daughters, left to right: May Clements (later Walker), Margaret Clements (later Tucker), Evelyn Clements (later Briggs) (sitting), Theresa Clements and Geraldine Clements (later Briggs), c.1916. © Theresa Clements' family.

"The day mother came"

In 1903 Clements, née Middleton, met William Clements (he was Aboriginal) and they married at Gundagai (see Figure 6.2), New South Wales. Her marriage certificate is a good example of the inaccuracy and lack of detail on early records of births, deaths and marriage experienced by Aboriginal people. As stated earlier, in her memoirs Clements says she was born at 'Ulupna Station': the marriage certificate declares she was born at 'Wupna, Vic'. The certificate gives her place of residence as Cummeragunja and her husband, William Clements, as a resident of Brungle (NSW). Although there is no birth date recorded for either of them, the marriage certificate recorded that they were both 22 years of age. Their witnesses were a James O'Reilly and a relative of William Clements; Elizabeth Clements could not sign her name and placed an X as her signature.

Theresa and William Clements had four daughters but William did not stay with Theresa and their children and thus Theresa became a single mother. She wrote: 'But our way of life didn't really suit him. He wanted to travel. He was a smart fellow and he liked admiration. He went to live in Sydney'. In her memoirs there is no mention of the Aboriginal missions Warangesda and Moonahcullah, but both places were important in her life. Warangesda was where she gave birth to her children and Moonahcullah is where she settled as a single mother to be with her sister who helped her look after her children. Here she lived on rations while working to provide food for her children.

Theresa Clements was known in the area of Maloga, Moonahcullah and Cummeragunja as a midwife and delivered babies to black and white women. Oral history in Aboriginal families descended from Maloga and Cummeragunja shows that midwifery was very common among Aboriginal women due to hospitals being quite a distance away. Aboriginal women had close links with each other because of the kinship between them and other women and their knowledge of the children that they assisted being born was extensive.

The most significant part of Nanny Theresa's life, that has impacted upon all her children, grandchildren and great grandchildren, and which took place at Moonahcullah Mission, is the forced removal of two of her daughters. It has become a part of our family's history and it is one of the most horrific stories that I have ever heard. Her daughter, Margaret Tucker, recorded this event in her autobiography in 1977[70] and Clements had noted it in her memoirs earlier:

> One day some men came from the Aborigines' Protection Board. They said they wanted to take my children away. I said, 'My children are well cared for. They were said to be taking all the clever children to educate them. It was the most terrible thing that ever happened to me when they took my two daughters'.[71]

Theresa Clements and her descendants, left to right: granddaughters Margaret Wirrpanda (née Briggs) and Leah Andrews (née Briggs); daughter Margaret Tucker (née Clements); granddaughter Geraldine Ives (née Briggs); daughter Evelyn Briggs (née Clements); and Theresa Clements (seated), 1955, Coburg, Melbourne, at the 21st birthday celebrations for Aboriginal Australian Lightweight champion, George Bracken. (Courtesy of AIATSIS, JACKOMOS.A04.BW-N03784_09)

The impact of this day would have affected Clements, emotionally and financially, for after this incident she focused upon finding her daughters and remaining in contact with them. Her granddaughter, Naomi Mayers, states 'My grandmother was delivering other people's babies and her own babies were taken away from her'. I have grown up hearing my grandmother, aunts and uncles say, 'She was very smart you know?', 'She was learned', 'She was a determined woman', or 'She never gave up', but I really did not understand how this was so until I began researching. After her two daughters, Margaret (Tucker) and May, were forcibly taken from her and sent to be trained as domestic servants at the Cootamundra Aboriginal Girls Training Home, it was not until they were in their late teens that they were allowed to return home to her, approximately six to eight years after they were taken. A family member stated: 'She [Clements] made friends with someone in the Aboriginal Protection Board who would inform her of their whereabouts. She wrote letters all the time pestering [the Board]'. My aunt Thelma stated that Clements and 'her daughters were close and she stayed in touch with all her grandchildren'. The photo above shows Clements with my mother and some of her daughters and granddaughters in Melbourne. Jones also illustrates Clements' bond with her family in her research on Tucker. Tucker wrote her autobiography titled *If Everyone Cared*; however, the original manuscript was titled *The Day Mother Came*.[72]

The Aborigines Protection Board instructed the Aboriginal servant children to write home to their families. Tucker's white mistress would check her letter before sealing the envelope and Tucker would have to post it. Tucker, who was being abused by her white mistress, would draw a story of the abuse she was suffering on the back of the envelope before she posted it. Tucker gave an account of Clements coming to see her at the white mistress's house. The mistress tried to stop Clements from visiting Tucker but she was no match for the determined mother:

> I stared at the person at the gate and my dullness cleared as I realised it was my mother. Oh the joy, I can feel it as I write. I experienced it. I kept thinking how? How did she find me? How did she manage it? All this in the space of a second. As I think of it now I cry, I cannot help it. I think of my wonderful Aboriginal mother finding her way from the bush. She had read my drawings — a figure chasing a smaller figure, hitting the small one on the head with a saucepan.[73]

Applying Clements today

Theresa is remembered fondly by her family. Tucker dedicates her book to her mother and throughout the book there are references to her mother telling stories to her children and teaching her family what she learnt while working in white people's homes. Tucker writes:

> When Mother was not working and was at home for a while, the days were delightful. She would teach us new games that she'd seen the white children playing. At nights we would sit around a big fire, and she would read stories to us by the fire light. The adults would sit and enjoy listening too.[74]

My Aunty Bev reflected on Theresa: 'Nanny was learned, she was very good at school and she was good at writing. She had a lot of friends too that she wrote to.' This learned experience assisted her immensely later in her life when she approached government agencies seeking access to her two daughters who were forcibly removed. Australian government policies for the removal of Aboriginal children separated Theresa from her daughters but she was fierce – and successful – in her attempts to have her family returned to her.

I first connected to great grandmother's writing in the 1990s when an aunt was rifling through the many, many papers that she had. My aunt was able to produce the most interesting papers that related to the history of Aboriginal people, organisations and events. It was fascinating to listen to her talk and produce the documents that supported her discussion. Many of these discussions, though, were teachings of Aboriginal politics of Aboriginal identity and land rights. During one of these teachings my aunt handed me a stapled small bundle and said 'Here, look – mum's mother wrote this.' My aunt had given me a copy of my great grandmother's memoirs titled '*From Old Maloga – Memoirs of an Aboriginal Woman*'. It was the most personal and immediate piece of writing I have ever read and have since considered it like a family heirloom. In preparation for this chapter I have found it extremely rewarding to revisit and engage with this chapter in various ways: first, because it is a legacy she has left for our family, and second, because the memoirs are a wonderful document that is written with an Aboriginal voice and on a personal level. I found myself closer to my great grandmother. Fellow Aboriginal scholar, Cindy Solonec, while researching her parents' marriage for her PhD on the social history of the Kimberley in Western Australia, found that her research began to connect to her great grandparent's lives in the same era. Solonec explains this intergenerational connection succinctly when she writes:

> As I progressed this study my predecessors started to emerge in an almost life like way and I began to know my great grandparents who had passed almost twenty years before I was born. It then became obvious to me that it was incumbent on me to give them a voice in a bid to unravel the complexities of my family's past. Thus, through the 'power of textuality' the past can speak to the now; and I began to bring my ancestors into the present.[75]

Like Solonec, I too felt closer to my great grandmother through my research and felt a responsibility to connect the past to the present. Solonec and I discussed many times the satisfaction of researching our own families; it created a personal connection, uniqueness and originality and thus authenticity in the research. This inspired us to continue to completion in the difficult times of academic writing and processes.

There is also another reason I have chosen to connect Theresa Clements' writing with my own; her memoirs are a public document and able to be downloaded easily and hence used widely. I first realised this when a student handed me a copy in the 1990s as it was being discussed in class. The student did not know my family connection and the feeling of disappointment of that moment still resonates with me today because what I considered to be a family heirloom was public property. Over time I realised that Clements' memoir was a legacy, an heirloom, and a historical piece of literature spoke to everyone. Haag lists my great grandmother's memoirs as the 'first Aboriginal female autobiography'.[76] This is a respectful acknowledgement of her writing.

My aunt Beverley recalls her grandmother visiting her at the convent she and her sister, Naomi, were staying at, and Clements was highly distressed when she left because of her own experiences with her daughters being institutionalised and alone:

> After our parents broke up we were put in a convent at Bendigo. Nanny Theresa would visit us when the rest of the family would and she used to cry for us when she was leaving. She used to say 'I'm not having my grandkids in that place. And she just came [back to the convent a short time later] and took us [away from the convent] without our mother knowing because she was that upset about us being in that place'.[77]

Another aunt, Laurel in personal communication for this paper, recalls:

> She would stay six months with each daughter and just stay with the grandkids. We were so so excited to see her — she would just turn up in a taxi with her little bag, she didn't tell anyone she would be coming, we would all yell out 'Nanny!' and run out the front door to greet her [laughs].[78]

No doubt Theresa was reflecting upon her own experience of her children being placed into institutions. What is clear is that she never wanted her children or grandchildren to be away from her or their families. She spent most of her senior years moving between her daughters' homes and spending time with her grandchildren.

Conclusion

In 1959 Clements died, three years before I was born. By that time there were lots of grandchildren and several great grandchildren. She is buried at Cummeragunja cemetery alongside her family. To me, her memoirs are a legacy to her family. In writing her memoirs she documented proof of our genealogy, history, culture and family rights to our traditional land. Her memoirs were a foundation for her family to undertake research on our genealogy and clan, the Dhulanyagen clan of the Ulupna people, Yorta Yorta, and document our connection to our traditional lands.

Clements' memoirs are a testimony of her life's influence over the succeeding generations of our family. The oral histories she passed down to her daughters and grandchildren have contributed to the strong Aboriginal identity that many of her direct descendants cherish today. Upon reflection of her life, I believe she never considered herself to be a victim but a survivor of forced change and hardship that was brought upon her because she was born Aboriginal. Her resilience to keep her family together will be admired and revered in her family's generations to come.

Reading personal memoirs of earlier times, such as that of my great grandmother, can give a wider understanding, when revisiting Australian history, of how people are shaped and how important their experiences are. Reading those memoirs alongside hearing the oral history of the family can correct undue outside influences in the writing, correct errors in official documents, and enrich the stories of our ancestors' lives.

Thanks to Andrew Butt for formatting Figure 6.2 and to Edith Bavin for reading this document.

CHAPTER 7

Aboriginal education, meritocratic scholarships and the Country Women's Association of NSW 1962–1972

Jennifer Jones

In April 1961 a member of the Country Women's Association (CWA) wrote to the NSW Director General of Education, Mr Wyndham, proposing to establish a scholarship for an Aboriginal school girl. The Director General suggested that the scholarship should target a girl proceeding from the Immediate Certificate exams in junior high school to the Leaving Certificate in senior high school. He applauded the CWA's initiative, saying it was 'indeed a worthy one' because Aboriginal students were grossly underrepresented amongst senior high school graduates in NSW. Wyndham noted, 'As far as we have been able to ascertain, six children of aboriginal blood have passed the Leaving Certificate examination since 1947, and we understand that there will be four candidates for the examination this year.'[1] Low Aboriginal school completion persisted despite Aborigines Welfare Board (AWB) efforts to ameliorate disadvantage, including the award of scholarships for Aboriginal pupils with the highest Intermediate Certificate result since 1946. Assisting philanthropic groups like the CWA to establish similar awards was viewed as a means to further encourage school progression. Aborigines Welfare Board policy was that 'every aboriginal child worthy of secondary education [is] to be given that opportunity',[2] yet as I argue below, lack of opportunity was not the only obstacle to Aboriginal achievement in NSW schools.

Aboriginal experience of education in NSW was characterised by exclusion, segregation and inferior delivery during much of the twentieth century. Consequently, most scholars in the field have focused upon histories of unequal opportunity. Foundational contributions by Huggonson, Harris and Fletcher drew attention to institutionalised racism and discrimination in public education.[3] Walden, Cole and Ramsland later focused upon assimilatory policies of forced removal and training for Aboriginal children.[4] In 2012, Quentin Beresford reiterated his view that the field still had not 'received the attention it deserves', arguing that more historical research will reveal how legacies of poor provision are manifest in intergenerational disadvantage and ongoing Aboriginal resistance 'to the potential benefits of education'.[5] Following Richard Broome, I suggest that resisting cultural absorption and pursuing education were not mutually exclusive choices for Aboriginal families. Rather, educational encounters in NSW schools were also 'shaped by Aboriginal people themselves through their own agency'.[6]

By examining the experience of two Aboriginal students who were awarded meritorious scholarships by the Country Women's Association of NSW in 1962 and 1966, this chapter traces Aboriginal student response to assimilatory pressures in their pursuit of education. The CWA provided endowments for Aboriginal children, including the CWA Susie McGrady scholarship, with the view that the selected scholars would demonstrate improvement, ambition and excellence as they climbed the meritocratic educational ladder.[7] Aboriginal recipients were, however, placed in positions of conflict if their progress through high school disappointed expectations, or when institutional priorities clashed with their own personal goals and cultural values. Comparing the experiences of two students who accepted CWA assistance also reveals how their schooling was impacted by reforms in the education and Aboriginal affairs sectors in this period of great political ferment. Aboriginal students were increasingly enabled to pursue personal aspirations and cultural priorities as a result of wider reform in the 1960s and 1970s.

Aborigines Welfare Board scholarships and bursaries

The Aborigines Welfare Board (AWB) first sought to ameliorate Aboriginal educational disadvantage by awarding annual scholarships to

NSW Aboriginal students who achieved high results in their final exams. This approach encountered difficulties, however, when Aboriginal families refused to accept AWB help. Ruby Langford Ginibi's father, for example, declined the offer of an AWB scholarship in 1948 to help Ruby complete the Leaving Certificate and to contemplate Teacher's College. Her father argued 'I'm not having any protection board put you through college. All the protection they've done so far is take people from their land and split up families'.[8] Other Aboriginal parents must have concurred, as poor uptake by targeted students in the period 1946 to 1951 prompted the AWB to replace the scholarship with a 'bursary' in 1952. The AWB explained this change as necessary because some parents were 'not prepared to allow their children — some of whom are intelligent and well qualified — to proceed to secondary schools for higher education'.[9] The new bursary was allocated according to financial need as well as academic capability, to 'selected children who possess the requisite educational standard to continue to a secondary education but whose parents are not able to afford the cost of maintaining them at school for that further period'.[10] Eligibility was further extended in 1958, by including students undertaking the Primary Final exam, 'to assist and encourage students to progress to a higher standard of education'.[11] Despite these accommodations, the majority of the capable students (64 per cent) who accepted the scholarship or bursary in the period 1947 to 1960 still left school without attaining a junior secondary qualification; eleven bursaries were relinquished, nine cancelled due to poor attendance and 28 scholars failed their Intermediate Certificate exams.[12] The progression of meritorious Aboriginal children through high school was clearly problematic, even after financial hardship was somewhat mitigated by the provision of monetary support and despite the development of meritocratic educational pathways.

Secondary education in NSW

The AWB's prioritisation of secondary education for 'worthy' Aboriginal students coincided with sweeping reform of secondary education in NSW that de-emphasised scholastic excellence as the primary measure of educational success. The reform program, known as the Wyndham

Scheme, drew upon pupil-centred 'New Education' and comprehensive schooling philosophies that envisaged generalist junior secondary education as providing 'tools of living and of citizenship' for the majority, not just the social elite or scholastically talented.[13] Upon completion of the primary school course, 'all pupils [would] proceed without examination to secondary education' and could aspire to gain a School Certificate and Higher School Certificate (HSC) regardless of their socioeconomic status or academic achievement.[14]

Prior to the Wyndham reforms, entrance examinations and scarcity of places restricted secondary education to members of the upper classes or scholarship applicants who excelled in the Qualifying Certificate exam.[15] Allocation to either an academic high school or post-primary vocational education was determined by results in this exam.[16] Secondary education was thus, in theory, accessible to all social classes because 'the talented portion of the population' were selected 'without reference to their origin'.[17] The idealised aim of secondary education in the pre-Wyndham era was to establish 'an aristocracy of intellect and character, [rather] than the maintenance of an exclusive caste founded upon birth or wealth'.[18] In reality, this inflexible system of limited high school entry failed to meet burgeoning community demand for a generalist education in the post-World War II period.[19] Harold Wyndham's scheme discarded the meritocratic 'educational ladder' scaled by few in favour of an educational 'conveyor belt' travelled by many.[20] He envisaged '[e]very child having a common experience, common knowledge and common skills to fit him or her to become a member of an adult community in which citizenship rights are not only common to all, but equal'.[21] Citizenship rights for Aboriginal people, including the right to an education, were not common or equal in the early 1960s. Campaigns to remove discriminatory legislation and to challenge and discourage informal colour-bar practises were just gaining momentum.[22]

Aborigines educational disadvantage in NSW

Aboriginal education in NSW had been characterised by legally segregated Aboriginal schools with a limited and inferior primary curriculum delivered by untrained AWB teacher–station managers, from 1916 to

1960.[23] Reforms began in 1940, when the AWB devolved responsibility for Aboriginal education to the NSW Education Department, and the appointment of teacher-managers was discontinued.[24] By 1945, the Education Department agreed to accept the admission of Aboriginal children whose parents were holders of exemption certificates.[25] Presentation of a medical certificate that attested to the child's 'health and personal cleanliness' was also required.[26] Exemption certificates therefore provided a potential pathway to school continuation, but as only 10 per cent of the eligible Aboriginal population applied for the hated exemption certificates between 1943 and 1964, the number of children accessing secondary education via this route must have been small.[27]

Equity was little improved after Aboriginal schools began to be staffed by trained teachers in 1947, as the majority of Aboriginal schools had no secondary facilities or specialist secondary teachers.[28] Most Aboriginal students remained stalled in the primary grades until they reached school-leaving age. Desegregation and compulsory transfer to secondary school in 1961 marked the end of formalised educational discrimination against Aboriginal pupils. Following these reforms, the AWB's annual report confidently announced that: 'Every aboriginal child is afforded the opportunity of attaining the educational standard which is open to white children. As a matter of fact aboriginal students are in a better position than their white counterparts, so far as aid in education is concerned.'[29] The AWB assumed that access to financial aid would deliver educational parity, but the experience of Aboriginal scholars suggests that such suppositions often conflicted with Aboriginal lived experience. The majority of Aboriginal families in NSW then lived in regional and rural areas,[30] and children thus progressed from the 'protected and familiar environment' of a small Aboriginal school, 'to a large academic high school [often] in a very different and unfriendly town'.[31] Unsurprisingly, the integration of Aboriginal children into mainstream high schools did not lead to immediate improvement in scholastic outcomes. Late enrolment, economic difficulties, discrimination and an alien environment continued to encourage irregular attendance and early school-leaving.

A NSW Teachers Federation survey of secondary schools, conducted in 1964, found that only nine per cent of all Aboriginal secondary students advanced beyond the second year of high school before they reached the legal leaving age.[32] It also found that 76 per cent of schools with significant Aboriginal enrolments rated 58 per cent of their Aboriginal pupils as slow learners.[33] Educators acknowledged that early school leaving among white children was not restricted to those with 'scholastic retardation', but included, 'a considerable number of pupils of undoubted talent' whose home values were misaligned with the middle-class values of the school.[34] Consistent Aboriginal underachievement was similarly viewed as reflecting 'quite intensive hitting back' at white institutions and values.[35] Many educators, however, continued to interpret hostility to white values as 'apathy', or an indication that 'Aborigines were less intelligent than Europeans'.[36] This focus upon the capacity of the individual learner, rather than upon structural inequalities or cultural differences, achieved a social-Darwinian 'naturalisation of unequal reward' by distracting attention from factors that continued to disadvantage Aboriginal students.[37] The early history of CWA Aboriginal scholarships reveals how academically capable Aboriginal pupils who failed to thrive in secondary school were held personally accountable for poorer-than-expected outcomes. As a white institution sponsoring Aboriginal scholarships, the CWA was flummoxed by the underachievement or withdrawal of talented students. The CWA's members also became frustrated when Aboriginal students exercised their agency and made choices about school attendance or continuation according to Aboriginal cultural priorities, including togetherness and reciprocity, despite CWA-imposed pressure to conform to mainstream values. As Richard Broome notes, Aboriginal resistance to white domination in southern Australia was undergirded by 'an unshakeable sense of being Aboriginal', which was expressed through daily practises and ways of being.[38] The two case studies discussed in this chapter confirm Broome's view that Aboriginal pursuit of betterment in the assimilation era required decisions every day 'about where their values and identity lay'.[39] Broome, however, concentrates upon either end of the 'polarity of responses' to the colonial condition, that of demonstrable 'despair or an attitude of defiance'. I draw attention to those who 'just got on with living', adopting tactics including patience and persistence to achieve culturally congruent material betterment.

Meritocracy and the CWA Susie McGrady Scholarship

The Country Women's Association developed an interest in the meritocratic assimilation of Aboriginal children as a consequence of another successful initiative, the establishment of Aboriginal CWA branches in rural NSW.[40] The first branch, known as Toomelah CWA, was formed at Boggabilla Aboriginal Station on the NSW–Queensland border in 1956.[41] The branch achieved state-wide impact when new Aboriginal members attended state conferences in 1958 and 1960, with the vivacious Foundation president of the branch, Susie McGrady, becoming somewhat of a celebrity amongst CWA representatives.[42] CWA members were shocked and saddened when Susie McGrady died suddenly in 1961, and calls were made to commemorate her life and achievements within the organisation. Gwydir CWA Group requested that a scholarship named the 'Susie McGrady Memorial Scholarship' be established in honour of her achievement as the 'first Aborigine...to actively participate in Association affairs'.[43] The Group also expressed the view that 'it would be nice if the scholarship could be awarded to a girl from Toomelah where a number of Mrs McGrady's grandchildren lived', because 'it would be an incentive to the holder to know that one of her own people had become a President of an Association branch'.[44] The CWA State President disagreed with the proposal to geographically target the scholarship. She argued that 'the resolution was a general one and there would be nothing to prevent the award of a scholarship to a girl from [elsewhere in the State], even if it was known as the Susie McGrady Scholarship'. The bid by Gwydir Group to award the scholarship in their local area was unsuccessful, and the inaugural award went to a child from a distant community. This decision would hold unforeseen implications for one of Susie McGrady's grandchildren, as discussed below, as Gwydir Group continued to nurture the ambition to sponsor the academic development of a child from Toomelah, leading to the creation of a targeted scholarship in 1966.

Applicants for the inaugural CWA Susie McGrady Scholarship were 'thoroughly investigated' by the AWB and the winner announced after enquiries established that her school work was 'satisfactory and her behaviour excellent'.⁴⁵ The successful candidate, Joanne Barry,⁴⁶ wrote to the CWA Executive thanking them for their support and informing them of her goals and interests:

> I would like to thank you and your association for the CWA Bursary which I received on 17th July. I am twelve years and I am in Form I at High School and am very interested in English, Social Studies, Mathematics and Art. I hope to attend the school for six years and get my Higher School Certificate and then either go teaching or nursing. I am also very interested in sport.⁴⁷

In her first-year exams, Joanne achieved an average percentage of 59.1 per cent, which disappointed AWB and CWA observers. The school principal encouraged Joanne Barry's sponsors to exercise patience, suggesting that 'Joanne will improve when she settles down in her new school environment'.⁴⁸ Joanne's second-form results, however, declined to 57.1 per cent. An AWB Welfare Officer was dispatched to inform Joanne and her family of the expected level of performance, 'stress[ing] on them the necessity...to apply herself more diligently to her study'.⁴⁹ Joanne Barry was reared in a large family who lived in a fringe settlement some kilometres outside the nearest small town. Family circumstances made it difficult for her to remain at high school without the CWA scholarship. Unfortunately, Joanne's results undermined the security of the award, as the 'extension of the bursary will be dependent on improvement in her application to study'.⁵⁰ Although the CWA determined that Joanne's report was 'more or less unsatisfactory', the scholarship was extended until her end-of-year results were known.⁵¹ Joanne's identification as a bright but underperforming student clearly placed her under pressure to fulfil external expectations.

In the 1960s researchers understood that the declining performance of a talented student drawn from underprivileged circumstances was linked to an increased awareness of their social location as they matured from childhood to adolescence. In 1964, Joanne was one of only five Aboriginal students enrolled at the regional high school of nearly 600 white students. Experts held that in such contexts Aboriginal children experienced regression:

Up to secondary school,...aboriginal children do intellectually as well as white children. But something happens at 12 years of age at secondary school. Some sort of consciousness develops about their so-called inferiority and I think at that point educationally they tend to slip back.[52]

In 1965, Joanne Barry's results continued to disappoint, as she achieved an average of just 50.1 per cent.[53] The borderline failure of the CWA scholarship holder prompted the organisation to make a direct appeal for a more concentrated effort, bypassing the AWB Welfare Officer. The Association sent Joanne an encouraging letter which emphasised the importance of education as an avenue for self-improvement: 'every lesson you learn at school helps you in later life. Education grows more and more important each year, and we are sure you will take good advantage of this'.[54] The ongoing decline of the Susie McGrady scholar's results placed the CWA in a position of philosophical conflict, as the award was established on the understanding that the child would demonstrate their merit via continuous improvement.

Joanne's teachers were still optimistic about her capability, noting that 'with maximum determined effort she could gain a reasonable Higher School Certificate'.[55] Under the new Wyndham Plan, Joanne was able to progress from form five to form six even though her results were 'not up to the standard expected of a bursary holder'.[56] At the end of form five, Joanne achieved an average mark of just 43.8 per cent. Upon reception of the news, the CWA Executive wrote her a letter that balanced encouragement and reproach:

> While being pleased that your conduct is so good, we were rather disappointed that you have not done better in your studies last year. Your teachers feel that you could do better and that you have the ability to really get ahead, and we in the Country Women's Association do hope that you will make a special effort this year to take full advantage of the scholarship which members have made possible for you.... We send you our very best wishes for 1967, and assure you that we are very happy to hear that you have a record of such excellent conduct. That is something special.[57]

After this intervention, which emphasised CWA members' sacrifice and Joanne's privilege and duty, the CWA did not receive further reports on her progress. On 16 January 1968, however, the CWA Head Office received a phone call from the CWA Group representative who had liaised with Joanne's high school.[58] She reported the sincere thanks of the headmaster, 'for allowing Joanne to take out the scholarship at his school. They are all very proud of her and will continue to advise CWA of her progress outside school'. Several days later, a letter from the AWB confirmed that Joanne had obtained four passes at Ordinary Level in the recent Higher School Certificate examination: 'It is understood that Joanne wishes to become a teacher, but it is unlikely that she will receive a teacher's scholarship. Thank you for your assistance given to Joanne throughout the past year.'[59] The school's pride in Joanne, who had joined the very small number of Aboriginal secondary school graduates, contrasts with the muted enthusiasm of the Aborigines Welfare Board, who emphasised her likely failure to qualify for further scholarships. This contrasting response clearly reveals the AWB's ongoing investment in meritocracy and the superseded 'education ladder'.

Wyndham's 'education conveyor belt' had ensured that senior secondary study was now open to all students regardless of performance. One result of this change to secondary education was that persistence was now rewarded as well as high achievement. Joanne's tenacity enabled her to pass the new Higher School Certificate, despite her declining grade averages and consequential pressure imposed by judgmental and disappointed institutional authority figures. That Joanne achieved the goals articulated in her 1962 letter, by gaining her HSC, suggests that she adopted effective tools to resist the imposition of meritocratic normativity, which — given her low grades — would have labelled her as having failed to meet the expectations of her sponsors or to realise her academic potential. Richard Broome suggests that successful Aboriginal resistance to white domination in southern Australia has historic expression in the demand for rights without cultural absorption.[60] Describing this duality as a 'radical hope' to be 'both in the new world, and of an Aboriginal one', Broome traces the activism of Aboriginal male public figures including William Cooper, Doug Nichols and Bill Onus. Joanne Barry's quiet persistence suggests that she refused the psychological inferiority commonly associated with Aboriginal femininity and poor grades. Aboriginal country girls were then imagined to be pre-modern, and were expected to be 'poor, sick, and forever on the verge of extinction'.[61] By contrast, in the assimilation era, Aboriginal culture held high regard for the capacity of women and their role as leaders in the longer term pursuit of Aboriginal goals and cultivation of Aboriginal values.[62] For Joanne, effective Aboriginal resistance took place geographically at the local high school and imaginatively in the mind.[63] Joanne subsequently completed her teacher education and gave career-long service in NSW schools.

As the inaugural Susie McGrady Scholarship holder, Joanne Barry achieved her educational aims within the constraints of her circumstances, and while resisting pressure from vested CWA and AWB interests. Although Joanne's results were judged to be inadequate according to the CWA's meritocratic values, systemic educational reform in NSW had made it possible for her to achieve her Higher School Certificate regardless. The Director General of Education, Vernon Truskett, had admitted in 1966 that bursary systems were poorly serving Aboriginal students like Joanne Barry:

> I do not like applying the word bursary to the needs of secondary education for aborigines. ...To me, a bursary, has a definite connotation: it is granted to people of outstanding abilities and skills. On the other hand, a number of aboriginal children are missing the opportunity of becoming good citizens because of this falling-off at the secondary education level...The only way we will overcome this problem in the next twenty years is to do something for the younger people – and not only a few but for most of them.[64]

In this period, the geographic and social location of the majority of Aboriginal students excluded access to secondary education. Locally available education did not extend 'beyond the leaving age marking the end of compulsory schooling', and students who aspired to complete high school 'needed to travel long distances' to major centres, or access the financial means to attend as residential boarders 'in order to access suitable secondary education'.[65]

The Carl McGrady Scholarship: Access to rural secondary education and school-term hostels

Distance and financial hardship placed secondary education out of the reach of most Aboriginal students in the 1960s, including Susie McGrady's grandchildren at Boggabilla. Until secondary school facilities were opened at Boggabilla in 1988, the nearest NSW state high school was at Moree, 115 kilometres to the south. Senior high school facilities were established in nearby Goondiwindi, Queensland, in the early 1960s, but Aboriginal students could not access this opportunity until after 1967.[67] The majority of post-primary school-age Aboriginal students continued to attend the primary school at Boggabilla Aboriginal Station, which catered for their secondary education 'with extremely limited facilities for this purpose'.[68] As one former student recalls:

> My older siblings and uncles [did] grade six for three years until they were fifteen and then they left. [Then] they actually introduced correspondence. So, my next couple of brothers started some form of secondary school via correspondence. ...Most primary school teachers didn't have the necessary skills to make correspondence work for the students. So, it just filled in time for the two or three years, depending on their age, until they left.[69]

Sympathetic observers interpreted this phenomenon as a regrettable 'wastage' of potential. When talented student Carl McGrady (one of Susie McGrady's grandsons) completed primary school, his teachers believed he had potential to further his education. They enlisted help from the local Anglican priest and the Gwydir CWA Group to establish a scholarship for Carl. This would pay for accommodation at St. Johns Hostel for Boys, a school-term hostel run by the Anglican Church in Armidale, and thus enable Carl to attend Armidale High School.

Access to secondary education in rural Australia was then characterised by the conveyance of children to centralised facilities.[70] Leading educator Frank Tate reported as early as 1937 that growing demand for secondary education was 'causing parents to realise that the central school... was the only practical method of giving country children a reasonable choice of courses'.[71] Grudging acceptance of centralised education facilities reflected the traditional opposition of Australian parents to regional consolidation. Rural parents had 'never taken kindly to any proposals to close their local one-teacher schools in favour of a large central school'.[72] Lobby groups including the CWA of NSW supported the education of rural children 'in their own communities', believing that rural decline or 'the drift of population' was exacerbated by centralisation.[73] Dogged lobbying by the CWA to establish secondary education for country children appeared to have a positive impact upon allocation of resources, as rural NSW was subsequently 'very well served in respect of secondary education' compared to other states.[74] The CWA of NSW also lobbied 'strenuously' for the provision of school bus services, which were provided free of charge after 1949. Where daily transport was impracticable, children attending state high schools made arrangements to board in private homes or in school-term hostels managed by philanthropic or religious groups. The CWA of NSW established seven hostels for girls from 1925, supported wholly by the CWA or jointly funded by the Department of Education after 1946.[75] As the CWA catered solely for girls, it was decided that an Anglican boy's hostel in Armidale, 330 kilometres to the south of Boggabilla, would offer the most proximate accommodation for Carl McGrady. Reverend Colin Wellard, then located at Boggabilla, recalls:

> When I was in Armidale as the Assistant Curate, I stayed at the Anglican Hostel for Boys. [Students] came in from all over the country to go to the high school. I thought we could raise sufficient money to get Carl in [the hostel] at least for the first twelve months, and go from there. So that is what we did.[76]

CWA branches in the Gwydir district, that had regretted the lost opportunity to administer the CWA Susie McGrady Scholarship exclusively for the advantage of local Aboriginal children, also supported the proposal:

> Mrs Barlow told the meeting about Carl McGrady of Toomelah, who is an above average school pupil. Mrs Barlow suggested that a scholarship fund be commenced within the group to help this boy further his education. The Church of England people at Boggabilla and the

Diocese of Armidale, along with the Aborigines Welfare Board could assist with books, etc. [I]t would cost approx $100 for the first year. The scholarship would be for three years at the Armidale Hostel.[77]

The Carl McGrady scholarship proved very appealing to Gwydir CWA members and the Group Treasurer soon noted a parallel decline in support for state-wide initiatives including the Susie McGrady Scholarship.[78] That the older scholarship was 'not receiving the support that it should' but 'branches were supporting the Carl McGrady scholarship very well' suggests that local causes garnered more significant and sustained support than the intangible outcomes of more distant appeals.[79]

Carl McGrady's response to his selection as a targeted local scholar was less enthusiastic than that of his CWA sponsors. He recalls, 'I was never asked anything about it. I just assumed that the whole world must have hated me to send me there, because it was hell'.[80] Carl commenced residence at St John's Hostel and schooling at Armidale High School in 1967, when he was 13 years old.[81] Only two other Aboriginal boys were then in residence at the hostel, with about 100 white children.[82] Carl McGrady, who had been 'just a little mission kid all my life', described the distant hostel as a completely alien environment, akin to being 'dropped on the moon'. Hostel life was characterised by a regimented routine which included after-school sport, nightly homework and study sessions.[83] In this controlled environment, Carl became 'a bit like a battery hen' as he was 'told what to do and when to do it twenty-four-seven...when the bell goes, you jump'.[84] Nevertheless, Carl McGrady was noted as making 'good progress...at the Armidale High School, where he came twenty-second out of thirty-seven in his form'.[85]

At the hostel, Carl was made aware of his inferior social rank as a Black student. Armidale High School and St John's Hostel then had reputations as 'the upper echelon of education in country NSW', attracting the children of 'well-to-do people...who couldn't afford bloody St Joey's Boys College [a prestigious private school], so the next best thing was to send them off to Armidale'.[86] Carl, who is a light-skinned Murri, recalls how his identity as an Aboriginal person initially undermined his social acceptability:

> [On the Mission] everyone was Black...we had shades of Murris [but] as far as we were concerned we were just mob kids; black, white or anything. ...So it was never a question [for me] until about two months into my stay, one of my little mates came running up to me [and] said, 'Carl, you know what [he] said?' and I said, 'No, what did he say', and he said, 'That you are a *fucking* black fella!' I said, 'So?'

Being labelled as 'Black' isolated Carl from some students, but fostered solidarity with others:

> It sort of distanced me, I suppose [but] I was almost adopted, if you like, by the older Murri fella. ...It was a living hell at the hostel and it got worse because of the fact that I was black. ...But I won all me mates back in the second term, because I was an exceptionally good footballer.[87]

For Carl McGrady, the greatest crisis of 1967 was not provoked by the fickle friendship of white boys: it came when he returned home for holidays. Carl became aware that he had changed in the majority-white hostel: 'The best part of my life was being a Murri kid on the mission. But going to Armidale and after that, it was taken away from me because I never went back to being a mission kid. I'd become this stressed out, stuck up bloody white fella almost.'[88] Carl realised that achieving success at high school was far less important to him than emulating his cultural role models at home, and he refused to return to Armidale:

> There was nothing in the whitefella's world that I wanted. All I knew was that I was going to leave school and be a shearer: my uncles and my pop and everybody else that I knew were [shearers]. ...I remember arguing with my Nan and Pop, that is who I lived with, that if they sent me back I would run away. I would not go back.[89]

Gwydir CWA Group later received a letter advising them that 'it was regretted that Carl McGrady would not be returning to Armidale, and no amount of persuasion would make him return'.[90]

Other former hostel residents have also described the clash between Aboriginal values and this white school environment. Terry Widders, who left St John's Hostel as soon as he reached the legal school-leaving age, argues that the experience produces a 'paradox'; secondary education emphasises pursuit of individualistic white-Australian cultural goals 'aimed at economic and social security' in a highly controlled environment, while Aboriginal education focuses on the 'growth of the individual' fostered by 'high nurturance...great autonomy in decision making and, subsequently, a growing sense of responsibility towards others'.[91]

Carl McGrady exercised cultural skills in autonomous decision making when he chose not to return to Armidale High School. Instead, he transferred to Goondiwindi High School until he was 'old enough to leave' and became a shearer.[92] Carl was aware, however, that his grandfather Ron McIntosh still held the hope that he might aspire to a professional career. Ron McIntosh was the Aboriginal leader whose networking skills had fostered the inaugural Aboriginal CWA branch on Boggabilla Aboriginal Station, in 1956.[93] His view was that 'there has to be a better way' for Aboriginal people; a way that harnessed mainstream opportunities and accommodated cultural integrity'.[94] Ron McIntosh was disappointed that Carl did not 'do [his] bit for the Black fellas' by completing his education. Their disagreement draws attention to divergent views on culturally congruent and effective pathways to educational success and employment then championed within Aboriginal communities. These views ranged from separatist Aboriginal Family Education Centres, which assisted Aboriginal people to 'educate our own children the way we want to' in local communities, including Boggabilla, through to the Aboriginal Family Resettlement Scheme, which sought educational and employment opportunities through voluntary mainstream integration in larger regional centres.[95] Carl McGrady's views on education eventually aligned with those of his grandfather Ron McIntosh, rewarding his patience:

> My Grandfather always said that I should/could have been a teacher. Every time I came home after I grew up, 'look at him still shearin: should have been a teacher'. ...When I finally went back and did teacher training, it made my Pop's heart skip a beat.[96]

A national financial aid scheme, instituted in 1970 by the federal government, made it possible for Carl McGrady to access higher education as an adult. Since graduation, Carl McGrady has served in school education and the Aboriginal affairs sectors, seeking 'a better way' for the Aboriginal community.

Commonwealth reform and educational access

Equitable access to secondary schooling was already theoretically extant for Aboriginal pupils when the CWA instituted two Aboriginal scholarships in 1962 and 1966. These awards acknowledged, however, that financial circumstances prevented Aboriginal children from completing secondary education. The majority of Aboriginal children would wait until after 1970 for a universal Aboriginal study grant scheme to provide assistance 'for primary and secondary education'. Until then, educational provision continued to be 'the responsibility of the States', despite constitutional reform in 1967 that enabled the Commonwealth to take responsibility for Aboriginal affairs.[97]

After 1967, the Commonwealth Government chose to target Aboriginal students entering tertiary education for financial assistance. The Aboriginal Study Grant Scheme (ASGS), instituted by the Office of Aboriginal Affairs in 1968, was immediately criticised for overlooking 'the gap which exists for Aboriginal scholars between the compulsory school ages and the stage at which the Commonwealth begins to support them through study grants at the post-secondary level'.[98] The scheme was reformed in January 1970 to create the Aboriginal Secondary Grants Scheme (ABSEG), and administrators soon noted that applications were 'lodged at a fast rate'; requests outstripping both expectations and funds budgeted to support Aboriginal secondary education.[99] By May 1970 ABSEG had received:

> Nine times as many requests for secondary school grants under the scheme introduced this year than [was] budgeted for, [reflecting the unfulfilled] desire for secondary education among Australian Aborigines.[100]

In NSW, for example, 994 students received ABSEG grants to enable high school study in 1971, whilst only 77 received ASGS grants for tertiary education.[101] This imbalance reflected both Aboriginal demand for high school education and low qualification rates for tertiary entry. It also suggests that Aboriginal people were prepared to seek school completion for their children, despite being well aware that Aboriginal customs and values were not shared or respected by educational institutions.[102]

Undertaking high school education in the 1960s required Aboriginal students to negotiate school environments designed to accommodate the cultural needs of the white majority. CWA scholarship holders Joanne Barry and Carl McGrady negotiated the disappointment of financial supporters who expected scholastic excellence and school completion as reward for their generosity. Reform of the NSW education system and federal Aboriginal affairs, which coincided with their secondary schooling, enabled these students to resist the assimilatory agenda of their scholarships. Sheer persistence saw Joanne Barry fulfil her personal and cultural goals, despite five years of critical surveillance and negative feedback from white authority figures. As an Aboriginal boarder at St John's school-term hostel, Carl McGrady experienced a total environment oriented towards non-Aboriginal values. He chose early leaving as an immediate means to maintain cultural fidelity. Carl later helped fulfil his grandfather's wider aspirations for Aboriginal community advancement: through a career in education. These histories reveal that while unequal opportunity hindered Aboriginal school completion, so too did the absence of Aboriginal customs and values in these educational environments. Both students responded to the constraints of their meritocratic scholarship, which aligned with mainstream cultural aspirations, by choosing available forms of Aboriginal resistance.

CHAPTER 8

A different courage
'Radical Hope' and the continuous strand of Aboriginal agency in Victoria

Richard Broome

When I began to write my latest book on Aboriginal History, *Fighting Hard, The Victorian Aborigines Advancement League* (2015), I pondered my argument. The League that was founded in 1957 was a significant and vital organisation in Aboriginal history, not only in Victoria, but during its first generation across Australia. Once Aboriginal people assumed control in late 1969 it became one of the most important contemporary expressions of Aboriginal political and cultural agency. As I researched the League's history I saw the League and its members were rooted deep into the history of Aboriginal activism in Victoria, a story I wanted to tell. This would set this organisation clearly in a historical context and make its history of wider relevance for readers.

What central idea or motif would hold this organisational history of agency together? While contemplating this I chanced upon a book by Jonathan Lear, an American philosopher. It was entitled *Radical Hope: Ethics in the Face of Cultural Devastation* (2006). Arrested by the sub-title, I consulted it. After consideration I decided to use Lear's idea of 'radical hope', albeit lightly, as the central theme in my book. I related it to my argument about Aboriginal activism and agency. I did not discuss Lear's book at any length in *Fighting Hard*, so I will take the opportunity now to do so, teasing out its connections to the situation in Victoria.

Plenty Coups and the Crow responses to cultural devastation

As a philosopher, Lear is interested in universal ideas, and in his book he explores the problem of what humans do when faced with the devastation of their culture. His discussion is enacted through a case study of Plenty Coups, the most esteemed leader of the Crow Native American people in the two generations around 1900.

Plenty Coups was born in 1848 — exactly 100 years before me — and was named by his mother Chiilaphuchissaalesh (Bull Goes into the Wind) before his grandfather, after a dream, renamed him Alaxchiiaahush (Many Achievements), having foreseen his grandson's long and prestigious life. Perhaps his grandfather had this vision out of hope that the Crow at this time might find a great leader. They faced many threats and perils, due partly to white incursion, but mostly because their traditional enemies, the Sioux, Cheyenne and others, were pressing them hard. Indeed, two decades before Plenty Coups' birth, over a thousand Sioux warriors launched a surprise attack on a Crow village near the Yellowstone River and destroyed several hundred lodges, killing half the population.[1] The Crow, much weakened, eventually threw their lot in with a lesser enemy, the US government, under the terms of the Fort Laramie Treaty in 1851. This gave the Crow control over 13 million hectares, centred on what became Montana and Wyoming. However, in subsequent treaties of 1868 and 1882, their land was reduced to less than one million hectares. By 1884 they had moved to a reservation. Alaxchiiaahush, who grew up in perilous times, soon became known as Plenty Coups.

What did his new name mean? The Crow lived by hunting buffalo on their territory and growing crops and tobacco. They enjoyed a good life, but because other groups pressed on their resources, they were also by circumstance a warrior people. Boys grew to be warriors and girls to be the wives of warriors and the proud mother of their children. A warrior tradition thrived, focussed on the coup stick. The coup stick was used to mark Crow territory in any military struggle beyond which any enemy could not go. The stick had to be defended, as it symbolised territory, and thus also came to symbolise bravery. Indeed, the highest valour was accorded a warrior who merely touched an enemy with the coup stick before killing him, thus endangering himself by such a flamboyant act. Alaxchiiaahush (Many Achievements) when only 16 took revenge for the death of his older brother by the Sioux. He surprised a Sioux warrior and, instead of killing him outright, took the harder path of collecting his scalp, thus condemning his opponent to a life of disfigured shame, testimony to a Crow victory over him. This and other deeds caused Alaxchiiaahush to be known as Plenty Coups — that is, many braveries or a man of much valour.[2]

Jonathan Lear investigates the question: what befalls a people when their culture suffers devastation? He is haunted by the words of Plenty Coups, who in the 1930s told his friend and biographer, a former hunter and trapper Frank B Linderman, that after the US government outlawed intertribal warfare, and after the buffalo disappeared, and after the Crow lost land and moved to a reservation: 'the hearts of my people fell to the ground, and they could not lift them up again. After this nothing happened. There was little singing anywhere'.[3] Indeed, in 1921 when Plenty Coups was chosen to represent Native American peoples at the ceremonial burial of the Unknown Soldier in Arlington National Cemetery, Virginia, he laid his coup stick and war bonnet on the sarcophagus.

What did this mean? Lear contemplates long and hard what Plenty Coups' action meant, what lay behind his words 'nothing happened', and universalises his situation. Plenty Coups' response parallels the words of emptiness spoken by Chief Joseph of the Nez Perce upon his surrender in Oregon to Colonel Miles on 30 September 1877. Wracked by defeat, his relatives dead, lost or fugitives, he said: 'Hear me my chiefs! I am tired, my heart is sick and sad. From where the sun now stands I will fight no more forever'.[4] His phrase 'no more forever' contains the finality and desolation of Plenty's Coups' statement: 'nothing happened'. Of course, the Crow and Nez Perce lived on, but Plenty Coups and Chief Joseph at first believed it might be a life of mere survival, not deep significance.

Lear maintains cultural devastation not only affects what a people might do, but also what they might be. It affects not so much a person's identity — for a people might continue on — but the ability of individuals to internalise and act out the group's ideals. This enactment of social roles might become constricted: indeed impossible. In the mid-nineteenth century the Crow, like other Native American peoples, were facing rapid change. There was a shift to hunting buffalo for the non-traditional export market in skins, intensified competition between groups over this trade, pressure from encroaching European settlers, and the loss and eventual demise of buffalo in the face of massive over-hunting.[5] After 1887, the US government banned intertribal warfare. By the time Plenty Coups was a youth, war and hunting were either diminished or no longer existed. How then can a Crow boy aspire to be a Crow man, enacted by being a hunter or warrior, when these roles are altered, gone or now make little sense in a changing world? And if one aspires to be a Crow chief, how can this occur when the basis of being a chief – that is, a great hunter and warrior – have vanished? Lear stresses that this was not in reality precisely what the Crow experienced, for we can never quite know what was in their minds, but Lear pursues the question to imagine what any human group might face and how they might respond.[6]

Lear argues that, in this situation, humans are not without hope, but what is needed is a new poet or visionary in the group who takes the past and projects it into 'vibrant new ways to live and to be'.[7] He suggested that Plenty Coups symbolically buried his coup stick and war bonnet, and told his story to Linderman, as a 'symbolic death'. This was to preserve tradition, by laying the foundation of a new life in a new way, 'in the hope of a future in which things – Crow things – might start to happen again'.[8]

In Plenty Coup's youth, young boys fasted, undertook sweat baths, and then went into the country for some days alone, in order to have dreams that might extend Crow wisdom and understanding. These dreams would be interpreted by the elders on their return. About 1857, Plenty Coups, then aged nine, undertook this ordeal in the context of a transforming world of many dangers to the Crow. The Sioux and Cheyenne were pressing hard; the whites were coming; smallpox had diminished the Crow and others; and the buffalo were being harvested at the astounding rate of 100,000 per year from the 1830s.[9] After two nights in the 'wilderness', and after he had lopped off a piece of finger by way of stress and a trance-like feeling – which was not unusual for Crow spiritual practice – he had an extraordinary dream. This dream, Lear argues, not only predicted the future but foresaw a changed world that allowed the Crow elders to face a 'radically different future'.[10]

In the dream, which he related to elders, Plenty Coups saw a Man-buffalo who led him to a cavity in the ground. Out of the hole came vast numbers of buffalo, which spread across the plains and then vanished. Then another vast herd came out of the hole, but they dispersed onto the plain and settled in groups. These animals had long tails, were spotted, and bellowed differently to buffalo. Then he was shown a vision of himself as an old man sitting against a tree. A mighty wind came and devastated the forest, knocking down every tree but one, which was the lodge of the Chickadee, a bird of little strength but much wisdom. The Chickadee in Crow culture was a listener, missed nothing, and was one who learned from others. The Man-buffalo declared to Plenty Coups: 'It is the mind that leads a man to power, not strength of body'.[11] Back in the council of elders, young Plenty Coups related his baffling dream. Yellow Bear, one of the wisest, stepped forward and declared:

> The dream of Plenty-coups means that the white man will take and hold this country and that their Spotted-buffalo will cover the plains...The tribes who have fought the white man have all been beaten, wiped out. By listening as the Chickadee listens we may escape this and keep our lands.[12]

The Crow realised that the way to face the future in an altered world was to form an alliance with the whites against their traditional enemies.

Lear argues that the Crow forged a new form of courage: that of listening and learning from one's enemies, and acting in a non-traditional way, not just to survive, but indeed thrive. Plenty Coups not only acted with the US Army against his traditional enemies, but presented himself for adult baptism, married in a church, negotiated for a reservation school, became a farmer and invited his people to be the same. Lear points to 'the radical form of hopefulness embedded in Plenty Coup's vision: that even with the death of traditional forms of Crow subjectivity, the Crow can nevertheless survive – and flourish again'.[13] This is the radical hope: to be Crow, but in a different way in a newly-emerging world. As Lear writes: 'this hope is radical in that it is aiming for a subjectivity that is at once

Crow and does not yet exist'.[14] Lear is at pains to argue that it is not a hope of mere optimism or an ill-founded confidence that things will work out, but an act of courageous hope based on fineness of decision making, good judgement, and belief in the power of prophesy. Jonathan Lear believes that we can learn something of human responses to cultural devastation by listening to the story of Plenty Coups.

Victorian Aboriginal responses to cultural devastation*

Aboriginal peoples in Australia faced similar problems to Native Americans. In the 1790s smallpox spread from the north into the central and western parts of what we now call Victoria, with what Noel Butlin argued were devastating consequences. Possibly 50 per cent of people died in the groups affected.[15] In 1834 the lands of the Gunditjmara were invaded by the Henty brothers who settled at Portland, and in 1835 John Batman and John Pascoe Fawkner heralded a pastoral invasion focussed on Melbourne, first from Van Diemen's Land and then NSW. Despite the efforts for a private treaty by John Batman and his entrepreneurial backers, this was declared null and void by Governor Richard Bourke and the native title of the people went unrecognised. Sheep bred for wool soon swarmed over traditional lands in possibly the fastest land grab in imperial history.[16] New diseases, white (and black) violence, displacement and malnutrition all caused a population crash as the estimated Victorian Aboriginal population of 10,000 in 1834 fell to 1907 in the two decades to 1853. This was a fall of over 80 per cent in less than 20 years.[17] Cultural devastation occurred as key elders died, causing a massive loss of knowledge in early Victoria, then called the Port Phillip District.

Melbourne was the port of entry and exit for the burgeoning pastoral industry, so the Woiwurrung and the Boonwurrung took the brunt of this invasion. They were two of five intermarrying cultural/linguistic groups of central Victoria who called themselves 'Kulin'. Within one year of settlement in 1836, Melbourne's settler population was about 400, equal to the combined numbers of the Woiwurrung and Boonwurrung, and rising. By 1842 there were over 6000 settlers in Melbourne and, by 1851, 23,000, with an equal number in the countryside. During this time the numbers of people in these two tribes plummeted, as they did in all groups across Victoria. The Assistant Protector of Aborigines, William Thomas, carefully estimated that the Woiwurrung and Boonwurrung people of Melbourne numbered 350 in 1836, 207 in 1839, and 59 in 1852: a fall of 83 per cent. Thomas recorded 135 deaths from all causes among these two groups from 1839 to 1859, and only 28 births.[18] The sadness of loss and death was ubiquitous. New ideas of private property, backed by guns and later by fencing, meant the original owners were increasingly excluded from their lands and resources. How did Melbourne's Indigenous leadership manage this population crash, inordinate disruption, and growing cultural devastation? I will look closely at the case of Billibellary, a Woiwurrung leader, who emerged as a key individual in these deliberations.

The Woiwurrung language group occupied the large area of the watersheds of the Yarra and Maribyrnong rivers, extending from Mt Baw Baw in the Dividing Range to the east, west to Mt Macedon and Lancefield. Five clans formed the Woiwurrung and one of these five clans, the Wurundjeri, named after a grub which resided in the white gum, was split into two: Wurundjeri-Baluk and Wurundjeri-Willam. The latter occupied the area north of Melbourne to present-day Kyneton, Lancefield, and Kilmore. The Wurundjeri-Willam, a large group, was further subdivided into three led by Borrunupton, his younger brother Billibellary, and Bebejan. Each of these men were *ngurangaeta*, or clan heads.[19]

Early popular imagination was that Aboriginal society was egalitarian, ruled by elders and devoid of big men. Even the eminent anthropologist William Stanner wrote in his famous essay 'The Dreaming' in 1953 that, in Aboriginal society, there was no idea of a 'formal chief, or a leader with authority over the persons of others...There are leaders in the sense of men of unusual skill, initiative, and force and they are given much respect; they may even attract something of a following; but one finds no trace of formal or institutionalised chieftainship'.[20] However, Stanner's work was based in northern Australia. Was the situation different in the south?

James Dawson, a Western District settler, published an ethnographic work *Australian Aborigines* in 1881, based on the oral evidence of Aboriginal informants, which Dawson commented was 'approved of by them before being written down'. Of leadership, Dawson wrote: 'every tribe has its chief, who is looked upon in the light of a father, and whose authority is supreme. He consults with the best men of the tribe, but when he announces his decision they dare not contradict or disobey him'. Dawson was told that succession was by inheritance to the oldest male child, if fit, and if there were no sons, to the chief's brothers and their line.[21] Diane Barwick, an anthropologist, deeply researched Victorian Aboriginal social structure through the works of Alfred Howitt and early Aboriginal Protectors, such as William Thomas and George Augustus Robinson. These men had drawn on conversations with William Barak and others. Barwick argued that clan heads existed who had 'executive authority' and led 'external affairs'. Some 'were so eminent that their wishes were obeyed by all clans comprising a -(w)urrung [equivalent to language groups/tribe], and their religious authority was acknowledged far beyond the region'.[22]

Barwick, who combed the Protectors' journals, declared 'officials who saw daily evidence of their leadership in the early 1840s had no doubt that Billibellary was the "paramount chief" among the southern Kulin', namely: the Wathaurung, Woiwurrung and Boonwurrung.[23] An imposing man of six feet, Billibellary, also known as Jika Jika and Jaga Jaga, was a signatory of the Batman Treaty with his elder brother in May 1835.[24] Billibellary was also a key decision-maker in not taking hostile action against Fawkner's party on the Yarra banks in October 1835, when the northern Kulin or Daungwurrung (Goulburn) people threatened to attack.[25]

Billibellary was the traditional owner of one of the most important Aboriginal mining sites in Victoria, the Mt William axe-head quarry near Lancefield. The stone axe was a key item of technology in Aboriginal society and the axe blanks from Mt William were the most prized. This was revealed by Isabel McBryde's analysis of their extensive distribution across central and Western Victoria, far in excess of axe-heads from other quarry sites.[26] Neighbouring groups wishing to procure axe-head blanks sent messages to Billibellary and his people, and items such as possum-skin rugs were exchanged for axe blanks. Barak, Billibellary's nephew, told the ethnographer Alfred Howitt a generation later that on one occasion in the early 1840s a theft at Mt William of axe-head blanks was discovered. Billibellary summoned the Wathaurung from their country west of the Werribee River in the Geelong area. They met at the

Werribee River and Billibellary's spokesman Bungerim asked: 'Did some of you send this young man to take tomahawk stone?' The Wathaurung elders denied it. However, Billibellary, through Bungerim, reminded all present of the protocols: 'When the people speak of wanting stone, the old men must send us notice'. To this the Wathaurung elders replied, 'That is all right, we will do so'. Billibellary's authority and ownership of the quarry was thus affirmed.[27]

In Billibellary's prime, the question of the day for Aboriginal people was what to do about the European incursion. It must have filled their campfire conversations and their talk became no doubt more anxious with each passing month. In the first year of the invasion, that is, by 1836, the Woiwurrung and Boonwurrung were outnumbered by new arrivals. The newcomers brought thousands of sheep, which began to munch through the native grasses and prized indigenous food sources, such as the staple yam daisy or murnong (*Microseris spp.*). Europeans observers believed that the majority of the yam fields in the sheep districts were eaten out within a few years.[28] In 1839 assisted immigration to Port Phillip commenced and, between 1839 and 1842, 12,000 assisted immigrants arrived in Melbourne. The number slowed during the mid-1840s depression and then sped up again after 1847. Thirty-one thousand came as assisted immigrants by 1851 and a further 60,000 unassisted. After gold was discovered, newcomers became a torrent, as almost 600,000 came in a decade.[29] This was without doubt a 'demographic takeover' as Alfred Crosby termed it, aided by European plants and animals.[30]

Billibellary and other Woiwurrung witnessed the transformation of their world, which appeared irreversible, as their numbers fell and the newcomers increased rapidly. By 1840 they were outnumbered tenfold, by 1843, a hundred-fold. Adjustments had to be made to this rapidly changing world. Billibellary discussed his people's future with his friend and Assistant Protector of Aborigines, William Thomas: the problems of alcohol-fuelled deaths, the poor survival rate of Aboriginal children and the failure of others to be born. He remarked to Thomas, '[B]lackfellows all about say that no good have them Pickaninneys now, no country for blackfellows like long time ago'.[31] It seemed an expression of despair and resignation, like Plenty Coups' view that 'nothing happened'.

However, Billibellary, like Plenty Coups, made decisive moves. He sent at least one of his sons, probably Simon Wonga, to the government school at Narre Narre Warren in 1841.[32] After some hesitation he led 21 men into the Native Police Corps in 1842, an offer of 'another kind of living' as Marie Fels, the historian of the Corps, writes.[33] Billibellary did not undertake active policing, and played only a ceremonial role, stating: 'I am King. I no ride on horseback; I no go out of my country; young men go as you say, not me'.[34] Younger Woiwurrung and Boonwurrung, most of them clan heads or their heirs, that is, men of influence, played an active role in the Corps. Marie Fels called this act of becoming police a 'creative and adaptive Aboriginal strategy', by which their power was enlarged into the white world.[35] And power to act in the black world extended as well.

The colonial frontier fostered alliances that may be surprising to those of us in the present, but settler and Kulin historical actors at the time accepted as unremarkable that Aboriginal men were in a policing role. However, the traditional enemies of the Kulin, or those who were *mainmet* or strangers to them, were less enamoured of this fact. Native troopers while on patrol in distant regions acted with deadly violence against traditional enemies, notably those in the Western District and the Gunai/Kurnai in Gippsland. Kulin policemen also killed Aboriginal strangers in Melbourne who were considered dangerous *mainmet*. As Marie Fels commented: '[I]n these cases primary consciousness triumphed over learned European consciousness: they acted as Aboriginal men not policemen'.[36] Such policing power was used against non-local Aboriginal people in the way that Plenty Coups and the Crow battled their traditional enemies alongside the US Army. Being Aboriginal first and policemen second also worked the other way, as policemen had 'difficulty' finding perpetrators of 'crimes' who were Kulin kin.[37]

Therefore, Billibellary like Plenty Coups, pursued realistic strategies about the new and powerful forces before him: learning English and discussing the world with William Thomas, forming new alliances and making sure the whites were never attacked under his watch in the Melbourne area, educating a son at a mission school, joining the Native Police and enlisting his son Culpendure as well.

Billibellary's realism was to what purpose? Plenty Coups spoke to Linderman of the Crow actions:

> The Crow were wiser [than other tribes]. We knew the white men were strong, without number in their own country, and that there was no good in fighting them.... Our leading chiefs saw that to help the white men fight their enemies and ours would make them our friends. We had always fought the three tribes, Sioux, Cheyenne and Arapahoe, anyway, and might as well do so now. The complete destruction of our old enemies would please us. Our decision was reached, not because we loved the white man who was already crowding other tribes into our country, or because we hated the Sioux, Cheyenne and Arapahoe, but because we plainly saw that this course was the only one which might save our beautiful country for us. When I think back my heart sings because we acted as we did. It was the only way open for us.[38]

The salvation of 'beautiful country' was the salvation of the meaning of life to hunters and gatherers worldwide. Such a philosophy emerged from living with nature to forge successfully a traditional life of plenty, which Marshall Sahlins called 'affluent'.[39]

It is certain that Billibellary remained unflinchingly Aboriginal in his identity and cultural actions. When stricken with a lingering lung infection he found meaning in the traditional aetiology of his sickness. Billibellary developed a 'slight cough' in late 1845 and was given European medicine. When his illness became severe, Billibellary consulted Aboriginal doctors. They advised that an up-country Aboriginal man had stolen some of Billibellary's hair as he slept, and now his *marmbulla* (kidney fat) was wasting, draining away his life force. Billibellary recalled waking from sleep some months earlier to see a strange Aboriginal man near his fire. He must have been the thief, seeking to work sorcery on Billibellary! Thomas was unable to dissuade his friend of his traditional view that sorcery caused his decline. On his death in late 1846, a Woiwurrung party headed north against the Daungwurrung people, seeking revenge as tradition demanded. So powerful were traditional ideas that the revenge party included a mission youth, who Thomas believed 'has learnt to know better'.[40]

Despite his life and death being surrounded by the webs of tradition, three years earlier Billibellary made a remarkable request. In late 1843 he declared to William Thomas: 'If Yarra blackfellows had a country on the Yarra, that they would stop on it and cultivate the ground'.[41] His desire to become a farmer was a massive shift and a personal re-enactment of the Neolithic revolution. Farming provided a new way of staying Aboriginal and close to the land of the Woiwurrung — their land. It was not a declaration that they would relinquish hunting and gathering altogether, but rather they would farm as well and enter the new world — to survive as Aboriginal. Like the early neoliths, they might practise both modes simultaneously.[42] And, like Plenty Coups and the Crow, he sought to keep his clan together and find a new way to be Aboriginal, since hunting and gathering was becoming — if not yet impossible — increasingly difficult. Billibellary's effort to foment a new way to be Aboriginal was a courageous decision, but one that was unfulfilled at his death. His request of 1843 for land on which to farm had emerged from the Aboriginal question of the day, no doubt the topic of countless earnest campfire conversations deep into the night — how to respond to their predicament and maintain tradition? How to balance continuity and change?

Unsurprisingly, Billibellary was not alone in such thinking, as Aboriginal people daily discussed their predicament. In January 1849, William Thomas wrote in his journal that Woiwurrung and Boonwurrung asked him to 'get us a country' and, in February, that 'they press me very hard for a country to locate themselves upon'. In March 1849, Benbow, a Boonwurrung elder, waited outside the Royal Hotel to see Governor Fitzroy who was receiving settler deputations while visiting Melbourne. William Thomas recorded that Benbow sought to 'ask him for country for the Western Port blacks'. Thomas gave him sixpence to dissuade him from bothering his Excellency, 'but he coolly pocketed the 6d & and said he would send up his [breast] brass plate' to announce his presence. Three Boonwurrung waited on the opposite side of the street and Thomas 'tried to bribe them to get Benbow away from the Hotel but to no purpose'.

Governor Fitzroy did not grant Benbow an audience and Thomas lamented that if Benbow had asked for assistance 'I would have endeavord (sic) to have gain'd him an interview'.[43]

The requests for land continued, many no doubt unrecorded. In August 1850 Thomas reported that the Woiwurrung, who he called 'the Yarra blacks', 'again point out the spot they would wish to locate upon. I again object [being too near white settlers], they reason the matter with some degree of art'.[44] A month later Thomas visited Woiwurrung people at their Bulleen camp, reporting: 'the blacks impatient for a station'.[45] In 1852 they finally gained 782 hectares at Warrandyte and in August the Boonwurrung 'selected the spot they would desire to have as a reserve', being about 340 hectares on the Mordialloc Creek.[46] These reserves were unstaffed and remained mostly as stopping over places. Thomas supplied tea, sugar, flour, tobacco and blankets annually to keep the people supplied and out of Melbourne, but reported the Boonwurrung used few of the rations, and the 'Yarra tribe have not desired aught but a little tobacco'.[47]

The Kulin continued to request land throughout the 1850s, intensely so in 1859. The climate of opinion proved more favourable by that time. A gold-rush population began to think of the Aboriginal remnant they believed were fading before their eyes and needed protection. After a decade of policy inaction, a parliamentary select committee led by Thomas McCombie tabled its report in February 1859, calling for reserves to provide the less than 2,000 Aboriginal people in Victoria with their own land for agricultural and de-pasturing purposes.[48]

In late February 1859, Billibellary's two surviving sons – Simon Wonga, now a clan head aged 35, and Tommy Munnering, aged 24 – visited their father's old friend William Thomas, who was now Guardian of the Aborigines. He was called by them 'Marminarta' or father. Billibellary's sons arrived with five Daungwurrung men and they all stayed at Thomas' Merri Creek home. The next morning Wonga, speaking for the Daungwurrung, said: 'Marminarta, I bring my friends Goulburn blacks they want a block of land in their country where they may sit down, plant corn, potatoes, etc. – and work like white men'. Thomas was pessimistic of success but spoke to the men for hours.[49] The Kulin men, accompanied by Thomas, met with the Surveyor-General of Lands. They requested a specific piece of land on the 'Nakkrom' (Acheron River) near Alexandra, where 'kangaroos and possums were abundant'. Regarding their use of the land, they stated: 'that blackfellows and lubras go look out food, but some always stop and turn up ground, and plant potatoes and food'. Thomas recommended that they be given 60 hectares each, in the form of about 2000 hectares for the group, together with some initial provisions, implements and advice from a 'steady, sober agricultural family'.[50]

On 7 March 1859 the same seven Kulin waited on Charles Duffy, the Minister of Lands. The *Argus* described them as 'robust and well-made men, apparently equal in physical power to the average of Europeans', and all between 173 and 183 cm. They wore 'coarse jumpers and trousers like sailors or labourers of an inferior class'. The *Argus* newspaper reported: 'their countenances were intelligent and animated. Their entrance into the board-room was made in an unembarrassed and quiet manner', where upon being seated they listened with attentiveness and 'an air of grave courtesy'. Duffy was moved by these dignified land-seekers, reflecting his own history of involvement in land and tenancy protests in Ireland. He sanctioned the proposals and was astonished that this group had been reduced from 600 to 32 in just 20 years. Duffy agreed to a grant 'for we are anxious to make any reasonable experiment in this direction'. The Kulin made 'exclamations, apparently of approval', and withdrew with a slight bow in Duffy's direction.[51]

In March 1863 and after several hindrances, Simon Wonga, William Barak and 20 other Woiwurrung squatted at a traditional camping site called 'Coranderrk' near Healesville. To consolidate their hold on this land, representatives of the group attended Governor Barkly's levee in May 1863, where they presented a loyal address to the 'Great Mother Queen Victoria', promising to 'live like white men almost', and gave weapons, rugs and baskets as presents for the soon-to-be-married Prince of Wales. They also spoke to Sir Henry Barkly about land. The Kulin thereafter considered the gazettal of 931 hectares of reserve land at Coranderrk in June 1863 as a gift from Queen Victoria, forming a powerful story of reciprocity: loyalty and fealty to a great kin in return for land of their own.[52] The promise to live 'almost' like white men was a clear affirmation that these nascent farmers also wanted to remain Aboriginal. It was their radical hope.

With the encouragement of Barak's friend John Green, other Kulin — Boonwurrung and Daungwurrung — came freely to settle at Coranderrk over succeeding months and years. As clan owners of the country, Simon Wonga and Barak led this new community, Wonga being pre-eminent until his death in 1875.[53] They worked with a will on land they believed to be theirs, dressing as, and building houses like, the labouring people of the district. Fences were erected, gardens laid out, and animals put to pasture with the mentoring of John Green, Coranderrk's manager. The Central Board for the Aborigines was at this stage helpful. In 1864 the Central Board reported: 'Wonga and Barak, who have made homes for themselves at Coranderrk, and who are now receiving instruction, are very intelligent men and in their behaviour would compare favourably with the better class of other races'.[54]

Barak, who became leader after 1875, displayed the flexibility of his uncle, Billibellary — and of course Plenty Coups. Barak had witnessed the signing of the Batman Treaty when a boy, joined the Native Police and became Christian under the mentoring of his friend John Green. And, as Diane Barwick explains, Barak married a Kurnai woman, whose people had been at enmity with the Woiwurrung; travelled to the Murray River, another site of traditional enemies; and with Simon Wonga fought for a school at Coranderrk and encouraged the people to farm.[55] These were all acts in the remaking of what it was to be Woiwurrung. Barwick first told the remarkable story of Coranderrk's agricultural successes in 1972, which included winning prizes for their hops at the Royal Melbourne Agricultural Show, and the Coranderrk people's pride in their farming success.[56] It was a story Barwick enriched immeasurably in her magnificent *Rebellion at Coranderrk* (1998). Others have since told the story in less depth but more manageable size.[57]

In 1880 William Barak, Coranderrk's most senior elder, travelled to the Maloga Mission on the Murray River to stay with kin, desperately also seeking a finer climate for his son David, who was declining from tuberculosis. While there, Barak told the Maloga people of Coranderrk's achievements in farming and Green's assurance that if they made a success of it, the land would remain theirs. The Maloga people listened intently and in July 1881 petitioned the NSW government, narrating how their tribal lands had been taken, over-run with sheep, and the native game reduced or exterminated, leaving them in 'beggary'. They were trained in agriculture by the missionaries Daniel and Janet Matthews, and wanted their own land 'to cultivate and raise stock', believing, like Billibellary, that 'we could, in a few years support ourselves by our own industry'. On the strength of Barak's story, they added: 'we more confidently ask this favour of a grant of land as our fellow natives in other colonies have proved capable of supporting themselves, where suitable land had been reserved for them'. Forty-two men, including Barak's son David who had stayed on at Maloga, signed the petition. Other petitions followed from Maloga men, including one from young William Cooper, until land was finally granted at Cummeragunja.[58]

On his return from Maloga, Barak faced a concerted attack by the Central Board, renamed the Aborigines Protection Board after new powers were granted it in 1869. The Board sought to close down the assertive Coranderrk community, which was also suffering from a tuberculosis outbreak, and shift its people to an allegedly healthier station on the Murray. The people resisted and Barak led a march of 20 Kulin men to Melbourne in March 1881 to petition the Premier Graham Berry. Berry received them sympathetically, but soon after his ministry fell from office. The Coranderrk people immediately petitioned the O'Loghlen Ministry for the return of Green, who had been replaced by Reverend Stahle in 1874, and the continuance of Coranderrk. O'Loghlen appointed a select committee to investigate Coranderrk.[59] The following month, Coranderrk's unloved current manager, Reverend Strickland, informed the Board that the Kulin 'men are in a state of revolt'.[60] During the inquiry 22 Coranderrk residents, including four women, answered more than 5000 questions, airing their grievances about the removal of John Green as manager, recent mismanagement including the poor state of the rations, and their commitment to farming.[61]

On the matter of land the people called for the continuance of Coranderrk. The real issue for the Kulin had always been land and freedom. As William Barak testified: 'The Government leave us here, give us this ground and let us manage here and get all the money'.[62] The petition signed by 46 Coranderrk people simply said: 'We want the Board and the Inspector, Captain Page, to be no longer over us. We want only one man here, and that is Mr John Green, and the station to be under the Chief Secretary; then we will show the country that the station could self-support itself'.[63] It was the 1843 dream of Billibellary reaffirmed yet again: to have land, to farm and be independent as a people. Those on other Victorian Aboriginal reserves had similar desires, and when they were attacked by the Board, they responded in a similar way.[64]

William Cooper was a Yorta Yorta man of Maloga who had petitioned for land in the 1880s, and later worked as a rural labourer when he left reserve life to be free of the Board's control. Cooper moved to Melbourne in 1933 when in his seventies, to pursue a concerted political campaign for Aboriginal rights. Within a year Cooper drafted a petition to the King, calling for royal protection to 'prevent the extinction of the aboriginal race and give better conditions for all', and to 'ensure an Aboriginal representative in parliament'.[65] By December 1934, Cooper, writing as honorary secretary of the Australian Aborigines' League, an Aboriginal political body he founded, claimed 3000 Aboriginal people had signed and 'signatures are still coming freely from all states'.[66] Cooper based his petition on a history of injustice, and his position as 'heir' to the 'original inhabitants'. He claimed civil rights as an Australian, but also as a descendant of the 'original Australians'. The League, whose membership was only open to Aboriginal people, ran meetings marked by Yorta Yorta songs and gum-leaf playing. The 'Day of Mourning' in 1938, conceived by William Cooper and Bill Ferguson's NSW-based Aborigines Progressive Association, continued the clarion call for citizens' rights for Aboriginal people across Australia, again set in a history of injustice and a clear determination to remain Aboriginal.

In this sense Cooper and others redefined Billibellary's radical hope to fit a new era in Australian life, by conceiving the Aboriginal future, not simply as farmers, but equal citizens fit for a life in, but not of, Australian society. Citizenship, formally framed as white in both theory and legislation, was now in Cooper's mind to include Aboriginal people.[67] Just as Plenty Coups re-imagined being Crow, Cooper re-imagined Aboriginal people across Australia as citizens. This was truly radical, as Aboriginal people were then in diverse stages of contact with white society across Australia, and few people were imagining citizenship for any of them. It was a hope, but one based on Australian democratic traditions and the emerging notions of human rights internationally, of which Cooper and others were all too well aware. The ageing Cooper mentored a crop of young Aboriginal people to follow him. Doug Nicholls (later Sir Doug), Bill Onus and others stood on the Yarra Bank hustings alongside Cooper, learning the trade. They later assumed control of the Australian Aborigines' League after Cooper's death in 1941.

Bill Onus certainly embraced this new version of the radical hope of his forefathers — to be citizen and Aboriginal at the same time. Onus openly resisted the assimilation policy that became *de rigeur* for governments in the 1950s, a policy which offered rights, but also demanded cultural absorption. In April 1957, he sent a ten-page statement to the Victorian Governor, Sir Reginald Alexander Dallas Brooks, circumventing the politicians, as Simon Wonga and William Barak had done a hundred years before. He reiterated the usual political demands for Aboriginal rights, but added that future Aboriginal citizens 'are constantly made to feel our inferiority. There is scarcely a waking moment of our lives that we are not made conscious of it, and this influences our whole lives'. Governments should fund a tourist industry focused on Aboriginal culture to boost their self-esteem, as 'there is no doubt that our biggest tourist attraction is the Aboriginal himself and his way of life'. Aboriginal people, Onus declared, had 'never completely surrendered our ways nor accepted yours... Even right here in Melbourne we still are Aborigines at heart. ...We do not wish to become white, rather it is our ardent desire to remain black.'[68]

In March 1957, Doug Nicholls, together with Stan Davey and several other white activists, formed a new organisation, the Victorian Aborigines Advancement League, to pursue welfare and advocacy issues. It was a coalition of black and white forces. This new League soon opposed the assimilation policy and led a campaign against the Aborigines Welfare Board, the successor in 1957 to the century-old Aborigines Protection Board. The League played a pivotal role in the demise of the Welfare Board in December 1967. After some tumultuous months of controversy the League itself was taken over in late 1969 by Aboriginal people in a bloodless 'black power' coup. Since then and to the present day, the League has sought to advocate and deliver services to the Indigenous community within a world of government grants, funding rules and accountability, and a continuing government penchant for mainstreaming. Nonetheless, radical hope survives within the hearts of its leaders, which exhibits a different sort of courage to the warrior tradition, one embraced by Billibellary.

Esme Bamblett, the current CEO of the League, explains how she deals with governments and their procedures that expect uniformity:

> We resist it [mainstreaming] in our own way, because we maintain culture, even *though* we run [government-funded] programmes, our whole idea is to maintain culture. If you look upstairs now, I've got photos of our heroes. There in the boardroom we have all the photos of all the people who've ever been on the Board, so we maintain culture by the very presence of those people. When people come here, we talk about culture, we talk about the history, talk about the struggle for rights, so we constantly tell people, when they come here, they *see* it, and they read it. ...Governments don't muck around with us in Victoria, like they used to, they're not game. We're outspoken, we're loud, and we're aggressive, [Aboriginal] Victorians are very *active* people.[69]

Today the League stands proudly as the oldest Aboriginal organisation in the country. This is much more than survival, the phase during which Plenty Coups said 'nothing happened'. Radical hope in its various forms — as imagined farmer or citizen — gave Aboriginal people a new and vibrant way to be Aboriginal, after much of their material and cultural life had been swept away. The Victorian Aboriginal community, like the Crow Nation, remain vibrant today. Former warriors, inspired by Billibellary, Barak, Cooper and others, shrugged off mere survival, being carried forward by a new and different courage.

CHAPTER 9
How do you teach Aboriginal history?
Maxine Briggs

I am an Indigenous Victorian Aboriginal woman born of the Yorta Yorta and Taungwurrung people and affiliated with the tribes of my great-grandparents. As the Koori librarian at the State Library of Victoria, I was invited to participate in the symposium titled 'Writing and Teaching Aboriginal History', an event to acknowledge the retirement of La Trobe University history professor, Richard Broome. Throughout his time at La Trobe, Richard produced a number of books that concentrated on the history and culture of Indigenous Victorian Aboriginal people. I salute Richard Broome for his contribution to the cause of greater public awareness of Aboriginal nationhood in his own backyard. Inspired by his work, I chose to give an informal presentation, based on my personal experiences, to inform the conversation.

As an elder in my family group, I write from a Victorian Aboriginal perspective, using our own references, oral tradition and cultural practice to express a grassroots/clan view. I also employ an Indigenous research paradigm and an Aboriginal cultural policy to frame the conversation. In this chapter I highlight the work of grassroots Aboriginal people who live at the coalface with the dispossessed and disenfranchised in our communities. It is the families of these people who often find that there are little to no appropriate services to respond to the complexity of their loved ones' needs. When they can't participate in mainstream society because the cultural gap is too great, there is no alternative for them. It is for those members of our families and communities that I write this chapter.

The focus for this chapter is the importance of Aboriginal culture to this country through the symbiotic relationship between the people and the land. Aboriginal cultural practice links people with the natural world and reinforces our connections and our responsibilities. Our worldview is relational and it requires that we live a life that respects our ancestors; they give us our identity and protect future generations, they give us meaning. The creation of the Australian nation shattered a system that had nurtured this land for 60,000 years. Since its beginnings, when Captain Cook planted the British flag on Aboriginal country on the basis that it was terra nullius — a land with no people, so described because to his eyes the land had not been worked or cultivated, thus allowing the British to take possession by stealth — our position has had to be protected. We have done so at great physical, social and spiritual cost to Aboriginal people.

My role as the Koori librarian at the State Library of Victoria (SLV) is custodial in nature; it is the job of the Koori librarian primarily to identify, manage and protect Aboriginal materials in the library's holdings. An Indigenous knowledge management system, which is based on an Indigenous research paradigm, ensures that the Aboriginal worldview is paramount in the design of any program that manages Indigenous information. This is achieved in concert with Aboriginal and Torres Strait Islander people and their communities through the ATSI Cultural Permission Program (CPP), which is the principle tool employed for achieving those outcomes. The CPP was designed along traditional Aboriginal kinship lines: direct descendants/clan are the senior authority then the descendant/clan communities have the secondary authority, and there are traditional owner corporations (established through native title) that in some circumstances may speak for all the clans in a language group. Ultimately though, the program was designed to put the authority for these records in the hands of descendants. The ATSI CPP is triggered when a photograph of an Aboriginal or Torres Strait Islander person is ordered from the SLV's online catalogue: a CPP form is created and a descendant is identified by the Koori librarian. Contact is then made with the descendant, they are introduced to the person ordering the photograph and then negotiations can begin. This process puts the authority into the hands of the Aboriginal descendant and it opens up discussion between the parties around the use of the image of their ancestor. It may be that the descendant will advise on the use of the image and the nature of the contextual information, and agreement must be reached before the order is completed.

The core component of my work is informed by the references to my cultural heritage. Indigenous Victorian people's connection to country is recorded in the archives from the colonial period and backed up by the photographs of our ancestors. The photographs are touchstones for us, they are a record of the lives of the ancestors and they are a record of highly sensitive moments of great significance that are critical to our lives. As I have said previously when talking about the heritage photographs: 'for Aboriginal people, the images represent the members of their bloodline at the point of impact, at the point where the future lives of their descendants was changed forever. This is the end of a complete way of life and the beginning of a dual existence.'[1]

We can use these photographs, and other records, to write honest histories of Australia, in which Aboriginal people and their worldview have survived despite more than two centuries of colonial onslaught. In this chapter I begin by discussing the links between the assimilation policy and histories that uphold the notion of terra nullius, and the damage caused to Aboriginal people by Australian histories that tell a peaceful story of settlement in which Aboriginal people barely exist. I then discuss some of the ways that both the colonial archive and an Aboriginal worldview can challenge these terra nullius stories and inform new kinds of Aboriginal histories.

Growing up on country

I believe that the Aboriginal voice and Aboriginal knowledge systems need to stand alone, without any outside influences that might steer and shape them, allowing us to return to the source of our strength. It is important to me, as an elder in my family group, to follow Aboriginal cultural practice by using our oral traditions with the authority of my ancestry, to speak from my heart about my own firsthand experience of this topic. These are my recollections of my life and my family's experiences.

Like many Aboriginal people who were born in the years after World War II, my family and I lived on an Aboriginal reserve or mission. Our mission, Cummeragunja, is situated on the banks of the Murray River on the border of Victoria and NSW. Cummeragunja was always home to a large number of the Yorta Yorta tribe, my paternal grandmother's people. My maternal grandmother was of the Taungwurrung tribe in central Victoria through her father; her mother was of the Wiradjuri tribe in central NSW. In the mission setting we lived very easily with the pre-invasion past because it was only a generation away and part of a continuum. My grandmother's mother had two brothers, one of whom was a practicing 'clever man' or medicine man until his death in 1943. Through the oral tradition, the stories told by our kin always kept us in touch with members of our family groups across the years in other generations.

Everyone knew everyone else on 'Cummera'. We knew what family groups we all came from because for the most part we were descendants of Yorta Yorta and living on Yorta Yorta country. But we also shared the mission with Aboriginal people from other tribal groups, such as my mother and her family, who were sometimes forced to live off country due to government policy. However, for us all, it was our little patch and we knew the land well. We fished for Murray cod and Murray perch and yabbies from the waters and hunted rabbits on the sandhill, we gathered mushrooms in the autumn and duck eggs when the river was in flood. Sometimes Mum would catch a native bee and attach a little feather to it, let it go and follow it to its hive and then smoke them out so she could get their honey for us. That was something she learned from her grandmother. My father, Hartley Briggs, worked with his brothers and cousins for the Forest Commission in the Barmah redgum forest: maintaining it and keeping a close eye on it, killing off the weeds, clearing the ground of fallen branches and the trees of broken limbs to prevent a build-up of fuel for bushfires. They were excellent bushmen, ensuring the good health of our rivers and the natural environment by following in the footsteps of their ancestors. We knew our world intimately and although we did not have a ceremonial life we had a cultural life, and it grounded us and bound us to the natural world and our place in it.

For my parents' generation, their education was not deemed to be important to the government or the mission managers, just as long as they could perform the duties required of them in service to white society. This is described in the unpublished writings of my mother, May Briggs-Walsh, in her recollections 'Stories and Memories of My Childhood', where she says: 'The mission school only went to grade four and we were not given the assistance to further our education, which was done by correspondence in our day. I believe it did come later but too late for us. Coming from a large family, we all went to work in our early teens. I went to work at the age of thirteen and a half.'[2] My mother worked as a domestic servant for well-to-do white families. Child care was the core of her duties, so she minded the children, provided emotional support to the wives and cooked meals for the family, washing and ironing their clothes and cleaning their houses. She came out of this experience wanting a better life for the next generation.

We had attended primary school on the mission and were isolated except for when we played sports against non-Aboriginal schools. All class levels were taught in the one school room and for the teachers it was usually their first year on the job. However, I didn't feel inadequate when we were later enrolled in a white primary school in a small town in dairy country, central Victoria, due mainly to my early Aboriginal education in our mission community.

In the 1960s the government introduced the assimilation policy that was supposed to create a level playing field for Aboriginal people. In order to be equal to non-Aboriginal people it required Aboriginal children to attend high school. The newly established Aboriginal Advancement League, guided by Pastor Doug Nicholls, set up a hostel for Aboriginal students in Nathalia, a small town that serviced the local dairy industry. We moved in to the hostel and my parents began their work as surrogate parents to Aboriginal children from across the state.

The then Minister for Territories, Paul Hasluck, expressed the agreement reached by the states at the 1961 Native Welfare Conference on the meaning of assimilation in this way:

> The policy of assimilation means in the view of all Australian governments that all aborigines and part-aborigines are expected eventually to attain the same manner of living as other Australians and to live as members of a single Australian community enjoying the same rights and privileges, accepting the same responsibilities, observing the same customs and influenced by the same beliefs, hopes and loyalties as other Australians.[3]

However, it did not provide all the protection and security for Aboriginal students that it proposed. It essentially took away our right to be Aboriginal, taking a toll on the Aboriginal students who were now forced to act white without the government educating the white educators about what that meant for us. Hasluck went on to talk about the way Aboriginal people would be assisted to assimilate:

> Thus, any special measures taken for aborigines and part-aborigines are regarded as temporary measures not based on colour but intended to meet their need for special care and assistance to protect them from any ill effects of sudden change and to assist them to make the transition from one stage to another in such a way as will be favourable to their future social, economic and political advancement.[4]

But that 'transition' was not what we wanted; it was what the government wanted and it failed to recognise our human rights – proving to be yet another effort to deprive us of our identity and our heritage, and serving only to inflict more damage on Indigenous people. This was cultural abuse; it was in essence what Portuguese sociologist Boaventura de Sousa Santos termed epistemicide, the process by which knowledge systems are killed.[5]

High school was a shock for me. I could not reconcile my worldview with the way Aboriginal people were represented in the teaching of Australian history. My ancestors were painted as less than human, possessing no religion, as savages who did not till the land and were therefore not masters of it, and their efforts to fight the invaders of their land were seen as merely a nuisance for the settlers. For my people, it was the white people who were the thieves, stealing our land and our way of life; they were the savages murdering our ancestors and destroying our country by imposing land management practices that degraded the natural world. There were no cultural references for Aboriginal children in the classroom; it wasn't Aboriginal history that was being taught – it was a white colonial history that only involved Aboriginal people when they intersected with settlers.

Recently, as I researched this topic, I interviewed a number of Aboriginal people in my community and was not surprised to find that my very much older cousins had had similar experiences to me in the classroom. I was shocked to learn that my own nephews and nieces had the same experiences as I did with the teaching of Aboriginal History in their school years of the mid 1990s. It has become apparent that the idea of terra nullius (a land without owners, effectively a land without people) was a concept applied to the 'conquest' of Australia by the British in 1788 and was still impacting us through all the generations of our people ever since. The fiction of terra nullius, as well as the Aboriginal cultures it ignores, needs to be taught to all Australian students in order for them to gain a deeper understanding of the situation for Aboriginal people. I don't know how many times I have been told by non-Aboriginal people that they are completely unprepared for how awkward they feel when they realise how little they know about Aboriginal culture. It is as though, by learning about Aboriginal culture and the way it works, they are woken from the great Australian dream where everyone gets a 'fair go' to a reality built on lies.[6]

Because of my upbringing in the 'gated' community that was the mission, when I left school I felt I was able to take on the world as a fully functioning human being, I felt equipped with all the life skills and resilience I had acquired from my Aboriginal heritage. I learned my ABCs too but I knew I would achieve whatever I set out to do based on the strength of my cultural heritage and the knowledge that I walk on Aboriginal land wherever I go in this country. With little assistance for Aboriginal people to remain on their country, the assimilation policy forced them to move into the towns to 'become white', but that brought with it many new challenges for the mob. These experiences inform my identity and the paradigm through which I view those issues that control and constrain the public persona of our people.

The Great Australian Silence: A colonising paradigm

After 230 years, Aboriginal people continue to suffer the consequences of colonisation, but it must not continue into the twenty-first century. Aboriginal people in the southeast and all over Australia are standing strong on country and building their cultural capacity to move forward and to contribute to society on their own terms. There are currently enormous efforts to recover and re-establish Aboriginal languages which were taken away from Aboriginal people in the aftermath of the invasion and during the generations since. When Aboriginal people operate on their own terms it can put them at a disadvantage in the dominant society because they are seen to be breaking the society's so-called social contract, a mechanism that ensures its citizens act only in the national interests. However, if they do not break this contract, Aboriginal people not only face a life as second-class citizens but they will forever have a dual existence, placing undue stress on their daily lives. The Victorian Aboriginal Health Service argues that the 'underlying causes of poor Indigenous health can be attributed to social and economic exclusion, unemployment, low income, poor housing and sanitation, poor education, and lack of adequate nutrition.'[7] I would add that all of these issues can be in some way attributed to the teaching of Aboriginal history.

The teaching of Aboriginal history in the education system in Australia has had a negative effect on the self-esteem of Aboriginal people, and on how they have been viewed and treated by non-Aboriginal Australians. It is necessary to deconstruct the historical context that created the curriculum in order to better understand its intent. Richard Broome's books *Aboriginal Australians* and *Aboriginal Victorians* have contributed to a better understanding of the true nature of Aboriginal society and how it was decimated by the cruelty of colonisation. Education by its very nature is a means by which the population is taught how to live in the society that is in control and so it was for the nation of Aboriginal tribes too, before colonisation. However, in any conflict, the winner writes the story and the losers have no option but to become participants in it.

I support the theory that the doctrine of terra nullius was employed by the colonisers as a device to dispossess the Aboriginal nation. As this doctrine has been embedded in the education of Australian children, Aboriginal people have suffered the consequences. In 1994, Aboriginal politician Linda Burney presented a paper called: 'An Aboriginal Way of Being Australian,' to the Citizenship Forum held by the Ideas for Australia Committee. In it she said:

One reason why I need to tell our story is that so few Non-Aboriginal people know anything about Aboriginal Australia or Aboriginal experiences.... As you may or may not know, the reason for this ignorance is that there was a conspiracy of silence about Aboriginal Australia through all the dark years of White Australia. Fundamentally, that silence started when Captain Cook landed on an uninhabited island of Cape York, planted the English flag and claimed the whole of eastern Australia as *Terra Nullius* – 'land belonging to no-one'.[8]

This silence is the unofficial policy of forgetting that underpins the notion of terra nullius. It is part of what could be called the social contract, a paradigm which underpins all market economies, with its silent rules, regulations and guidelines. It was employed to keep all Australians ignorant, not only of the painful story of our shared history, but of how this policy of forgetting has deliberately prevented a true understanding of Aboriginal nationhood in this country. Aboriginal nationhood was possibly not easily recognisable to the untrained eye of the uneducated convict class, but it was blatantly ignored by an invading force that not only felt themselves to be superior but were bent on colonising in spite of their official orders and despite what their experienced eyes could see.

In the first instance, sickness arrived on the wind and smallpox was its name; it killed thousands of Aboriginal people. It weakened their resistance and it heralded the terror that was to come in the form of genocidal attacks perpetrated by the invaders who followed the smallpox plague. Some people today argue that this was no natural disaster but something very deliberate and cruel, and that it was germ warfare practiced on an unsuspecting and ill-equipped population. Watkin Tench, an officer on the First Fleet, was aware of bottles of smallpox that were carried on his ship, 'The Supply'.[9] On the frontier, widespread arsenic poisonings and massacres were carried out by the new arrivals, based on flimsy excuses to reduce the population and clear the land for their own purposes. Aboriginal people lived through a holocaust of sorts, with raiding parties of whites murdering large groups of Aboriginal people in response to the killing of one of their own.

The churches also played a part in this 'policy of forgetting' and their contribution must be considered too because, while missions provided some protection for Aboriginal people, it came at a great cost. When residents of these missions could not continue their cultural responsibilities in caring for country, in some part because their numbers had been so greatly reduced by the invasion and also as it was still dangerous for Aboriginal people to try to live on country due to squatters taking over traditional Aboriginal lands as their own. Moreover, there was a breakdown of cultural connections as people were, some would say deliberately, removed from one mission to other missions away from their own lands. Aboriginal people were convinced by the church that education into white culture was their only option for survival as they learned how to live in a white world and to adopt a white way of life. However, that view is today being challenged by Aboriginal people themselves.

From invasion and throughout the following 100 years, mission life sought to ensure that Aboriginal culture, in its traditional state, could not survive. Aboriginal people in Victoria and southeastern Australia bore the brunt of the initial onslaught. They were persuaded, often very cruelly, to stop speaking their language and to stop practicing their culture. They could not continue to maintain and preserve a cultural life as free people and they could no longer carry out their ceremonial responsibilities. But, in a range of circumstances, they endured. It is my personal view that some of the cultural practices may not have survived if the tourist trade had not provided an economic opportunity for them to persist. Possum-skin cloaks were made for a financial return along with woven fibre baskets, boomerangs and personal artworks by Aboriginal elders, amongst other things. Some of these were collected by cultural institutions such as the Museum of Victoria, the National Gallery of Victoria and local historical societies and can now form the basis for cultural revival programs.

Disproving histories: Recovering from the archive

In the years since Mabo and the Native Title Act, there has been a developing awareness in the Australian population of the rights of Indigenous people to their traditional lands to practice their culture. The impact that these insights have had on the teaching of Aboriginal history has been enormous, as history teachers have had to re-evaluate the curriculum. However, this process has not been easy. When we talk about Aboriginal history in education, we are dealing with a topic that is not an easy fit in terms of the history of non-Aboriginal people in this country. Since Europeans' arrival in 1788, there have been cover-ups and lies in respect to the treatment of the original inhabitants. These continued in the 1990s, when the Howard Government argued against a 'black armband' view of history that it believed created uncertainty (for non-Aboriginal Australians). Opposing views fed into the 'history wars', a battle amongst anthropologists and historians over the histories of invasion and settlement. Robert Manne has argued that the history wars 'could not have broken out' if 'the Great Australian Silence had not been a potent ingredient in our political culture for a century or more, and if there had not existed in Australian society a deep yearning for a history in which no serious crimes against the Aborigines had been committed'.[10]

At this point I would like to acknowledge the work and writings of Aboriginal people that I drew from in writing this chapter, including Kevin Gilbert, Hyllus Maris, Bill Neidjie, Rosalie Kunoth-Monks and May Briggs-Walsh, as well as academics like Henry Reynolds, Richard Broome, Bruce Pascoe, Bill Gammage, Jonathan Lear, and others like Diane Barwick and her benefactor Bill Stanner: scholars who mined the archives of the cultural institutions. They opened up the hidden histories of our ancestors contained in the photograph, the manuscript, the old maps and rare book collections of libraries and museums that hold the studies of Aboriginal life produced by the 'settlers' in the colonial period. We have a shared history from the colonial period of the nineteenth century through to the twenty-first century and much of that history is detailed in Australia's collecting institutions.

There is proof throughout the colonial record that Aboriginal people loved the land and took care to preserve it for future generations. They always had a spiritual connection to their country that has helped people to maintain it by honouring their responsibilities. In the eastern states, this country was known as Bandiana before it was called Australia, it was continuously sung and danced and painted through the ceremonies that kept the sacred places strong and healthy. Drawing from the colonial records, it is easy to disprove the notion of terra nullius by instead exposing an intelligent and thoughtful program of farming practices that were directly connected to Aboriginal spiritual and ceremonial life, such as the songlines system.

Aboriginal history in the future: Creative adaptation on our terms

This is a personal perspective in which I have used Aboriginal references to examine the ontology of 'terra nullius' and its impact on the teaching of Aboriginal History in education. At the heart of Australian history, this doctrine of terra nullius sanctioned the 'settlement' of this country by an invading force, a force that stripped away ownership laws and cultural stewardship from Aboriginal people, relegating them to savagery and thereby justifying occupation by a so-called superior society. Though the 1992 Mabo High Court decision ushered in an era of 'honest histories', before that time the methodology for teaching Australian history had been basically unchanged since the colonial era, although some historians, including Richard Broome, did have an impact in the classroom in the 1980s.

As Aboriginal people in Australia we are compelled to straddle two worlds and yet it is not the same for people of the dominant society. For the dominant society, they continue to exist in a place of privilege, they only need to understand one culture, their own, and that needs to change. Today, Aboriginal people are well educated in the world of the market society in which we live, and we also know more about the world of our ancestors than ever before because we are now researching our own histories through the archives and applying our own references to what we find. More than 50 years since those days when Australian history was bathed in a banal, insidious overtone of white superiority and entitlement, it is Aboriginal people who will change the dynamic and restore the balance because it matters to us. Aboriginal and non-Aboriginal Australians are from worlds of very different cultural values and historical perspectives. This is an issue between the Aboriginal nation and the settler nation and we will need to work together at a local level to achieve a beneficial outcome for future generations.

A way forward in the teaching of Aboriginal history must be in a space where Aboriginal people drive the process: this might involve Aboriginal people teaching students ways of caring for country as a subject. It may even mean that Aboriginal people consider adoption of non-Aboriginal locals into the tribe or clan as a means of ensuring that Australians embrace the lore of the land. The Aboriginal worldview must be recognised and understood by those people in government who make decisions because it is they who decide the form of our education system, they who write the curricula and develop the subjects.

As an Aboriginal person I will always write from our perspective and will always use our oral tradition. An Aboriginal perspective is relational, it requires that we move forward together and by engaging people of all ages in the discussion you show proper respect for Aboriginal values. In all the discussions that I had with family and other community members, it became apparent that all the immediate generations around me had the same experiences in the classroom. The importance of identifying ways to inculcate the Aboriginal worldview and infuse the teaching of Aboriginal history with Aboriginal references must be a high priority, with Aboriginal people employed as policy makers in the mainstream educational system. Those people who teach the children of Australia about Aboriginal history must understand that this can only be done in concert with Aboriginal people.

Using the Aboriginal worldview and incorporating an Indigenous research paradigm in the telling of Aboriginal history by Aboriginal people can create a stronger society for everyone living on country. An Aboriginal worldview is relational in nature: the clan-based society that exists in Australia is testament to this. There is a physical relationship that exists between a clan in the kinship system and their land, through the plants and animals that provide their sustenance, the trees and rocks that provide their shelter. There is a spiritual connection to all of these elements through the totem paradigm which links them to other clans from their language group through the Dreaming and its stories. The songlines and the trade routes connect a clan to other clans in their and other language groups across the country. An Indigenous research paradigm deals with the relationship between Aboriginal people and their knowledge system, which incorporates traditional values in the ownership of information.

Up until now we have been adapting our lives to the needs of the dominant society in order to gain a respected place in it. But after all this time and all those generations jumping through hoops, still we have the lowest life expectancy of any other group in Australia, an incarceration rate that continues to grow and suicide numbers that now include children. With all the educated, qualified and well paid Indigenous people in high positions in mainstream society, on the ground nothing much has changed for the majority of Aboriginal people. It is clear now that we must embrace our own worldview and employ the knowledge systems developed by our ancestors over millennia to ensure a better life for our youth. Some Aboriginal people will thrive in the wider community but they will always need to touch the ground and all that that entails, and that will require the presence of Aboriginal cultural custodians who are fully immersed in, and deeply connected to, traditional Aboriginal governance systems and cultural practice.

The negotiation of a national treaty is currently under discussion, while others are pushing for constitutional recognition. At the same time we are all trying to come to terms with Native Title and the many layers of complexity that it has already added to our lives. We must prepare for the second coming of the white man in our world — but this time at our invitation and on our terms. Aboriginal culture is generous in its philosophies and its relationships, it was always so but it may be that from now on we will proceed with extreme caution.

It is time now to build keeping places and knowledge centres on country where our people can restore their spirit through their cultural connections. Many young Aboriginal people have told me that they feel a deep disconnection from their people and their culture, which in turn creates high levels of anxiety and despair. Building the capacity of the clans and their communities is the priority now. We need to have dedicated places where we can gather in our clan/family groups, or as individuals, developing our craft or studying historical records returned from collecting institutions. Our cultural custodians must develop policies created with traditional Aboriginal values that will guide both our art practice in the wider community and our cultural practice in our own inner community. Using guiding principles from the Dreaming stories to find solutions is an example of cultural practice that is drawn from the Aboriginal worldview. It will take time and effort to restore the Aboriginal worldview to its proper place in our daily lives but it will be a labour of love and I look forward to undertaking that quest.

Appendix
Richard Broome's publications on Aboriginal history

Books
Aboriginal Australians: Black Response to White Dominance, 1788–1980, George Allen & Unwin, Sydney, 1982.

Aboriginal Australians: Black Responses to White Dominance, 1788–1994, Allen & Unwin, Sydney, 1994, revised 2nd edn.

Sideshow Alley (with Alick Jackomos), Allen & Unwin, Sydney, 1998.

Aboriginal Australians: Black Responses to White Dominance, 1788–2001, Allen & Unwin, Sydney, 2002, revised 3rd edn.

Aboriginal Victorians: A History Since 1800, Allen & Unwin, Sydney, 2005.

'A Man of All Tribes': The Life of Alick Jackomos (with Corinne Manning), Aboriginal Studies Press, Canberra, 2006.

Aboriginal Australians: A History Since 1788, Allen & Unwin, Sydney, 2010, completely revised 4th edn.

Fighting Hard: The Victorian Aborigines Advancement League, Aboriginal Studies Press, Canberra, 2015.

Book chapters
'Aboriginal Pioneers', in *The Victorians: Arriving*, Fairfax, Syme & Weldon, Sydney, 1984, pp. 1–16.

'Voices Beside the Creeks', in *Coburg: Between Two Creeks*, Lothian, Melbourne, 1987, pp. 4–16.

'The Struggle for Australia: Aboriginal-European Warfare 1770-1930', in *Australia: Two Centuries of War and Peace*, eds M McKernan and M Browne, Australian War Memorial in association with Allen & Unwin, Canberra, 1988, pp. 92–120.

'Victoria', in *Contested Ground: Australian Aborigines under the British Crown*, ed. A McGrath, Allen & Unwin, Sydney, 1995, pp. 121–67.

'Historians, Aborigines and Australia: Writing the National Past', in *In the Age of Mabo: History, Aborigines and Australia*, ed. B Attwood, Allen & Unwin, Sydney, 1996, pp. 54–72.

'Collaborations on Writing a Popular Photographic History of Aboriginal Tent Boxers: A Duet' (with Alick Jackomos), in *Work in Flux*, eds E. Greenwood, K. Neumann and A. Sartori, History Department, Melbourne University, Melbourne, 1995, pp. 83-91.

'"No One Thinks of Us": The Framlingham Aboriginal Community in the Great Depression', in *Through Depression and War: The United States and Australia*, eds P Bastien and R Bell, Australian and American Fulbright Commission & Australian and New Zealand American Studies Association, Sydney, 2002, pp. 62-81.

'The Statistics of Frontier Conflict', in *Frontier Conflict: The Australian Experience*, eds B Attwood and SG Foster, National Museum of Australia, Canberra, 2003, pp. 88-98.

'Aboriginal People and Government in Victoria', in *Walata Tyamateetj: A Guide to Government Records about Aboriginal People in Victoria*, Public Records Office of Victoria, Melbourne, 2014, pp. 11-15.

'Aboriginal Melbourne', in *Remembering Melbourne 1850-1960*, ed. R Broome with R Barnden, D Garden, D Gibb, E Jackson and J Smart, Royal Historical Society of Victoria, Melbourne, 2016, pp. 10-13.

'Mallee Country and Deep Time' (with Andrea Gaynor), in *Australia's Mallee Country: Land, People and History*, eds R Broome, C Fahey, A Gaynor and K Holmes, Monash University Press, Melbourne, forthcoming.

'Aboriginal Homelands', in *Australia's Mallee Country: Land, People and History*, eds R Broome, C Fahey, A Gaynor and K Holmes, Monash University Press, Melbourne, forthcoming.

'Pastoral Adventurers', in *Australia's Mallee Country: Land, People and History*, eds R Broome, C Fahey, A Gaynor and K Holmes, Monash University Press, Melbourne, forthcoming.

'Camping and Working on Country', in *Australia's Mallee Country: Land, People and History*, eds R Broome, C Fahey, A Gaynor and K Holmes, Monash University Press, Melbourne, forthcoming.

Richard Broome, "Aborigènes", in *101 Mots pour comprendre l'Australie*, eds by Peter Brown and Jean-Yves Faberon, Centre de documentation pédagogique de la Nouvelle-Calédonie (CDP-NC), Noumea forthcoming March 2018.

Articles

'Professional Aboriginal Boxers', *Aboriginal and Islander Identity* 3, 1979, pp. 28-31.

'Professional Aboriginal Boxers in Eastern Australia, 1930-1979', *Aboriginal History* 4, no. 1/2, 1980, pp. 48-71.

'Victoria's Boxing Champs', *Aboriginal News* 3, no. 9, 1980, pp. 24-6.

'The Aboriginal Resistance', *Australia: Issues and Images*, History Teachers' Association of NSW, 1981, pp. 1-10.

'Thoughts on Aboriginal-European Culture Contact', *Readings in Senior History: Australian* 5, 1985, pp. 1-8.

'Why Use Koori', *La Trobe Library Journal* 11, no. 43, 1989, p. 5.

'Tracing the Humanitarian Strain in Black-White Encounters', *La Trobe Library Journal* 11, no. 43, 1989, pp. 37-8.

'Constructing Kooris in the 20th Century Victorian Press', *La Trobe Library Journal* 11, no. 43, 1989, p. 43.

'Should We Call a Koori, a "Koori"?', *Australian Historical Association Bulletin* 68, 1991, pp. 43-6.

'Aboriginal Workers on South-Eastern Frontiers', *Australian Historical Studies* 26, no. 103, 1994, pp. 202-20.

'Aboriginal Victims and Voyagers: Confronting Frontier Myths', *Journal of Australian Studies* 18, no. 42, 1994, pp. 70-7.

'Enduring Moments of Aboriginal Dominance: Aboriginal Performers, Boxers and Runners', *Labour History* 11, no. 69, 1995, pp. 171-87.

'Theatres of Power: Tent Boxing circa 1910-1970', *Aboriginal History* 20, 1996, pp. 1-23.

'Dangerous and Marvellous Encounters: Early Aboriginal and European Contacts in the Plenty and Melbourne Regions', *Plenty Valley Papers* 2, ed. L Ellem, Latrobe University and Plenty Valley Arts Inc., Melbourne, 1996.

'Windows on Other Worlds: The Rise and Fall of Sideshow Alley', *Australian Historical Studies* 29, no. 112, 1999, pp. 1-22.

'Seeking Mulga Fred', *Aboriginal History* 22, 1998, pp. 1-23.

'Entangled Histories: The Politics and Ethics of Writing Indigenous Histories', *Melbourne Historical Journal* 33, 2005, pp. 6-12.

'"There were Vegetables every Year Mr Green was Here"': Right Behaviour and the Struggle for Autonomy at Coranderrk Aboriginal Reserve', *History Australia* 3, no. 2, 2006, pp. 43.1-43.16.

'At the Grass Roots of White Support: Victorian Aboriginal Advancement League Branches 1957-1972', *La Trobe Library Journal*, no. 85, 2010, pp. 141-56.

'Changing Aboriginal Landscapes of Pastoral Victoria, 1830-1850', *Studies in the History of Gardens & Designed Landscapes* 31, no. 2, 2011, pp. 88-96.

'The Great Australian Transformation: An Argument About Our Past and its History', *Agora* 48, no. 4, 2013, pp. 16-24.

'Doing Aboriginal History', *Agora* 49, no. 2, 2014, pp. 40-9.

'Environmental History and the Port Phillip Frontier', *Agora* 51, no. 2, 2016, pp. 9-17.

'The 1969 Aboriginal Takeover of the Victorian Aborigines Advancement League – Indigenous and Black Power Inspirations', *Agora* 51, no. 3, 2016, pp. 12-22.

'Murray Mallee: A Riverine Geography of Aboriginal Labour', *Agricultural History* 91, no. 2, 2017, pp. 150-70.

Appendix

Articles in dictionaries and encyclopedias

'Aborigines', in *Australians: A Historical Dictionary*, eds G Aplin, SG Foster and M McKernan, Fairfax, Syme & Weldon, Sydney, 1987, pp. 4-7.

'Boxing', in *Oxford Companion to Australian Sport*, eds W Vamplew et al., Oxford University Press, Melbourne, 1992, pp. 64-70.

'Richards, Randell William (Ron)', in *Oxford Companion to Australian Sport*, eds W Vamplew et al., Oxford University Press, Melbourne, 1992, pp. 287-8.

'Rose, Lionel', in *Oxford Companion to Australian Sport*, eds W Vamplew et al., Oxford University Press, Melbourne, 1992, p. 308.

'Sands, Dave', in *Oxford Companion to Australian Sport*, eds W Vamplew et al., Oxford University Press, Melbourne, 1992, p. 308.

'Aboriginal Australians', in *Dictionary of Race and Ethnic Relations*, eds E Cashmore et al., Routledge, London, 3rd edn, 1994, pp. 1-4; 4th edn, 1996, pp. 1-4; 5th edn, pp. 1-4.

'Jerome, Jerry (1874-1943)', in *Australian Dictionary of Biography*, vol. 14, Melbourne University Press, Melbourne, 1996, pp. 566-7.

'Massacres', in *The Oxford Companion to Australian History*, eds G Davison, J Hirst and S Macintyre, Oxford University Press, Melbourne, 1998, p. 415; 2nd edn, 2001, p. 418-419.

'Boxing', in *The Oxford Companion to Aboriginal Art and Culture*, eds S Kleinert and M Neale, Oxford University Press, Melbourne, 2000, pp. 546-7.

'Sands, David (1926-1952)', in *Australian Dictionary of Biography*, vol. 16, Melbourne University Press, Melbourne, 2002, pp. 174-5.

'Aboriginal Australians', in *Encyclopedia of Race and Ethnic Studies*, ed. E Cashmore, Routledge, London, 2004, pp. 1-3.

'Bennett, Elliott (1924-1981)', in *Australian Dictionary of Biography*, vol. 17, Melbourne University Press, Melbourne, 2007, pp. 85-6.

'Buckley, William (1780-1856)', *Oxford Dictionary of National Biography*, Oxford University Press, 2004, viewed 11 January 2017, <http://www.oxforddnb.com/view/article/3870>, doi:10.1093/ref:odnb/3870.

'Pemulwoy (c.1760-1802)', *Oxford Dictionary of National Biography*, Oxford University Press, 2004, viewed 11 January 2017, <http://www.oxforddnb.com/view/article/65442>, doi:10.1093/ref:odnb/65442.

'Aboriginal Melbourne', in *The Encyclopedia of Melbourne*, eds A Brown-May and S Swain, Cambridge University Press, Melbourne, 2005, pp. 2-5.

'Koori', in *The Encyclopedia of Melbourne*, eds A Brown-May and S Swain, Cambridge University Press, Melbourne, 2005, pp. 391-2.

'Aboriginal', in *The Routledge Companion to Race and Ethnicity*, eds SM Caliendo and CD McIlwain, Routledge, London, 2011, pp. 95-7.

'Nicholls, Sir Douglas Ralph (Doug) (1908-1988)', in *Australian Dictionary of Biography*, vol. 18, Melbourne University Press, Melbourne, 2012, pp. 219-21.

Booklets and edited books

Aboriginal People of Victoria, Aboriginal and Torres Strait Islander Commission, Canberra, 1990, p. 15.

The Colonial Experience: The Port Phillip District, 1834–1850 (with Alan Frost), La Trobe University Studies in History, Melbourne, 1997.

The Colonial Experience: The Port Phillip District, 1834–1850 (with Alan Frost), La Trobe University Studies in History, Melbourne, 2nd edn, 1999.

Aboriginal People of Victoria, Aboriginal and Torres Strait Islander Commission, Canberra, revised and updated edn, 2002.

The Colonial Experience: The Port Phillip District and Victoria 1834–1860, La Trobe University Studies in History, Melbourne, 3rd edn, 2008.

The Colonial Experience: The Port Phillip District and Victoria 1834–1860, La Trobe University Studies in History, Melbourne, 4th edn, 2016.

Newspaper feature articles

'The Aboriginal Resistance', *Sydney Morning Herald*, 30 June 1981, p. 14.

'The Five Ages of Victoria – The Aborigines', *The Age*, 10 November 1984.

Notes

Foreword

1   I explore this model in *Roving Mariners: Australian Aboriginal Whalers and Sealers in the Southern Oceans 1790-1870*, SUNY Press, New York, 2012.

Chapter 1

1   See, e.g., R Broome, *Aboriginal Victorians: A History Since 1800*, Allen & Unwin, Sydney, 2005, pp. 3-4; I Lee, *The Logbooks of the 'Lady Nelson' with the Journal of her First Commander Lieutenant James Grant*, Grafton & Co, London, 1915, pp. 137-9. Mark McKenna has since documented an earlier engagement, alluded to by Broome, on Kurnai country in Gippsland in 1797. See M McKenna, *From the Edge: Australia's Lost Histories*, Miegunyah Press, Melbourne, 2016, pp. 21-2.

2   E Scott, 'The Early History of Western Port, Part One', *Victorian Historical Magazine* 6, no. 1, September 1917, pp. 15-16; R Broome, *Coburg: Between Two Creeks*, Lothian, Melbourne, 1987, p. 15; Broome, *Aboriginal Victorians*, p. 4.

3   R Broome 'Tracing the Humanitarian Strain in Black-White Encounters', *La Trobe Library Journal* 1989, p. 37.

4   I Clendinnen, *Dancing with Strangers*, Text, Melbourne, 2003.

5   Broome's work on biography and family history includes R Broome and C Manning, *A Man of All Tribes: The Life of Alick Jackomos*, Aboriginal Studies Press, Canberra, 2006.

6   This research was published in a number of places, including R Broome, 'Professional Aboriginal Boxers in Eastern Australia, 1930-1979', *Aboriginal History* 4, no. 1/2, 1980, pp. 49-72.

7   R Broome, 'Rewriting *Aboriginal Australians* Thirty Years On', paper presented to the La Trobe University History Seminar, 29 August 2008. See, e.g., CD Rowley, *The Destruction of Aboriginal Society*, Penguin Books, Harmondsworth, 1972; D Barwick, 'Coranderrk and Cumeroogunga: Pioneers and Policy', in *Opportunity and Response: Case Studies in Economic Development*, eds T Scarlett Epstein and DH Penny, C Hurst, London, 1972; P Biskup, *Not Slaves Not Citizens: The Aboriginal Problem in Western Australia, 1898-1954*, University of Queensland Press, Brisbane, 1973; RHW Reece, *Aborigines and Colonists: Aborigines and Colonial Society in New*

South Wales in the 1830s and 1840s, Sydney University Press, Sydney, 1974; R Evans, K Saunders and K Cronin, *Exclusion, Exploitation and Extermination: Race Relations in Colonial Queensland*, Australia and New Zealand Book Co, Sydney, 1975; H Reynolds, 'The Other Side of the Frontier: Early Aboriginal Reactions to Pastoral Settlement in Queensland and Northern New South Wales', *Historical Studies, Australia and New Zealand* 17, no. 66, 1976; A McGrath, 'Aboriginal Women Workers in the Northern Territory, 1911-1939', *Hecate* 4, no. 2, 1978.

8   R Broome, *Aboriginal Australians: Black Response to White Dominance, 1788-1980*, George Allen & Unwin, Sydney, 1st edn, 1982, p. 6.
9   R Broome, 'Entangled Histories: The Politics and Ethics of Writing Indigenous Histories', *Melbourne Historical Journal* 33, 2005, pp. 7, 9.
10 Broome, 'Rewriting *Aboriginal Australians* Thirty Years On'.
11 *Koorie*, Koorie Cultural Heritage Trust, Melbourne, 1991, pp. 19-20.
12 R Broome, 'Aboriginal Victims and Voyagers: Confronting Frontier Myths', *Journal of Australian Studies* 18, no. 42, 1994, pp. 71-2.
13 Broome, 'Aboriginal Victims and Voyagers', pp. 72, 74, 77.
14 WEH Stanner, 'Continuity and Change among the Aborigines (1958)', in *White Man Got No Dreaming: Essays 1938-1973*, Australian National University Press, Canberra, 1979, pp. 48-9, 63.
15 R Broome, 'Aboriginal Workers on South-Eastern Frontiers', *Australian Historical Studies* 42, 1994, p. 204.
16 Broome, *Aboriginal Victorians*, p. 52.
17 GC Spivak, *A Critique of Postcolonial Reason: Toward a History of the Vanishing Present*, Seagull Books, Calcutta, 1999, p. 130.
18 M Foucault, 'The Ethics of the Concern for Self as a Practice of Freedom', in *Ethics: Subjectivity and Truth*, The New Press, New York, 1997, p. 283.
19 J Butler, 'Precarious Life, Vulnerability, and the Ethics of Cohabitation', *Journal of Speculative Philosophy* 26, no. 2, 2012, pp. 141-2; I Clendinnen, *Tiger's Eye: A Memoir*, Scribners, New York, 2000, p. 191.
20 M Langton, *"Well I heard it on the Radio and I saw it on the Television...": An essay for the Australian Film Commission on the politics and aesthetics of filmmaking by and about Aboriginal people and things*, Australian Film Commission, North Sydney, 1993, p. 32.
21 Foucault, p. 284.
22 R Broome, *Aboriginal Australians: A History Since 1788*, Allen & Unwin, Sydney, 4th edn, 2010, p. 80.
23 Ibid., pp. 84-5.
24 Ibid., p. 144.
25 R Broome, *Fighting Hard: The Victorian Aborigines Advancement League*, Aboriginal Studies Press, Canberra, 2015.

26 R Broome, '"There were Vegetables every Year Mr Green was Here": Right Behaviour and the Struggle for Autonomy at Coranderrk Aboriginal Reserve', *History Australia* 3, no. 2, 2006.

27 Broome, *Aboriginal Australians*, 2010, pp. 16, 34-5; Broome, *Aboriginal Victorians*, p. 52.

28 Broome, *Aboriginal Australians*, 2010, pp. 1-2; JH Wootten, *Royal Commission into Aboriginal Deaths in Custody: Report of the Inquiry into the Death of Malcolm Charles Smith*, Australian Government Publishing Service, Canberra, 1989.

29 Broome, *Aboriginal Australians*, 2010, p. 2.

30 On imagining Aboriginal people within the nation, see R Broome, *Aboriginal Australians: Black Responses to White Dominance*, Allen & Unwin, Sydney, 2nd edn, 1994, p. 7.

Chapter 2

1 R Broome, *Aboriginal Australians: Black Response to White Dominance, 1788-1980*, George Allen & Unwin, Sydney, 1st edn, 1982.

2 See, e.g., WK Hancock, *Australia*, Ernest Benn, London, 1930; CMH Clark, *A Short History of Australia*, Mentor Books, New York, 1963; FK Crowley (ed.), *A New History of Australia*, Heinemann, Melbourne, 1974.

3 R Broome, *Aboriginal Australians: A History Since 1788*, Allen & Unwin, Sydney, 4th edn, 2010.

4 See, e.g., P Corris, *Aborigines and Europeans in Western Victoria*, Australian Institute of Aboriginal Studies, Canberra, 1968; F Robinson and B York, *The Black Resistance*, Widescope, Melbourne, 1977; MF Christie, *Aborigines in Colonial Victoria 1835-86*, Sydney University Press, Sydney, 1979.

5 Christie, *Aborigines in Colonial Victoria*, p. 1.

6 Ibid., p.7.

7 Ibid., p. 51.

8 Ibid., p. 57.

9 Ibid., pp. 44-50.

10 Ibid., p. 69.

11 Ibid., p. 78.

12 WEH Stanner, *After the Dreaming: Black and White Australians – An Anthropologist's View*, Australian Broadcasting Commission, Sydney, 1969; WEH Stanner, 'The History of Indifference Thus Begins', *Aboriginal History* 1, no. 1-2, 1977, pp. 1-11; D Barwick, 'Changes in the Aboriginal Population of Victoria, 1863-1966', in *Aboriginal Man and Environment in Australia*, eds DJ Mulvaney and J Golson, Australian National University Press, Canberra, 1971; D Barwick, 'Coranderrk and Cumeroogunga:

Pioneers and Policy', in *Opportunity and Response: Case Studies in Economic Development*, eds TS Epstein and DH Penny, C Hurst, London, 1972; KR McConnochie, *Realities of Race: An Analysis of Race and Racism and their Relevance to Australian Society*, ANZ Book Co, Sydney, 1973; H Reynolds, 'The Other Side of the Frontier: Early Aboriginal Reactions to Pastoral Settlement in Queensland and Northern New South Wales', *Historical Studies, Australia and New Zealand* 17, no. 66, 1976, pp. 50-63.

13   Broome, *Aboriginal Australians*, 1982, p. 24.
14   Ibid., pp. 42-4.
15   Ibid., p. 44
16   Ibid.
17   Ibid., p. 39
18   Ibid., p. 42.
19   Ibid., p. 45.
20   Ibid., pp. 50-1.
21   R Broome, 'The Struggle for Australia: Aboriginal-European Warfare, 1770-1930', in *Australia: Two Centuries of War & Peace*, eds M McKernan and M Browne, Australian War Memorial/Allen & Unwin, Canberra, 1988, pp. 92-120.
22   Ibid., p. 93.
23   Ibid., p. 94.
24   Ibid.
25   Ibid.
26   Ibid., p. 102.
27   Ibid., p. 111.
28   Ibid.
29   Ibid., pp. 111-12.
30   Ibid., pp. 112-13.
31   Ibid., p. 114.
32   Ibid., pp. 94-5.
33   Ibid., p. 104.
34   Ibid., pp. 96-103.
35   See, e.g., R Price, *The Making of Empire: Colonial Encounters and the Creation of Imperial Rule in Nineteenth Century Africa*, Cambridge University Press, Cambridge, 2008.
36   Broome, 'The Struggle for Australia', pp. 117-8.
37   I have not been able to access a copy of the catalogue or the map. See Rosemary West, 'The Killing Times', *The Age* (Melbourne), 5 March 1994, p.3.

Notes

38 R Broome, 'Aboriginal Victims and Voyagers: Confronting Frontier Myths', *Journal of Australian Studies* 18, no. 42, 1994, pp. 70-7.
39 Ibid., pp. 70-1.
40 Ibid., p. 72.
41 Ibid.
42 Ibid., p. 73.
43 B Nance, 'The Level of Violence: Europeans and Aborigines in Port Phillip, 1835-1850', *Historical Studies* 19, no. 77, 1981, pp. 532-52. See especially p. 540.
44 Broome, 'Aboriginal Victims and Voyagers', pp. 73-4.
45 Ibid., p. 74.
46 Ibid., p. 77.
47 Ibid., pp. 75-7.
48 R Broome, 'Victoria', in *Contested Ground: Australian Aborigines under the British Crown*, ed. A McGrath, Allen & Unwin, Sydney, 1995, pp. 121-67.
49 Ibid., p. 121.
50 Ibid.
51 Ibid., pp. 126-7.
52 Christie, *Aborigines in Colonial Victoria*, p. 27.
53 Broome, 'Victoria', p. 128.
54 Ibid., pp. 128-9.
55 Ibid., p. 128.
56 Ibid., p. 129.
57 Ibid., p. 130.
58 K Windschuttle, 'The Myths of Frontier Massacres in Australian History, Parts I, II and III', *Quadrant* 44, nos 10-12, 2000, pp. 8-21, 17-24, 6-20.
59 L Ryan, 'Settler Massacres on the Port Phillip Frontier, 1836-1851', *Journal of Australian Studies* 34, no. 3, 2010, p. 258.
60 ID Clark, *Scars in the Landscape: A Register of Massacre Sites in Western Victoria, 1803-1859*, Aboriginal Studies Press, Canberra, 1995; R Broome, 'The Statistics of Frontier Conflict', in *Frontier Conflict: The Australian Experience*, eds B Attwood and SG Foster, National Museum of Australia, Canberra, 2003, pp. 88-98.
61 Broome, 'The Statistics of Frontier Conflict', p. 94.
62 R Broome, *Aboriginal Victorians: A History Since 1800*, Allen & Unwin, Sydney, 2005, p. 81.
63 Ibid., p. 70.
64 Ibid., pp. 71-9.
65 Ibid., p. 81.

66 Broome, *Aboriginal Australians*, 2010.
67 Ibid., pp. 2–3.
68 Ibid., pp. 28–9.
69 Ibid., p. 41.
70 Ibid.
71 Christie, *Aborigines in Colonial Victoria*, p. 29.
72 Broome, *Aboriginal Australians*, 2010, p. 45.
73 Ibid., p. 46.
74 Ibid., p. 55.

Chapter 3

1 For recent examples of the use of paternalism to discuss Aboriginal policy, see B Stephens and M Tyler, 'Paternalism is not working', *Canberra Times*, 10 February 2016, pp. 1, 4; J Taylor, 'ACBF: Consumer advocates disappointed by Federal Court decision on Aboriginal funeral insurance', ABC News, 5 July 2016, viewed 1 December 2016, <http://www.abc.net.au/news/2016-07-05/federal-court-aboriginal-community-benefit-fund-funeral-insuranc/7570508>; M Strom, 'A royal commission isn't enough', *Sydney Morning Herald*, 27 July 2016, p. 17; A Aikman, 'Widen welfare rules to all jobless, says Tony Abbott', *The Australian*, 6 October 2016; K Murphy, 'Linda Burney: funding cuts delayed reporting of Don Dale abuses', *The Guardian (Australia)*, 18 November 2016, viewed 1 December 2016, <https://www.theguardian.com/australia-news/2016/nov/18/linda-burney-funding-cuts-delayed-reporting-of-don-dale-abuses>.

2 R Broome, *Aboriginal Australians: Black Response to White Dominance, 1788–1980*, George Allen & Unwin, Sydney, 1st edn, 1982; R Broome, '"There were Vegetables every Year Mr Green was Here": Right Behaviour and the Struggle for Autonomy at Coranderrk Aboriginal Reserve', *History Australia* 3, no. 2, 2006. Broome has applied his definition of paternalism systematically to a non-mission context in 'Not Strictly Business: Freaks and the Australian Showground World', *Australian Historical Studies* 40, 2009, pp. 328, 331.

3 L Bamblett, 'Aboriginal Australians: A History since 1788', *Australian Aboriginal Studies*, no. 2, 2010, pp. 131–2. See also M Nakata, *Disciplining the Savages, Savaging the Disciplines*, Aboriginal Studies Press, Canberra, 2007, pp. 2, 216.

4 W Johnson, 'On Agency', *Journal of Social History* 37, no. 1, 2003, pp. 118, 121.

5 See, for example, N Pearson, *Our Right to Take Responsibility*, Noel Pearson and Associates, Cairns, 2000.

Notes

6   Rev. LB Salmans, 'Some reasons for prayer for missionaries', in *The Gospel in All Lands*, Journal of the Methodist Episcopal Church Missionary Society, vol. 20, 1899, p. 537.

7   Rev CS Sanders, 'The Training of a Native Ministry on Foreign Missionary Ground', in *The Hartford Seminary Record*, eds WS Pratt and AL Gillett, Hartford Seminary Press, Hartford, 1901, p. 163.

8   M McKenzie, *The Road to Mowanjum*, Angus & Robertson, Sydney, 1969, pp. 4, 282.

9   CD Rowley, *The Destruction of Aboriginal Society*, Penguin Books, Harmondsworth, 1972, p. 4; MF Christie, *Aborigines in Colonial Victoria 1835–86*, Sydney University Press, Sydney, 1979, pp. 180–1, 183. For other historical accounts which took a similar approach, see J Harris, *One Blood: 200 Years of Aboriginal Encounter with Christianity: A Story of Hope*, Albatross Books, Sutherland, 1990 and RC Thompson, *Religion in Australia: A History*, Oxford University Press, Melbourne, 2002, 52-X, 78-Y.

10 Broome, *Aboriginal Australians*, 1982, pp. 104–5.

11 R Broome, *Treasure in Earthen Vessels: Protestant Christianity in New South Wales Society 1900–1914*, University of Queensland Press, Brisbane, 1980.

12 Broome, *Aboriginal Australians*, 1982, p. 105.

13 P Wolfe, 'Nation and MiscegeNation: Discursive Continuity in the Post-Mabo Era', *Social Analysis: The International Journal of Social and Cultural Practice*, no. 36, 1994, pp. 96–7.

14 A McGrath, *Born in the Cattle*, Allen & Unwin, Sydney, 1987, p. 99. See also ED Genovese, *Roll Jordan Roll: The World the Slaves Made*, Pantheon Books, New York, 1974, pp. 3–7.

15 B Attwood, *The Making of the Aborigines*, Allen & Unwin, Sydney, 1989, pp. 25–6.

16 Ibid., pp. 26–7

17 J Kociumbas, 'Introduction', in *Maps, Dreams, History: Race and Representation in Australia*, ed. J Kociumbas, Department of History, University of Sydney, Sydney, 1998, pp. 28, 39–40.

18 Wolfe, pp. 100, 106.

19 Ibid., p. 99.

20 Johnson, p. 115.

21 R Broome, *Aboriginal Victorians: A History since 1800*, Allen & Unwin, Sydney, 2005, p. 128.

22 Ibid., p. 127.

23 Ibid.

24 See C McLisky, 'Managing Mission Life, 1869–1886', in *Settler Colonial Governance in Nineteenth-Century Victoria*, eds L Boucher and L Russell, Aboriginal Studies Press, Canberra, 2015, pp. 121–3.

25 Broome, 'Right Behaviour', p. 43.3
26 Ibid, p. 43.4.
27 Ibid, p. 43.13.
28 M Stephens, *White Without Soap: Philanthropy, Caste and Exclusion in Colonial Victoria, 1835–1888: A Political Economy of Race*, University of Melbourne Custom Book Centre, Melbourne, 2010, pp. 154–85, passim.
29 N Loos, *White Christ, Black Cross: The Emergence of a Black Church*, Aboriginal Studies Press, Canberra, 2007, p. 99.
30 In focusing on the work of missionaries to protect Aboriginal people from the brutality of other colonists, Loos did also point to some 'positive aspects of the mission policy of paternalistic protection'. Ibid., p. 111. See also A O'Brien, *Philanthropy and Settler Colonialism*, Palgrave Macmillan, Basingstoke, 2015, pp. 82, 113.
31 J Lydon, 'Imagining the Moravian Mission: Space and Surveillance at the Former Ebenezer Mission, Victoria, Southeastern Australia', *Historical Archaeology* 43, no. 3, 2009, p. 13.
32 J Mitchell, *In Good Faith? Governing Indigenous Australia Through God, Charity and Empire, 1825–1855*, ANU ePress, Canberra, 2011, p. 122.
33 Ibid., p. 6.
34 Noel Pearson's honours thesis, written in 1986 but not published until 1998, is one exception to this. It is, however, rarely cited. See N Pearson, 'Guugu Yimidhirr History: Hope Vale Lutheran Mission (1900–1950)', in *Maps, Dreams, History: Race and Representation in Australia*, ed. J Kociumbas, Department of History, University of Sydney, Sydney, 1998, pp. 131–238.
35 EA Povinelli, 'Indigenous politics in late liberalism', in *Culture Crisis: Anthropology and Politics in Aboriginal Australia*, eds J Altman and M Hinkson, UNSW Press, Sydney, 2010, pp. 23–4.
36 E Kowal, 'Responsibility, Noel Pearson and Indigenous Disadvantage in Australia', in *Responsibility*, eds G Hage and R Eckersley, Melbourne University Press, Melbourne, 2012, p. 48; D Martin, 'Reforming the Welfare System in Remote Aboriginal Communities: An Assessment of Noel Pearson's Proposals', in *Competing Visions*, eds T Eardley and B Bradbury, Social Policy Research Centre, University of New South Wales, Sydney, 2002, p. 318; E Watt, 'The Implementation of the Capabilities Approach in Cape York: Can Paternalism be a Pre-condition for Participation?', *Development Bulletin*, no 75, 2013, p. 39.
37 T Rowse, *Rethinking Social Justice: From 'Peoples' to 'Populations'*, Aboriginal Studies Press, Canberra, 2012, pp. 146–53. See also T Neale, 'Staircases, Pyramids and Poisons: The Immunitary Paradigm in the Works of Noel Pearson and Peter Sutton', *Continuum* 27, no. 2, 2013.

38 Pearson, 'Guugu Yimidhirr History', pp. 134–5.
39 Ibid, pp. 135, 180.
40 Ibid., pp. 135, 139, 222 (emphasis in original). Compare K Close-Barry, 'Land, Labour and Ambivalence: Lutheran Missionaries Managing Land Disputes at Cape Bedford Mission', *Journal of Religious History* 41, no. 2, 2017, p. 214.
41 It is interesting to note that Pearson cited Broome's early work favourably. See Pearson, 'Guugu Yimidhirr History', 144.
42 S Boym, *The Future of Nostalgia*, Basic Books, New York, 2001, p. xiii.
43 J Dlamini, *Native Nostalgia*, Jacana, Johannesburg, 2009. See also L Rademaker, '"We want a good mission not rubbish please": Aboriginal Petitions and Mission Nostalgia', *Aboriginal History* 40, 2016.
44 N Pearson, 'White Guilt, Victimhood and the Quest for a Radical Centre', *Griffith Review* 16, 2007, pp. 26–8.
45 Ibid., pp. 27–8; N Pearson, 'On the Human Right to Misery, Mass Incarceration and Early Death', *Arena Magazine* 56, 2001–2, p. 23.
46 N Pearson, 'Family' (2000), in *Up from the Mission: Selected Writings*, Black Inc, Melbourne, 2009, pp. 14–15.
47 N Pearson, 'Hope Vale Lost' (2006), in *Up from the Mission*, pp. 139–42.
48 N Pearson, 'Mabo: Towards Respecting Equality and Difference', in *Voices from the Land: 1993 Boyer Lectures*, ABC Books, Sydney, 1994, p. 93.
49 On the overlapping categories of race and family in establishing a paternalist order, see A McClintock, *Imperial Leather: Race, Gender and Sexuality in the Colonial Contest*, Routledge, New York, 1995, p. 45.
50 A McGrath, 'The State as Father: 1910–60', in P Grimshaw et al., *Creating a Nation*, Penguin Books, Melbourne, 1994, pp. 279–96. Note that McGrath suggests that this era ends in 1960, though this may simply be an effect of the determining periodisation at work in the overall book to which she was contributing.
51 N Pearson and M Gibson, 'The Peoples of the North: Anthropology and Tradition' (1987), in Pearson, *Up from the Mission*, p. 27.
52 Rowse, p. 153.
53 Pearson, *Our Right to Take Responsibility*, p. 84. Welfare reform represented part of a four-point plan that also included access to traditional subsistence resources, developing community economies; and engaging in the real market economy. Ibid., p. 83.
54 N Pearson, 'The Welfare Pedestal' (2007), in *Up from the Mission*, p. 287.
55 See V Hughes, 'Progress from the Grass Roots', *The Australian*, 29 July 2003; S Rintoul, 'Cape resists Pearson on grog', *The Australian*, 23 July 2003, p. 1; 'Pearson hits back at critics of his radical welfare plan', AAP

News Wire, 20 June 2007; P Morley and T Chilcott, 'Communities confused and activists go on the attack', *Courier Mail* (Brisbane), 30 June 2007.

56 For Pearson's opposition, see P Dodson and N Pearson, 'The Dangers of Mutual Obligation', *The Age* (Melbourne), 15 December 2004, p. 17. On the Howard Government embrace of mutual obligation, see P Mendes, 'Welfare Reform and Mutual Obligation', in *Howard's Second and Third Governments: Australian Commonwealth Administration, 1998–2004*, eds C Aulich and R Wettenhall, UNSW Press, Sydney, 2005, pp. 138–9.

57 N Pearson, 'Ladder of Obligation', *The Age*, 5 August 2005, p. 13.

58 Ibid.

59 T Abbott, 'Paternalism Reconsidered', *Quadrant* 50, no. 9, 2006, pp. 30–2; T Abbott, 'Few Aboriginal communities can govern themselves', *The Age*, 21 June 2006, p. 15.

60 Abbott, 'Paternalism Reconsidered', p. 33.

61 PME Lorcin, 'Imperial Nostalgia; Colonial Nostalgia: Differences of Theory, Similarities of Practice?', *Historical Reflections* 39, no. 3, 2013, p. 103.

62 'Brough rejects "new paternalism" call', *ABC Premium News*, 23 June 2006.

63 M Metherell, 'No thank you, greets Abbott's call for new paternalism', *Sydney Morning Herald*, 22 June 2006, p. 3.

64 E Roy and T Calma, 'Aboriginal leader says paternalism not the solution to disadvantage', ABC Radio, AM, 21 June 2006, viewed 1 December 2016, <http://www.abc.net.au/am/content/2006/s1667988.htm>.

65 'Pearson warns against return to paternalism', AAP News Wire, 22 June 2006.

66 N Pearson, 'The Welfare Pedestal', p. 289. By 2008, this welfare reform had further graduated into a 'New Deal'. See N Pearson, 'The Cape York Agenda' (2008), in *Up from the Mission*, p. 280.

67 'Pearson defends radical welfare plan', *Sydney Morning Herald*, 20 June 2007, <http://www.smh.com.au//national/pearson-defends-radical-welfare-plan-20070620-jfz.html>.

68 R Wild and P Anderson, *Ampe Akelyernemane Meke Mekarle, 'Little Children Are Sacred': Report of the Northern Territory Board of Inquiry into the Protection of Aboriginal Children from Sexual Abuse*, Department of the Chief Minister, Darwin, 2007.

69 P Karvelas, 'Moved by Pearson's passion', *The Australian*, 23 June 2007, pp. 1, 6.

70 M Hinkson, 'In the Name of the Child', in *Coercive Reconciliation: Stabilise, Normalise, Exit Aboriginal Australia*, eds J Altman and M Hinkson, Arena Publications, Melbourne, 2007, p. 5. On the implementation of the Northern Territory Intervention, see D Howard-Wagner and B Kelly, 'Containing Aboriginal Mobility in the Northern Territory: From "Protectionism" to "Interventionism"', *Law Text Culture* 15, 2011.

And see generally *The Intervention: An Anthology*, eds R Scott and A Heiss, Concerned Australians, Sydney, 2015.

71 M Brough, Transcript of National Press Club Address, ABC Channel 2, 15 August 2007; M Hinkson, 'Media Images and the Politics of Hope', in *Culture Crisis: Anthropology and Politics in Aboriginal Australia*, eds J Altman and M Hinkson, UNSW Press, Sydney, 2010, p. 230; P Karvelas, 'Right to tribal law scrapped', *The Australian*, 6 August 2007.

72 See, e.g., 'Beyond Handouts', *The Australian*, 4 July 2007; S Kearney, 'Rough road ahead', *The Australian*, 24 July 2007.

73 JC Altman, 'The Howard Government's Northern Territory Intervention: Are Neo-Paternalism and Indigenous Development Compatible?', Centre for Aboriginal Economic Policy Research, Topical Issue 16/2007, viewed 1 December 2016, <http://caepr.anu.edu.au/sites/default/files/Publications/topical/Altman_AIATSIS.pdf>; M Bamblett, 'Please listen to us, PM', *The Age*, 27 June 2007; P Briggs, 'Policing alone won't bridge a great divide', *The Age*, 28 June 2007. For further critical comment in the print media, in the days after the Intervention was announced, see, e.g., M Fraser and L O'Donoghue, 'Without respect, this will not stand', *Crikey*, 22 June 2007, <https://www.crikey.com.au/2007/06/22/malcolm-fraser-and-lowitja-odonoghue-without-respect-this-will-not-stand/>; 'Pearson lashes out at critics of Howard plan', *The Age*, 27 June 2007; R Hagen, 'A return to the past is no answer', *The Age*, 29 June 2007; P Dodson, 'An entire culture is at stake', *The Age*, 14 July 2007. In scholarly work, see, e.g., *Coercive Reconciliation: Stabilise, Normalise, Exit Aboriginal Australia*, eds J Altman and M Hinkson, Arena Publications, Melbourne, 2007; A Lattas and B Morris, 'The Politics of Suffering and the Politics of Anthropology', in *Culture Crisis: Anthropology and Politics in Aboriginal Australia*, eds J Altman and M Hinkson, UNSW Press, Sydney, 2010, p. 62; S Maddison, *Beyond White Guilt: The Real Challenge for Black-White Relations in Australia*, Allen & Unwin, Sydney, 2011, p. 79; S Bielefeld, 'History Wars and Stronger Futures Laws: A Stronger Future or Perpetuating Past Paternalism?', *Alternative Law Journal* 39, no. 1, 2014.

74 N Pearson, 'An end to the tears', *The Australian*, 23 June 2007, 17.

75 See, e.g., Secretariat of National Aboriginal and Islander Child Care Inc, '"Ending Paternalism: New Leadership, New Partnerships" SNAICC Welcomes Appointment of Jenny Macklin, MP to Indigenous Affairs Portfolio', *Aboriginal & Islander Health Worker Journal* 32, no. 3, 2008, p. 21; M Schubert, 'Apology brings positive change', *The Age*, 13 February 2009, p. 19.

76 Quoted in C Overington, 'A zealot's fight to lift people up', *The Australian*, 25 August 2012, p. 16.

77 Ibid., p. 16.

78 Pearson, *Our Right to Take Responsibility*, p. 21.
79 Ibid, p. 84 (emphasis in original).
80 See M Langton, 'Trapped in the Aboriginal Reality Show', *Griffith Review* 19, 2008, p. 156.
81 R Williams, *The Country and the City*, Oxford University Press, New York, 1973, p. 12.
82 See for example Marcia Langton's critique of reconciliation (which she associates with self-determination): 'The rhetoric of reconciliation is a powerful drawcard — like the bearded woman at the old sideshow... It almost allows "the native" some agency and a future. I say "almost" because, in the end, "the native" is not allowed out of the show, forever condemned to perform to attract crowds', Langton, p. 162. This debate replicates to some extent disputes over the relationship between the law and the will that took place among Neuendettelsau missionaries, of whom George Schwartz was one. See D Midena, 'The Wonders of Conversion: Objectivity and Disenchantment in the Neuendettelsau Mission Encounter in New Guinea, 1886-1930', PhD thesis, University of Copenhagen, 2015. Our thanks to Daniel Midena for this insight.

Chapter 4

1 K Boddy, *Boxing: A Cultural History*, Reaktion Books, London, 2008, p. 7
2 R Broome, 'Professional Aboriginal Boxers in Eastern Australia, 1930-1979', *Aboriginal History* 4, no. 1/2, 1980, pp. 48-71; R Broome, 'Theatres of Power: Tent Boxing circa 1910-1970', *Aboriginal History* 20, 1996, pp. 1-23; R Broome with A Jackomos, *Sideshow Alley*, Allen & Unwin, Sydney, 1998, pp. 167-90; R Broome, 'The Australian Reaction to Jack Johnson, Black Pugilist, 1907-9', in *The Best Ever Australian Sports Writing: A 200 Year Collection*, ed. D Headon, Black Inc., Melbourne, 2001, pp. 532-45.
3 Broome, 'Professional Aboriginal Boxers'.
4 Broome, 'Theatres of Power', p. 1.
5 Ibid, p. 2.
6 Broome, 'Professional Aboriginal Boxers', p. 53.
7 HL Bingham and M Wallace, *Muhammad Ali's Greatest Fight: Cassius Clay vs. the United States of America*, Robson Books, London, 2004, pp. 114-15.
8 J Maynard, *Fight for Liberty and Freedom*, Aboriginal Studies Press, Canberra, 2007, pp. 18-35. The research for this essay is the foundation for a planned new book to be titled 'The Life and Times of Jack Johnson in Australia 1907-1908'.
9 Broome, 'The Australian Reaction to Jack Johnson', p. 537.

Notes

10 Ibid., pp. 532-3.
11 P Corris, *Lords of the Ring: A History of Prize-fighting in Australia*, Cassell, Melbourne, 1980, p. 94.
12 Ibid., p. 94.
13 J Johnson, *Jack Johnson: In The Ring and Out*, National Sports Publishing, Chicago, 1927, p. 166.
14 *Brisbane Courier*, 23 February 1909, p. 6.
15 *Dalby Herald*, 23 July 1910, p. 3.
16 *Sydney Morning Herald*, 6 January 1909, p. 9.
17 H Goodall, *Evans Head History Report for the Application for a Native Title Determination*, Report, No NG 6034, pp. 70-1.
18 Ibid.
19 Ibid.
20 *Queensland Times*, 18 July 1910, p. 7.
21 Broome, 'Professional Aboriginal Boxers', p. 68.
22 W Maxwell, *F.B. Eyes: How J. Edgar Hoover's Ghostreaders Framed African American Literature*, Princeton University Press, New Jersey, 2015, p. 32.
23 Broome, 'Professional Aboriginal Boxers', p. 53.
24 D Booth and C Tatz, *One Eyed: A View of Australian Sport*, Allen & Unwin, Sydney, 2000, p. 107.
25 Unsourced clipping held at the Broome Historical Society Newspaper Files.
26 GC Ward, *Unforgivable Blackness: The Rise and Fall of Jack Johnson*, Pimlico, London, 2006, pp. 302-306
27 N Fleischer, 'The Ring: Boxing: The Twentieth Century', in *Ring Chronicle of Boxing*, eds S Farhood and S Weston, Hamlyn, London, 1993, p. 21.
28 JC Oates, *On Boxing*, Harper, New York, 2006, p. 250.
29 *Sydney Morning Herald*, 31 December 1908, p. 8.
30 *The Sun* (Kalgoorlie), 24 July 1910, p. 8.
31 DF Branagan and TG Vallance, 'David, Sir Tannatt William Edgeworth (1858-1934)', in *Australian Dictionary of Biography*, vol. 8, Melbourne University Press, Melbourne, 1981.
32 *The Evening News* (Sydney), 22 June 1910, p. 7.
33 *The Sun* (Kalgoorlie), 24 July 1910, p. 8.
34 *The Evening News*, 22 June 1910, p. 7.
35 *The Sun*, 24 July 1910, p. 8.
36 *Cairns Morning Post*, 19 February 1909, p. 5.
37 *Windsor and Richmond Gazette*, 16 July 1910, p. 14.
38 Ward, preface.

39 *The Negro World* (New York), 25 January 1930.
40 Maxwell, p. 26.
41 *The Evening News*, 9 March 1910.
42 Broome, 'The Australian Reaction to Jack Johnson', pp. 232-3.
43 *The Newsletter: An Australian Paper for Australian People* (Sydney), 25 June 1909.
44 *The Windsor and Richmond Gazette*, 16 July 1910, p. 14.
45 Ibid.
46 *The Newsletter*, 16 July 1910.
47 *The Windsor and Richmond Gazette*, 16 July 1910, p. 14.
48 Ibid.
49 Oates, p. 235.
50 Ibid.
51 *The Age* (Melbourne), 28 December 1908, p. 5.
52 Oates, p. 245.
53 Federal Surveillance of African Americans (1917-1925), Microfilm 7.21417 No. 586, Lamont Library, Harvard.
54 'Booing Adam Goodes: Australians Must Unite Against Racism', *The Age*, 1 August 2015; '"Racist" boo row rages as Adam Goodes sits out', *The Australian*, 30 July 2015.
55 *The Guardian*, 24 January 2016.
56 M Ali, 'Foreword', in S Fradetta, *Jack Johnson*, Branden, Boston, 1990.

Chapter 5

1 The map was actually published by WC Ferguson, 'Mokare's Domain', in *Australians to 1788*, eds DJ Mulvaney and PJ White, Fairfax, Syme and Weldon, Sydney, 1987, pp. 121-45.
2 T Shellam, *Shaking Hands on the Fringe: Negotiating the Aboriginal World at King George's Sound*, UWA Publishing, Crawley, WA, 2009.
3 A Collie, 'Anecdotes and Remarks Relative to the Aborigines at King George's Sound', *Perth Gazette and Western Australian Journal*, 5 July 1834.
4 G Molloy, 'Letter from Georgiana Molloy to Mrs Kennedy, 29 May 1833', Cumbria Archive Centre, UK, CAC KEN 3/28/9.
5 After Gyalliput's return from Swan River to King George's Sound, he travelled again two months later. When the schooner stopped off at Augusta overnight, Gyalliput decided to stay with the Wardandi people, and became a dependent of John Molloy's for several months before travelling overland back to King George's Sound. See G Molloy, 'Letter'. See also T Shellam, 'Manyat's "sole delight": Travelling Knowledge in Western Australia's Southwest, 1830s', in *Transnational Lives: Biographies of Global Modernity, 1700-present*, eds D Deacon, A Woollacott and P

Notes

Russell, Palgrave Macmillan, Basingstoke, 2010, pp. 121–32.
6   R Broome, 'Aboriginal Victims and Voyagers: Confronting Frontier Myths', *Journal of Australian Studies* 18, no. 42, 1994, pp. 70–7.
7   K Scott, 'Not so Easy: Language for a Shared History', *Griffith Review* 47, 2015, p. 202.
8   N Green, 'King George's Sound: The Friendly Frontier', in *Archaeology in ANZAAS 1983*, ed. M Smith, Western Australian Museum, Perth, 1983, pp. 68–74.
9   RM Lyon, 'Letter from RM Lyon to Frederick Robinson, 1 January 1833', *Swan River Papers*, State Records Office of WA (SRO WA), vol. 10, pp. 116–17.
10 FC Irwin to Lord Viscount Goderich, 26 January 1833 in *Report on the Select Committee on Aborigines (British Settlements), with the minutes of evidence*, F Cass, London, 1968 [1837], Appendix no. 4, item no. 7, p. 132.
11 GF Moore, 25 January 1833, *The Millendon Memoirs: George Fletcher Moore's Western Australian Diaries and Letters, 1830–1841*, Hesperian Press, Perth, 2006, p. 197.
12 FC Irwin, 'Letter from Francis Chidley Irwin to Peter Brown', 22 January 1833, SRO WA, CSR 26/75.
13 I have written about the daily experience of these two voyages at Swan River in Shellam, *Shaking Hands on the Fringe*, Chapter 8.
14 *Perth Gazette*, 26 January 1833, p. 15.
15 Ibid.
16 *Perth Gazette*, 19 January 1833, p. 10.
17 South West Aboriginal Land and Sea Council (SWALSC), J Host and C Owen, *"It's Still in my Heart, this is my Country": The Single Noongar Claim History*, UWA Publishing, Crawley, WA, 2009, p. 103; M Roe, 'Morgan, John (1792?–1866)', *Australian Dictionary of Biography*, 1967, viewed 18 February 2016, <http://adb.anu.edu.au/biography/morgan-john-2479/text3331>.
18 Quoted in CT Stannage, *The People of Perth: A Social History of Western Australia's Capital City*, City of Perth, Perth, 1979, p. 41.
19 T Flannery, 'Introduction', in *The Life and Adventures of William Buckley: Thirty Two Years a Wanderer amongst the Aborigines of the then Unexplored Country round Port Phillip*, Text, Melbourne, 2002, pp. ix–xlvi.
20 Ibid., p. xiii.
21 Ibid., p. 6.
22 J Morgan, 'Letter from Morgan to Hay, 28 January and 3 February 1833', *Swan River Papers*, SRO WA, vol. 15, pp. 50–65.
23 As SWALSC, Host and Owen have noted, '[t]he *bidi* followed lines of easiest movement, along the banks of rivers and through mountain

passes. Thousands of smaller pathways linked these main routes. The Noongar had many words to describe them and distinguished several grades of track, just as lanes are distinguished from avenues and streets from highways.' SWALSC, Host and Owen, pp. 284–5.
24 Shellam, *Shaking Hands on the Fringe*, p. 141.
25 DJ Mulvaney and N Green (eds), *Commandant of Solitude: The Journals of Captain Collet Barker*, Melbourne University Publishing, Melbourne, 1992, pp. 302–4.
26 P Carter, 'Dark with an Excess of Bright: Mapping the Coastlines of Knowledge', in *Mappings*, ed. D Cosgrove, Reaktion Books, London, 1999, p. 128.
27 The six Nyungar seasons are *Birak, Bunuru, Dieran, Makuru, Djilba* and *Kambarang*. Within these seasons are further specific seasonal markers, denoted by the arrival of salmon at King George's Sound, for example, or the sound of frogs. See Shellam, *Shaking Hands on the Fringe*, Chapter 1.
28 D Turnbull, *Maps are Territories: Science is an Atlas*, Deakin University Press, Melbourne, 1989, p. 51.
29 C Bracknell, 'Kooral Dwonk-katitjiny (listening to the past): Aboriginal Language, Songs and History in South-western Australia', *Aboriginal History* 38, no. 1, 2015, pp. 1–18.
30 Morgan, 'Letter from Morgan to Hay, 28 January and 3 February 1833'.
31 See Merriam Webster dictionary online, accessed 5 July 2016, <http://www.merriam-webster.com/dictionary/hams>.
32 For a discussion about the production of Bennelong's letter see P Van Toorn, 'Wild Speech, Tame Speech, Real Speech', *Southerly* 67, nos 1–2, 2007, pp. 174–8.
33 Ibid, pp. 174–8.
34 Barker, 17 June 1830, in Mulvaney and Green (eds), *Commandant of Solitude*, p. 307. As Mulvaney and Green note, Barker's comment on the hearth was a 'significant early recognition of the Aboriginal identification of the family hearth as the basic social unit'.
35 B Gammage, *The Biggest Estate on Earth: How Aborigines made Australia*, Allen & Unwin, Sydney, 2011, p. 139.
36 Barker, 1 February 1830, in Mulvaney and Green (eds), *Commandant of Solitude*, p. 254.
37 Ibid.
38 RM Lyon, 'A Glance at the Manners, and Language of the Aboriginal Inhabitants of Western Australia; with a Short Vocabulary, 23 March 1833', *Perth Gazette*, 20 April 1833.
39 *Perth Gazette*, 7 September 1833.

Notes

40 T Ballantyne, 'Strategic Intimacies: Knowledge and Colonisation in Southern New Zealand', *Journal of New Zealand Studies*, no 14, 2013, pp. 8-9.
41 Ibid., p. 8.
42 Ian Keen has noted that many early colonial observers acknowledged Aboriginal people's customary territoriality. I Keen, 'The Interpretation of Property on the Australian Colonial Frontier', in *Indigenous Participation in Australian Economies: Historical and Anthropological Perspectives*, ed. I Keen, ANU ePress, Canberra, 2010, pp. 45-8.
43 K Scott, 'From Drill to Dance', in *Decolonising the Landscape: Indigenous Cultures in Australia*, eds K Schaffer and B Neumeier, Brill Academic Publishers, Amsterdam, 2014, pp. 5-6.
44 Scott, 'From Drill to Dance', p. 6
45 I Clendinnen, 'Reading Mr Robinson', in *The Cost of Courage in Aztec Society*, Cambridge University Press, Cambridge, 2010, pp. 203-4.
46 Ibid., p. 204.
47 GF Moore, *Diary of Ten Years Eventful Life of an Early Settler in Western Australia; and also a descriptive vocabulary of the language of the Aborigines*, M Walbrook, London, 1884, p. 162.
48 *Perth Gazette*, 19 January 1833, p. 10.
49 FC Irwin to Lord Viscount Goderich, 10 April 1833, Appendix no. 4, item no. 7, p.134.
50 Molloy, 'Letter from Georgiana Molloy to Mrs Kennedy, 29 May 1833'.
51 A Lester and Z Laidlaw, 'Indigenous Sites and Mobilities: Connected Struggles in the Long Nineteenth Century', in *Indigenous Communities and Settler Colonialism: Land Holding, Loss and Survival in an Interconnected World*, eds A Lester and Z Laidlaw, Palgrave Macmillan, Basingstoke, 2015, p. 7.
52 Ibid., p. 8.
53 K Fox, 'Globalising Indigeneity?: Writing Indigenous Histories in a Transnational World', *History Compass* 10, no. 6, 2012, p. 431.
54 See also Dianne Austin-Broos' work on the Arrente people's desire to have their songs and histories recorded on paper. D Austin-Broos, *Arrente Present, Arrente Past: Invasion, Violence and Imagination in Indigenous Central Australia*, University of Chicago Press, Chicago, 2009, Chapter 3.
55 Clendinnen, p. 208.
56 Quoted in M Dunn, 'Aboriginal Guides in the Hunter Valley, New South Wales', in *Brokers and Boundaries: Colonial Exploration in Indigenous Territory*, eds T Shellam, M Nugent, S Konishi and J Cadzow, ANU Press, Canberra, 2016, p. 75.
57 Ibid., p. 76.
58 SWALSC, Host and Owen, p. 94.

59 Gyalliput's map recently featured in the National Archives of the UK publication: R Mitchell and A James, *Maps: Their Untold Stories – Map Treasures from the National Archives*, Bloomsbury and the National Archives, London, 2015.

Chapter 6

1 J Jones 'Indigenous Life Stories', *Life Writing* 1, no. 2, 2004, pp. 209-18.
2 G Hennessy, 'Character Above Colour: Fast Track to Assimilation? Margaret Tucker MBE and the Politics of Assimilation', *Social Alternatives* 21, no. 1, 2002, p. 62.
3 J Andrews, *Bringing Up Our Children: Aboriginal Families in Victoria*, AIATSIS, Canberra, 2000; J Andrews, 'Bringing Up Our Yorta Yorta Children', in *Contexts of Child Development Culture, Policy and Intervention*, eds G Robinson et al., Charles Darwin University Press, Darwin, 2008, pp. 23-35; J Andrews, 'Where's All the Community? Kinship, Mobility and Identity Revisited in Aboriginal Melbourne', PhD Thesis, La Trobe University, 2015; M Dodson 'The End in the Beginning: Re(de)finding Aboriginality', in *Blacklines: Contemporary Critical Writing by Indigenous Australians*, ed. M Grossman, Melbourne University Press, Melbourne, 2003; B Fredericks, '"We don't leave our identities at the city limits": Aboriginal and Torres Strait Islander People Living in Urban Localities', *Australian Aboriginal Studies*, no. 1, 2013, pp. 4-16.
4 J Andrews, 'Where's All the Community?'; A Moreton-Robinson, *Talkin' Up to the White Woman: Aboriginal Women and Feminism*, University of Queensland Press, St Lucia, 2000; M Nakata, 'Introduction to the Special Issue: Engaging with Indigenous Knowledge, Culture and Communities', *Australian Academic and Research Libraries* 45, no. 2, 2014, pp. 78-80; B Carlson, *The Politics of Identity: Who Counts as Aboriginal Today?*, Aboriginal Studies Press, Canberra, 2016.
5 S Maddison, 'Indigenous Identity, "Authenticity" and the Structural Violence of Settler Colonialism', *Identities: Global Studies in Culture and Power* 20, no. 3, 2013, pp. 288-303.
6 R. Broome, *Aboriginal Australians: A History Since 1788*, Allen & Unwin, Sydney, 4th edn, 2010.
7 J Andrews, 'Where's All the Community?'
8 T Clements, *From Old Maloga, (The Memoirs of an Aboriginal Woman)*, Fraser & Morphet, Melbourne, n.d.
9 *The Members of the Yorta Yorta Aboriginal Community v The State of Victoria & Ors* [1998] 1606 FCA (18 December 1998), [82]; Clements, *From Old Maloga*, p. 1.

Notes

10 R Pitty, 'A Poverty of Evidence: Abusing Law and History in *Yorta Yorta v Victoria* (1998)', *Australian Journal of Legal History* 5, no. 1, 1999, pp. 41-61; W Atkinson, '"Not One Iota" of Land Justice: Reflections on the Yorta Yorta Native Title Claim 1994–2001', *Indigenous Law Bulletin* 5, no. 6, 2001, p. 21.

11 Beverley Briggs, personal communication, April 2016.

12 Pitty, 'A Poverty of Evidence', p. 60.

13 Sharon Atkinson née Miller, personal communication, May 2016.

14 P Read, *Charles Perkins: A Biography*, Viking, Melbourne, 1990; P Read, *The Stolen Generations: The Removal of Aboriginal Children in New South Wales 1883 to 1969*, New South Wales Ministry of Aboriginal Affairs, Sydney, 1984. See also P Read, F Peters-Little and A Haebich (eds), *Indigenous Biography and Autobiography*, ANU ePress, Canberra, 2008.

15 C McLisky, 'The Location of Faith: Power, Gender and Spirituality in the 1883–84 Maloga Mission Revival', *History Australia* 7, no. 1, 2010; D Barwick, J Urry and D Bennett, 'A Select Bibliography of Aboriginal History and Social Change: Theses and Published Research to 1976', *Aboriginal History* 1, no. 2, 1977, p. 127.

16 P Read, F Peters-Little and A Haebich (eds), *Indigenous Biography and Autobiography*.

17 In 1903 Theresa Middleton married George Clements and in 1904 their first child, Margaret (later Margaret Tucker), was born. In 1910 my grandmother, their youngest daughter Geraldine (later Geraldine Briggs), was born. If the memoirs were written in the 1930s my grandmother would have been in her early 20s, and with young children. However, in the memoirs Clements states that her daughters were already married and she had adult grandchildren and a great grandson. 'An Aboriginal Girl's Plea for Understanding' by Margaret Tucker, produced in the 1930s, was fleetingly referred to in Clements' memoirs, indicating that the memoirs had already been written. In 1939, the famous Cummeragunja Walk Off occurred and Theresa Clements stated she had also participated, writing: 'It is more than ten years since things got so bad on Cummeragunja that we couldn't stand it. A lot of us come off'. This situates the writing of the memoirs in the 1950s. Clements also refers to her 'first great grandson', who was born in 1954, indicating the memoirs were written after this. My aunt Frances states that it is very possible that Theresa Clements was supported by her granddaughter, Molly Dyer, daughter of Margaret Tucker. Aunt Frances states: 'Molly was well educated and very smart.' Clements, n.d., p. 7.

18 J Jones, 'Indigenous Life Stories'.

19 Clements, *From Old Maloga*, p. 8.

20 Ibid., p. 2.
21 Yarmuk is a Yorta Yorta word meaning cousin; H Bowe, L Peeler, and S Atkinson, *Yorta Yorta Language Heritage*, Department of Linguistics, Monash University, Melbourne, 1998. Thwaites wrote a tribute to Clements on her passing titled 'For Yarmuk, Elder of the Ulupna Tribe'; M Thwaites, 'For Yarmuk, Elder of the Ulupna Tribe', viewed 11 January 2017, <http://thwaites.com.au/wp/for-yarmuk-elder-of-the-ulupna-tribe/>. See also M Tucker, *If Everyone Cared: Autobiography of Margaret Tucker*, Ure Smith, Sydney, 1977; A Morgan and G Bostock, *Lousy Little Sixpence*, motion picture, Sixpence Productions, 1984.
22 A good reputation secured continual or seasonal work for Aboriginal people in rural Victoria. Theresa states that the men on Maloga did seasonal shearing work (p. 4). Barwick's 1963 research on seasonal employment also identified this information through her Aboriginal informants and families, whose travel routes for regular seasonal employment were based on the reputations they had acquired through their connections to Aboriginal reservations. D Barwick, 'A Little More Than Kin: Regional Affiliation and Group Identity among Aboriginal Migrants in Melbourne', PhD Thesis, The Australian National University, 1963.
23 K Schilling, 'Mister Maloga (Book Review)', *Australian Aboriginal Studies*, no. 2, 1994, p. 96.
24 Clements, *From Old Maloga*, p. 2.
25 Ibid, p. 3.
26 M Bin-Sallik, 'Cultural Safety: Let's Name It!', *Australian Journal of Indigenous Education 32*, 2003, p. 22.
27 Clements, *From Old Maloga*, p. 4. James later married a Yorta Yorta woman, Ada Cooper, who was the sister of William Cooper.
28 Ibid; R Broome, *Aboriginal Victorians: A History Since 1800*, Allen & Unwin, Sydney, 2005, p. 308.
29 W Atkinson, 'The Cummera Walk Off and the Return to Base Camp Politics', 2009, viewed 11 January 2017, <https://waynera.files.wordpress.com/2010/10/cummerawalkoff-doc.pdf>; Morgan and Bostock, *Lousy Little Sixpence*; B Attwood and A Markus, *Thinking Black: William Cooper and the Australian Aborigines Advancement League*, Aboriginal Studies Press, Canberra, 2004.
30 The Federation of Aboriginal & Torres Strait Islander Languages & Culture Corporation, 'October 1998: Aretha Briggs and David Wirrpanda, viewed 11 December 2017, <http://archive.li/N7ajA>, 'The Lyrics to Bura Fera', We Want to Walk With You, 2016, viewed 11 January 2017, <http://towalkwithyou.com/the-lyrics-to-bura-fera/>; Broome, *Aboriginal Victorians*, p. 280; W Blair, *The Sapphires*, motion

picture, Hopscotch Entertainment, Sydney, 2012.
31. Atkinson, 'The Cummera Walk Off'; Morgan and Bostock, *Lousy Little Sixpence*; Attwood and Markus, *Thinking Black*.
32. Clements, *From Old Maloga*, p. 4.
33. R Hagen, 'Ethnographic Information and Anthropological Interpretations in a Native Title Claim: The Yorta Yorta Experience', *Aboriginal History* 25, 2001, p. 225.
34. Bin-Sallik, 'Cultural Safety'.
35. Aunty Frances Matthysson, personal communication, 2016.
36. McLisky, 'The Location of Faith'.
37. Clements, *From Old Maloga*, p. 8.
38. McLisky, 'The Location of Faith', p. 08.12.
39. Broome, *Aboriginal Victorians*, p. 127.
40. Morgan and Bostock, *Lousy Little Sixpence*.
41. Corranderrk Aboriginal Reserve was highly successful in growing vegetables and hops. The Reserve had won awards for its hops.
42. D Barwick, 'Coranderrk and Cummeroogunga: Pioneers and Policy', in *Opportunity and Response: Case Studies in Economic Development*, eds. TS Epstein and DH Penny, C Hurst & Co, London, 1972; D Barwick, *Rebellion at Coranderrk*, eds LE Barwick and RE Barwick, Aboriginal History Inc, Canberra, 1998; R Broome, '"There were Vegetables every Year Mr Green was Here": Right Behaviour and the Struggle for Autonomy at Coranderrk Aboriginal Reserve', *History Australia* 3, no. 2, 2006.
43. Broome, *Aboriginal Victorians*, p. 262.
44. P Seidel, 'Native Title: The Struggle for Justice for the Yorta Yorta Nation', *Alternative Law Journal* 29, no. 2, 2004, p. 71.
45. Atkinson, 'The Cummera Walk Off', p. 2.
46. Ibid; Broome, *Aboriginal Victorians*, p. 262.
47. Atkinson, 'The Cummera Walk Off', p. 2.
48. W Atkinson, 'Not One Iota: The Yorta Yorta Struggle for Justice', PhD Thesis, La Trobe University, 2000; R Broome, *Fighting Hard: The Victorian Aborigines Advancement League*, Aboriginal Studies Press, Canberra, 2015.
49. Atkinson, 'The Cummera Walk Off', p. 1.
50. Seidel, 'Native Title'.
51. Clements, *From Old Maloga*, p. 4.
52. Later this was to go against Aboriginal people in the Yorta Yorta Native Title case, when Justice Olney ruled this evidence meant that any traditional rituals were eroded and assimilation had occurred – effectively striking out the Yorta Yorta people's connection to tribal lands.

53 N Cato, *Mister Maloga: Daniel Matthews and His Maloga Mission*, University of Queensland Press, Brisbane, 1976; N Cato 'Matthews, Daniel (1837-1902)', *Australian Dictionary of Biography*, 1975, viewed 11 January 2017, <http://adb.anu.edu.au/biography/matthews-daniel-4170>.
54 H Goodall, 'Land in Our Own Country: The Aboriginal Land Rights Movement In South-Eastern Australia 1860 to 1914', *Aboriginal History* 14, no. 1/2, 1990, p. 6; Attwood and Markus, *Thinking Black*. Maloga Mission was struggling to survive by 1895.
55 Morgan and Bostock, *Lousy Little Sixpence*. It should be noted that there were two organisations with similar names: the first was the Australian Aborigines Progressive Association, established in Sydney in 1925 by Aboriginal Fred Maynard; the other one was the Aborigines Progressive Association, established by Jack Patten. See J Maynard, 'Fred Maynard and Marcus Garvey: Storming the Urban Space', in *Exploring Urban Identities and Histories*, eds C Hansen and K Butler, AIATSIS, Canberra, 2013, pp. 153-9.
56 Schilling, *Mister Maloga*.
57 Broome, *Aboriginal Victorians*, p. 262.
58 FL Davis, 'Colouring within the Lines: Settler Colonialism and the Cummeragunja Aboriginal Station, 1888-1960s', PhD thesis, Arts, School of Historical Studies, The University of Melbourne, 2010.
59 Schilling, *Mister Maloga*.
60 Atkinson, 'The Cummera Walk Off'.
61 Clements, *From Old Maloga*, p. 6.
62 Ibid., p. 4
63 B Attwood et al., *A Life Together, A Life Apart: A History of Relations between Europeans and Aborigines*, Melbourne University Press, Melbourne, 1994.
64 Ibid.
65 Ibid., p. 15.
66 Ibid., p. 16; Morgan and Bostock, *Lousy Little Sixpence*.
67 H Goodall, *Invasion to Embassy: Land in Aboriginal Politics in NSW, 1770-1972*, Allen & Unwin, Sydney, 1996, pp. 247-58.
68 Atkinson, 'The Cummera Walk Off'.
69 Ibid.
70 Tucker, *If Everyone Cared*, pp. 90-5.
71 Clements, *From Old Maloga*, p. 6.
72 J Jones, 'As Long as She Got her Voice: How Cross-cultural Collaboration Shapes Aboriginal Textuality', *Altitude* 5, 2005, p. 4.
73 Tucker, *If Everyone Cared*, pp. 121-2.
74 Ibid, p. 65.

Notes

75 JT Solonec, 'Shared Lives on *Nigena* Country: A Joint Biography of Katie and Frank Rodriguez, 1944-1994', PhD Thesis, University of Western Australia, 2015, p. 8.
76 O Haag, 'From the Margins to the Mainstream: Towards a History of Published Indigenous Australian Autobiographies and Biographies', in *Indigenous Biography and Autobiography*, eds P Read, F Peters-Little and A Haebich, ANU ePress, Canberra, 2008, pp. 5-28.
77 Beverley Briggs, personal communication, 2016.
78 Laurel Robinson, personal communication, 2016.

Chapter 7

1 Letter, HS Wyndham to Mrs Barlow, 28 April 1961, Country Women's Association of NSW (hereafter CWA of NSW), Sydney, Secretariat Files, Box 017.
2 *Annual Report* of the Aborigines Welfare Board (hereafter AWB) for the year ended 30 June 1948, Parliament of NSW, 7 April 1949, p. 6.
3 JW Harris, 'The Education of Aboriginal Children in New South Wales Public Schools since 1788: Part 1', *Aboriginal Child at School* 6, no. 4, 1978; JW Harris, 'The Education of Aboriginal Children in New South Wales Public Schools since 1788: Part 2', *Aboriginal Child at School* 6, no. 5, 1978; D Huggonson, 'Towards a History of Aboriginal Education in New South Wales', *Aboriginal Child at School* 12, no. 5, 1984; JJ Fletcher, *Clean, Clad and Courteous: A History of Aboriginal Education in New South Wales*, J Fletcher, Melbourne, 1989.
4 I Walden, '"That Was Slavery Days": Aboriginal Domestic Servants in New South Wales in the Twentieth Century', *Labour History*, no. 69, 1995; A Cole, 'Unwitting Soldiers: The Working Life of Matron Hiscocks at the Cootamundra Girls Home', *Aboriginal History* 27, 2003; J Ramsland, 'The Aboriginal Boys' Training Home, Kinchela, 1924-1970, and the Development of a Culture of Physical Fitness and Sport', *Journal of Educational Administration and History* 38, no. 3, 2006.
5 Q Beresford, 'Separate and Unequal: An Outline of Aboriginal Education', in *Reform and Resistance in Aboriginal Education*, eds Q Beresford, G Partington and G Gower, UWA Publishing, Crawley, 2012, p. 85.
6 R Broome, *Aboriginal Australians: A History Since 1788*, Allen & Unwin, Sydney, 4th edn, 2010, p. 32.
7 Meritocracy holds that individuals who are clever and hardworking can advance up the social hierarchy regardless of their class positioning at birth. The application of the common-sense equation 'intelligence + effort = merit' enables the formation of a hierarchy based on merit

and purportedly replaces the 'aristocracy of birth' with an 'aristocracy of talent'. See M Young, *The Rise of Meritocracy 1870–2033: An Essay on Education and Equality*, Penguin, Harmondsworth, 1958, p. 94.
8. RL Ginibi, *Don't Take Your Love to Town*, Penguin, Melbourne, 1988, pp. 37–8.
9. *Annual Report* of the AWB for the year ended 30 June 1952, Parliament of NSW, 15 September 1953, p. 4.
10. The second and final recorded scholarship was awarded in 1950. *Annual Report* of the AWB for the year ended 30 June 1950, Parliament of NSW, 3 May 1951, p. 14; *Annual Report* of the AWB for the year ended 30 June 1952, Parliament of NSW, 15 September 1953.
11. *Annual Report* of the AWB for the year ended 30 June 1958, Parliament of NSW, 10 December 1958, p. 4.
12. *Annual Report* of the AWB for the year ended 30 June 1961, Parliament of NSW, 30 November 1961, p. 5. A total of 75 students had received financial assistance since inception of the scheme. Of the 27 Aboriginal students who passed the Intermediate Certificate (36 per cent of bursary holders), only 12 continued to the Leaving Certificate (16 per cent of bursary holders); 6 graduating between 1947 and 1960 (50 per cent pass rate). By comparison, 93,268 non-Aboriginal students graduated with a Leaving Certificate between 1947 and 1960, a 75.6 per cent pass rate. (Calculations based on NSW year book figures 1947–1960; see Government Statistician, *The Official Year Book of New South Wales*, Bureau of Statistics, Sydney, 1947–61.)
13. J Hughes, 'The Development of the Comprehensive School in New South Wales: The Influence of Harold Wyndham and the 1957 Wyndham Report', *Education Research and Perspectives* 28, no. 2, 2001, p. 16.
14. Australian Council for Educational Research, *Review of Education in Australia 1955–1962*, Australian Council for Educational Research, Melbourne, 1964.
15. A Barcan, 'The Transition in Australian Education', in *Australian Education in the Twentieth Century*, eds J Cleverley and J Lawry, Longman, Melbourne, 1972, p. 195; C Campbell and H Proctor, *A History of Australian Schooling*, Allen & Unwin, Sydney, 2014, p. 109.
16. A Barcan, *A Short History of Education in New South Wales*, Martindale Press, Sydney, 1965, p. 208.
17. Report of the Commissioners, Mainly on Secondary Education, Legislative Assembly of New South Wales, 1904, p. 10.
18. Ibid., p. 10.
19. Australian Council for Educational Research, p. 124.
20. Barcan, 'The Transition in Australian Education', p. 180.

Notes

21 Hughes, 'The Development of the Comprehensive School in New South Wales', p. 8.

22 For campaigns addressing structural reform see S Taffe, *Black and White Together: FCAATSI: The Federal Council for the Advancement of Aborigines and Torres Strait Islanders 1958–1973*, University of Queensland Press, Brisbane, 2005; J Chesterman and B Galligan, *Citizens without Rights: Aborigines and Australian Citizenship*, Cambridge University Press, Cambridge, 1997. For efforts to dismantle the 'petty apartheid' of country towns see J Jones, *Country Women and the Colour Bar: Grass Roots Activism and the Country Women's Association*, Aboriginal Studies Press, Canberra, 2015.

23 A Barcan, *Two Centuries of Education in New South Wales*, New South Wales University Press, Kensington, 1988, p. 202.

24 *Annual Report* of the AWB for the year ended 30 June 1955, Parliament of NSW, 13 October 1955, p. 4.

25 *Annual Report* of the AWB for the year ended 30 June 1946, Parliament of NSW, 23 October 1947, p. 4.

26 *Annual Report* of the AWB for the year ended 30 June 1947, Parliament of NSW, 22 April 1948, p. 6.

27 Between 1943 and 1964 there were only 1500 applications from a population of 14,000. H Goodall, 'New South Wales', in *Contested Ground: Australian Aborigines under the British Crown*, ed. A McGrath, Allen & Unwin, Sydney, 1995, p. 90.

28 *Annual Report* of the AWB for the year ended 30 June 1947.

29 *Annual Report* of the AWB for the year ended 30 June 1963, Parliament of NSW, 9 April 1964, p. 9.

30 CD Rowley, *Equality by Instalments: The Aboriginal Householder in Rural New South Wales, 1965 and 1980*, Australian Institute of Aboriginal Studies, Canberra, 1982.

31 M Einfeld, J Killen and K Mundine, *Toomelah Report: Report on the Problems and Needs of Aborigines Living on the New South Wales–Queensland Border*, Human Rights Australia, Belrose, Sydney, 1988, p. 44.

32 G Phelan, 'A Survey of Aboriginal Children in NSW Secondary Schools', NSW Teachers Federation, p. 4, NSW State Records, Department of Education, Aboriginal Children education and living conditions, File no. 67/21137.

33 Ibid, p. 4.

34 HS Wyndham et al., *Report of the Committee Appointed to Survey Secondary Education in New South Wales*, Legislative Council, New South Wales, Sydney, 1957, pp. 44, 54; RW Connell, 'Working-class Families and the New Secondary Education', *Australian Journal of Education* 47, no. 3, 2003, p. 236.

35 Lippman quoted in C Guiness, 'What Motivates the High School Student?', in *Aboriginal Education: The Teacher's Role*, ed. T Roper, National Union of Australian University Students, North Melbourne, 1969, p. 125.
36 Lippman quoted in Guiness; Phelan, 'A Survey of Aboriginal Children in NSW Secondary Schools', p. 5.
37 S Themelis, 'Meritocracy through Education and Social Mobility in Post-war Britain: A Critical Examination', *British Journal of Sociology of Education* 29, no. 5, 2008, pp. 430–3.
38 Broome, *Aboriginal Australians*, pp. 230–1
39 Ibid., 229.
40 Jones, *Country Women and the Colour Bar*.
41 Boggabilla Aboriginal Station is also known locally as Toomelah Mission.
42 Jones, *Country Women and the Colour Bar*, p. 33.
43 Minute, Executive committee meeting 7 Nov 1961, Aboriginal Scholarships folder, CWA of NSW, Potts Point.
44 Ibid.
45 Letter, AWB to CWA, 20 July 1962, Aboriginal Scholarships folder, CWA of NSW, Potts Point.
46 A pseudonym has been used to protect the privacy of the inaugural scholarship holder. All identifying details have been altered.
47 Letter, Joanne Barry to CWA Executive, 6 August 1962, Aboriginal Scholarships folder, CWA of NSW, Potts Point.
48 Report on Joanne Barry, 20 July 1962, Aboriginal Scholarships folder.
49 Letter, AWB to CWA, 27 September 1963, Aboriginal Scholarships folder.
50 Ibid.
51 CWA State Executive to Superintendent of Aborigines Welfare, 16 October 1963, Aboriginal Scholarships folder.
52 Parliament of New South Wales, *Report from the Joint Committee of the Legislative Council and the Legislative Assembly upon Aborigines Welfare*, Parliament of New South Wales, Sydney, 1967, p. 17.
53 Report on Joanne Barry, 19 July 1965, Aboriginal Scholarships folder.
54 Letter, CWA to Joanne Barry, 25 July 1966, Aboriginal Scholarships folder.
55 Report on Joanne Barry Form 5, half yearly exam 1966, Aboriginal Scholarships folder.
56 Report on Joanne Barry, Yearly examinations 1966, Aboriginal Scholarships folder.
57 Letter, CWA to Joanne Barry, 22 March 1967, Aboriginal Scholarships folder.
58 Memo of telephone call, Group Representative to CWA headquarters, 16 January 1968, Aboriginal Scholarships folder.

Notes

59 Letter, AWB to CWA, 11 January 1968, Aboriginal Scholarships folder.
60 R Broome, *Fighting Hard: The Victorian Aborigines Advancement League*, Aboriginal Studies Press, Canberra, 2015, p. 23.
61 Langton quoted in C Driscoll, *The Australian Country Girl: History, Image, Experience*, Ashgate, Farnham, UK, 2014, p. 83.
62 Broome, *Aboriginal Australians*, p. 227
63 C McKinnon, 'Indigenous Music as a Space of Resistance', in *Making Settler Colonial Space: Perspectives on Race, Place and Identity*, eds T Banivanua-Mar and P Edmonds, Palgrave Macmillan, New York, 2010, p. 258.
64 Parliament of New South Wales, *Report from the Joint Committee*, p. 94.
65 C Campbell, 'Comprehensive Government High School', *Dictionary of Educational History in Australia and New Zealand (DEHANZ)*, 2014, viewed 20 January 2016, <http://dehanz.net.au/entries/comprehensive-government-high-school/>.
66 Einfeld, Killen and Mundine, p. 44.
67 Ibid., p. 43.
68 Ibid.
69 Carl McGrady, interview with the author. When Aboriginal children from Toomelah and Boggabilla were finally allowed to proceed to high school across the state border in Goondiwindi, they encountered an overtly racist educational culture exemplified by the provision of different blackboards for the use of Aboriginal and non-Aboriginal students. See Einfeld, Killen and Mundine, p. 45.
70 B Bessant, 'Rural Schooling and the Rural Myth in Australia', *Comparative Education* 14, no. 2, 1978, p. 128.
71 F Tate, 'Rural School Administration', in *The Rural School in Australia*, ed. PR Cole, Melbourne University Press, Melbourne, 1937, p. 85.
72 Ibid.
73 H Townsend, *Serving the Country: The History of the Country Women's Association of New South Wales*, Doubleday, Sydney, 1988, p. 183.
74 Ibid., Twenty-five rural high schools provided children with an education in their own NSW district by 1936. HS Wyndham, 'Statistics', in *The Rural School in Australia*, ed. PR Cole, Melbourne University Press, Melbourne, 1937, p. 224.
75 At Inverell, Narrandera, Moree, Mudgee, Murwillumbah, Narrabri and Tumut. Townsend, p. 183.
76 Colin Wellard, interview with the author.
77 Minute, Gwydir Group Council meeting 17 August 1966, CWA of NSW, Potts Point.
78 Minute, Gwydir Group Council meeting, 1 August 1967.
79 Ibid.

80 Carl McGrady, interview with the author.
81 Minute, Gwydir Group Council meeting 15 March 1967.
82 At least three other Aboriginal boys had lived at the hostel to attend Armidale High School in previous years: Neville Thorne, Terry Widders and Raymond Beale, for example, were resident in 1962-1963. See 'Pete's Page', *Dawn*, 10, Aborigines Welfare Board of NSW, Sydney, 1962.
83 Ibid.
84 Carl McGrady, interview with the author.
85 Minute, Gwydir Group Council meeting, 27 March 1968.
86 Carl McGrady, interview with the author.
87 Ibid.
88 Ibid.
89 Ibid.
90 Minute, Gwydir Group Council meeting, 27 March 1968.
91 T Widders, 'What Education Means to Me: An Aboriginal's Perspective', *The Aboriginal Child at School* 2, no. 1, 1974.
92 Carl McGrady, interview with the author.
93 Jones, *Country Women and the Colour Bar*, pp. 13-14.
94 Carl McGrady, interview with the author.
95 P Hickey quoted in BH Watts, *Aboriginal Futures: Review of Research and Developments and Related Policies in the Education of Aborigines*, Education Research and Development Committee, Canberra, 1981, p. 541; Dawn Dennison, interview with the author; IS Mitchell and JE Cawte, 'The Aboriginal Family Voluntary Resettlement Scheme: An Approach to Aboriginal Adaptation', *Australian and New Zealand Journal of Psychiatry* 11, no. 1, 1977.
96 Carl McGrady, interview with the author.
97 Press Release, 'Study Grants for Aboriginals', 19 November 1968, Aborigines – Aboriginal Secondary Grant Scheme Commonwealth Department of Education and Science, 71/25471, State Records of NSW, Sydney.
98 'Proposed Aboriginal Secondary Grants Scheme', Office of Aboriginal Affairs, 12 January 1970, MS 4167, Papers of Barrie Dexter, AIATSIS Library, Canberra.
99 Memo, 'Aboriginal Study Grants Scheme Estimated Expenditure 1969-70', Department of Education and Science to Director Office of Aboriginal Affairs, 23 February 1970, Papers of Barrie Dexter.
100 'Aborigines Seek Higher Education', *The Financial Review*, 14 May 1970.
101 Register: Aboriginal Education Commonwealth Secondary Scholarship Grants, 5 July 1971, Aborigines – Aboriginal Secondary Grant Scheme

Commonwealth Department of Education and Science, 71/25471, State Records of NSW, Sydney.

102   See, e.g., D Foley, 'Indigenous Epistemology and Indigenous Standpoint Theory', *Social Alternatives* 22, no. 1, 2003; LI Rigney, *Indigenist Research and Aboriginal Australia*, Ashgate, Hampshire, 2006; M Nakata et al., 'Decolonial Goals and Pedagogies for Indigenous Studies', *Decolonization: Indigeneity, Education & Society* 1, no. 1, 2012, for a discussion of Indigenous Australian intellectual sovereignty, and the ways in which school curriculum and underlying theories of knowledge perpetuate colonial domination.

Chapter 8

1   J Lear, *Radical Hope: Ethics in the Face of Cultural Devastation*, Harvard University Press, Cambridge, Mass, 2006, pp. 22-7.
2   Ibid., pp. 12-20.
3   Quoted in Ibid., p. 2.
4   Quoted in 'The surrender of Joseph', *Harper's Weekly* 21, no. 1090, 17 November 1877, p. 906, viewed 25 February 2016, <https://content.lib.washington.edu/aipnw/surrenderofjoseph.html>.
5   See A Isenberg, *The Destruction of the Bison: An Environmental History, 1750-1920*, Cambridge University Press, Cambridge, 2000, chaps. 3-4.
6   Lear, *Radical Hope*, p. 45.
7   Ibid., p. 51.
8   Ibid., p. 52.
9   Isenberg, *The Destruction of the Bison*, pp. 103-6.
10 Lear, *Radical Hope*, p. 68.
11 Ibid., p. 71.
12 Quoted in Ibid., p. 72.
13 Ibid., p. 99.
14 Ibid., p. 104.
15 N Butlin, *Our Original Aggression*, Allen & Unwin, London, 1983. See also R Broome, *Aboriginal Victorians: A History Since 1800*, Allen & Unwin, Sydney, 2005, pp. 6-9.
16 Broome, *Aboriginal Victorians*, chaps. 1-5.
17 For a discussion of depopulation see Ibid., pp. 90-3.
18 For settler Melbourne, see R Broome, *The Victorians: Arriving*, Fairfax, Syme & Weldon, Sydney, 1984, pp. 21, 23, 58; J Boyce, *1835: The Founding of Melbourne and the Conquest of Australia*, Black Inc., Melbourne, 2011. For Aboriginal population numbers see Broome, *Aboriginal Victorians*, pp. 91-3.

19 D Barwick, 'Mapping the Past: An Atlas of Victorian Clans 1835–1904', *Aboriginal History* 8, part 2, pp. 122, 124.
20 W Stanner, 'The Dreaming', in *White Man Got No Dreaming: Essays 1838–1973*, Australian National University Press, Canberra, 1979, p. 39.
21 J Dawson, *Australian Aborigines. The Languages and Customs of Several Tribes of Aborigines in the Western District of Victoria, Australia*, Melbourne, George Robertson, 1881, reprinted AIATSIS, Canberra, 1991, pp. iii, 5.
22 Barwick, 'Mapping the Past', pp. 107–8.
23 Ibid., p. 108.
24 Ibid., p. 124.
25 On the impending attack see Fawkner's diary from October 1835 to August 1836 in CP Billot (ed.), *Melbourne's Missing Chronicle*, Quartet Books, Melbourne, 1982; JP Fawkner, 'Reminiscences', State Library of Victoria, MS 8528; AW Greig, 'Some New Documentary Evidence Concerning the Foundation of Melbourne', *Victorian Historical Magazine* 12, no. 4, 1928, pp. 109–117. On Billibellary's opposition see William Thomas, Quarterly Report June–August 1846, Public Record Office Victoria, Victorian Public Record Series (VPRS) 4410, unit 3; and D Bunce, 'Australasiatic Reminiscences' in his *Travels with Dr Leichhardt*, Oxford University Press, Melbourne, 1979 [1859], pp. 64–79.
26 I McBryde, 'Wil-im-ee Moor-ring: Or, Where do Axes Come From?', *Mankind* 11, 1978, pp. 354–82.
27 AW Howitt, *The Native Tribes of South-east Australia*, Aboriginal Studies Press, Canberra, 1996 [1904], pp. 340–1.
28 R Broome, 'Changing Aboriginal Landscapes of Pastoral Victoria, 1830–1850', *Studies in the History of Gardens & Designed Landscapes* 31, no. 2, 2011, pp. 93–4.
29 Broome, *The Victorians: Arriving*, pp. 47–50, 72.
30 A Crosby, *Germs, Seeds and Animals: Studies in Ecological History*, ME Sharpe, New York, 1994, chap. 1.
31 Thomas, Quarterly Report, September–December 1843, VPRS, 4410, unit 3.
32 Noble Keenan's journal, Blue Books and Accounts [1844–1849], School Records for Aborigines in the Westernport and Melbourne Districts, Public Record Office Victoria, VPRS 26, p. 6.
33 M Fels, *Good Men and True: The Aboriginal Police of Port Phillip District 1837–1853*, Melbourne University Press, Melbourne, 1988, p. 51.
34 Quoted in Ibid., p. 53.
35 Ibid., p. 227.
36 Ibid., p. 101.
37 Ibid., pp. 101–6, 139–41.

Notes

38   Quoted in Lear, *Radical Hope*, pp. 141-2.
39   M Sahlins, 'The Original Affluent Society', in *Stone Age Economics*, Routledge, London, 2nd edn, 2004.
40   Thomas, Quarterly Report, June-August 1846. On sorcery see B Nance, 'The Level of Violence: Europeans and Aborigines in Port Phillip, 1835-1850', *Historical Studies* 19, no. 77, 1981, pp. 532-49.
41   Thomas, Quarterly Report, September-December 1843.
42   See discussion in J Diamond, *Guns, Germs and Steel: A Short History of Everybody for the Last 13,000 Years*, Vintage, London, 1998, chap. 6.
43   W Thomas, *The Journal of William Thomas, Assistant Protector of the Aborigines of Port Phillip & Guardian of the Aborigines of Victoria 1839-1867*, Volume two: 1844 to 1853, ed. M Stephens, Victorian Aboriginal Corporation of Languages, Melbourne, 2014, p. 370.
44   W Thomas, 29 August 1850, Weekly Report 26 August-1 September 1850; Registered Inward Correspondence to the Superintendent of Port Phillip District from W Thomas, Guardian of Aborigines and ES Parker, Assistant Protector of Aborigines Public Record Office Victoria, VPRS 2893, unit 1, 1850/55.
45   Thomas, 21 September 1950, Weekly Report 16-22 September 1850; VPRS 2893, unit 1, 1850/58.
46   Thomas, Monthly Report August 1850; VPRS 2893, unit 1, 1850/56.
47   Half-yearly Special Return, Aborigines – Counties of Bourke, Mornington and Evelyn, 30 June 1853 in *Victoria Parliamentary Papers*, 1853-54, 'Aborigines', C, no. 33a, p. 16.
48   'Report of the Select Committee of the Legislative Council on the Aborigines', 1859, *Victoria Parliamentary Papers, Legislative Council*, 1858-9, D8.
49   See D Barwick, *Rebellion at Coranderrk*, eds LE Barwick and RE Barwick, Aboriginal History Monograph 5, Canberra, 1998, pp. 39-40.
50   *Argus*, 8 March 1859.
51   Ibid.
52   Barwick, *Rebellion at Coranderrk*, pp. 66-7. See also J Lydon, 'The Experimental 1860s: Charles Walter's Images of Coranderrk Aboriginal Station, Victoria', *Aboriginal History* 26, 2002, pp. 82-5.
53   Barwick, *Rebellion at Coranderrk*, pp. 75, 107.
54   Board for the Protection of Aborigines, 'Fourth Report of the Central Board Appointed to Watch over the Interests of the Aborigines in the Colony of Victoria', *Victoria Parliamentary Papers*, 1864, No. 19, p. 5.
55   Barwick, *Rebellion at Coranderrk*, p. 255.

56 D Barwick, 'Coranderrk and Cumeroogunga: Pioneers and Policy', in *Opportunity and Response: Case Studies in Economic Development*, eds TS Epstein and DH Penny, C Hurst, London, 1972, pp. 50-61.

57 B Attwood, *Rights for Aborigines*, Allen & Unwin, Sydney, 2003, chap. 1; Broome, *Aboriginal Victorians*, chap. 9; G Nanni and A James, *Coranderrk: We Will Show the Country*, Aboriginal Studies Press, Canberra, 2013, chap. 1.

58 *Daily Telegraph* (Sydney), 5 July 1881 reprinted in N Cato, *Mister Maloga: Daniel Matthews and His Maloga Mission*, University of Queensland Press, Brisbane, 1976, pp. 387-8.

59 For the Kulin deputations to Berry see *Argus*, 30 March 1881, and to Grant reprinted in 'Coranderrk Aboriginal Station: Report of the Board Appointed to Inquire into, and Report upon, the Present Condition and Management of the Coranderrk Aboriginal Station: Together with the minutes of evidence (Coranderrk Inquiry Report)', *Victoria Parliamentary Papers*, 1881-82, no. 5, p. 58.

60 Quoted in Leitinger, 'The Board, the Parliament and the Aborigines', BA Hons thesis, La Trobe University, 1991, p. 45.

61 See Barwick, *Rebellion at Coranderrk*, chaps. 10-12; Broome, *Aboriginal Victorians*, chap. 9; R Broome, '"There were Vegetables every Year Mr Green was Here": Right Behaviour and the Struggle for Autonomy at Coranderrk Aboriginal Reserve', *History Australia* 3, no. 2, December 2006, pp. 43.1-43.16.

62 Barak, in Coranderrk Inquiry Report, pp. 9-10, Q. 398.

63 Ibid., p. 98.

64 For defiance at Lake Condah see J Critchett, *Untold Stories, Memories and Lives of Victorian Kooris*, Melbourne University Press, Melbourne, 1998, chaps. 6 and 8; for a strike at Ebenezer see Board for the Protection of Aborigines, 'Nineteenth Report of the Board for the Protection of the Aborigines in the Colony of Victoria', *Victoria Parliamentary Papers*, 1884, no. 1, p. 14; for other unrest see M Christie, *Aborigines in Colonial Victoria, 1835-86*, Sydney University Press, Sydney, 1979, p. 182.

65 *Argus*, 26 October 1937.

66 Letter to the *Argus*, 5 December 1934.

67 See J Chesterman and B Galligan, *Citizens without Rights: Aborigines and Australian Citizenship*, Cambridge University Press, Melbourne, 1997.

68 Policy of the Australian Aborigines League, signed by W. 'Bill' Onus, 4 April 1957, Victorian Aborigines Advancement League papers, State Library of Victoria, MS 13721, Box 178, Folder named 'Bryning Estate'.

69 Quoted in R Broome, *Fighting Hard: The Victorian Aborigines Advancement League*, Aboriginal Studies Press, Canberra, 2015, p. 219.

Notes

Chapter 9

1 M Briggs, J Lydon and M Say, 'Collaborating: Photographs of Koories in the State Library of Victoria', *The La Trobe Journal* 85, 2010, p. 120.

2 May Briggs-Walsh, 'Stories and Memories of My Childhood', unpublished manuscript, n.d., copy in possession of author.

3 P Hasluck and Department of Territories, Australia, *The Policy of Assimilation; Decisions of Commonwealth and State Ministers at the Native Welfare Conference, Canberra, January 26th and 27th, 1961*, AJ Arthur, Commonwealth Government Printer, Canberra, 1961, p. 1.

4 Ibid.

5 B de Sousa Santos, *Epistemologies of the South: Justice Against Epistemicide*, Paradigm, Boulder, CO, 2014.

6 There are many books published by Australian authors that examine this shared but invisible history with all its brutal, genocidal and shameful episodes.

7 Victorian Aboriginal Health Service, 'History – pre 1967', viewed 19 December 2016, <http://www.vahs.org.au/history-pre-1967/>.

8 L Burney, 'An Aboriginal way of Being Australian', *Australian Feminist Studies* 9, no. 19, 1994, p. 17.

9 W Tench, *A Complete Account of the Settlement at Port Jackson, in New South Wales*, G Nicol, London, 1793, p. 18.

10 R Manne, 'The History Wars', *The Monthly*, November 2009.

References

Unpublished works

Andrews, J, 'Where's All the Community? Kinship, Mobility and Identity Revisited in Aboriginal Melbourne', PhD Thesis, La Trobe University, 2015.

Atkinson, W, 'Not One Iota: The Yorta Yorta Struggle for Justice', PhD Thesis, La Trobe University, 2000.

Barwick, D, 'A Little More than Kin: Regional Affiliation and Group Identity Among Aboriginal Migrants in Melbourne', PhD thesis, Australian National University, 1963.

Briggs-Walsh, M, 'Stories and Memories of My Childhood', unpublished manuscript, n.d.

Broome, R, 'Rewriting *Aboriginal Australians* Thirty Years On', paper presented to the La Trobe University History Seminar, 29 August 2008.

Davis, FL, 'Colouring within the Lines: Settler Colonialism and the Cummeragunja Aboriginal Station, 1888-1960s', PhD thesis, University of Melbourne, 2010.

Leitinger, S, 'The Board, the Parliament and the Aborigines', BA Hons thesis, La Trobe University, 1991.

Midena, D, 'The Wonders of Conversion: Objectivity and Disenchantment in the Neuendettelsau Mission Encounter in New Guinea, 1886-1930', PhD thesis, University of Copenhagen, 2015.

Solonec, JT, 'Shared Lives on *Nigena* Country: A Joint Biography of Katie and Frank Rodriguez, 1944-1994', PhD thesis, University of Western Australia, 2015.

Manuscripts and archival papers

Country Women's Association of New South Wales Archive, Potts Point, Sydney.

Dexter, B, Papers, AIATSIS Library, Canberra, MS 4167.

Fawkner, JP, 'Reminiscences', State Library of Victoria, MS 8528.

Federal Surveillance of African Americans (1917-1925), Microfilm, Lamont Library, Harvard University.

Reference

Irwin, FC, 'Letter from Francis Chidley Irwin to Peter Brown', 22 January 1833, State Records Office of Western Australia, CSR 26/75.

Lyon, RM, 'Letter from RM Lyon to Frederick Robinson, 1 January 1833', Swan River Papers, State Records Office of WA, vol. 10.

Molloy, G, 'Letter from Georgiana Molloy to Mrs Kennedy, 29 May 1833', Cumbria Archive Centre, UK, CAC KEN 3/28/9.

Morgan, J, 'Letter from Morgan to Hay, 28 January and 3 February 1833', Swan River Papers, SRO WA, vol. 15.

Noble Keenan's journal, Department of Aborigines Account Book, Schools Board August 1841–January 1843, VPRS 26.

Phelan, G, 'A Survey of Aboriginal Children in NSW Secondary Schools', NSW Teachers Federation, p. 4, NSW State Records, Department of Education, Aboriginal Children education and living conditions, File no. 67/21137.

Policy of the Australian Aborigines League, signed by W. 'Bill' Onus, 4 April 1957, Victorian Aborigines Advancement League papers, State Library of Victoria, MS 13721.

Press Release, 'Study Grants for Aboriginals', 19 November 1968, Aborigines – Aboriginal Secondary Grant Scheme Commonwealth Department of Education and Science, 71/25471, State Records of NSW, Sydney.

Register: Aboriginal Education Commonwealth Secondary Scholarship Grants, 5 July 1971, Aborigines – Aboriginal Secondary Grant Scheme Commonwealth Department of Education and Science, 71/25471, State Records of NSW, Sydney.

Thomas, W, Quarterly Report June–August 1846, Public Record Office Victoria, Victorian Public Record Series (VPRS) 4410, unit 3.

Thomas, W, 29 August 1850, Weekly Report 26 August–1 September 1850, VPRS 2893, unit 1, 1850/55.

Thomas, W, Monthly Report August 1850, VPRS 2893, unit 1, 1850/56.

Thomas, W, 21 September 1950, Weekly Report 16–22 September 1850, VPRS 2893, unit 1, 1850/58.

Government documents

The Members of the Yorta Yorta Aboriginal Community v The State of Victoria & Ors [1998] 1606 FCA (18 December 1998).

Parliament of New South Wales, *Report from the Joint Committee of the Legislative Council and the Legislative Assembly upon Aborigines Welfare*, Parliament of New South Wales, Sydney, 1967.

'Pete's Page', *Dawn*, 10, Aborigines Welfare Board of NSW, Sydney, 1962.

Report of the Aborigines Welfare Board, NSW, 1947–61.

Report of the Commissioners, Mainly on Secondary Education, Legislative Assembly of New South Wales, 1904.

Victoria Parliamentary Papers, 1853–84.

Wyndham, HS et al., *Report of the Committee Appointed to Survey Secondary Education in New South Wales*, Legislative Council, New South Wales, Sydney, 1957.

News sources

AAP News Wire, 2007

ABC Premium News, 2006

ABC Radio, 2006

The Age (Melbourne), 1908–2015

The Argus (Melbourne), 1859–1937

The Australian, 2003–16

Brisbane Courier, 1909

Cairns Morning Post, 1909

Canberra Times, 2016

Courier Mail (Brisbane), 2007

Crikey, 2007

Dalby Herald, 1910

The Evening News (Sydney), 1910

The Financial Review, 1970

The Guardian (Australia), 2016

The Negro World (New York), 1930

The Newsletter: An Australian Paper for Australian People (Sydney), 1909–10

Perth Gazette, 1833

Perth Gazette and Western Australian Journal, 1834

Queensland Times, 1910

The Sun (Kalgoorlie), 1908

Sydney Morning Herald, 1908–2016

Windsor and Richmond Gazette, 1910

Published works

Abbott, T, 'Paternalism Reconsidered', *Quadrant* 50, no. 9, 2006.

Altman, J and M Hinkson (eds), *Coercive Reconciliation: Stabilise, Normalise, Exit Aboriginal Australia*, Arena Publications, Melbourne, 2007.

Andrews, J, *Bringing Up Our Children: Aboriginal Families in Victoria*, AIATSIS, Canberra, 2000.

——, 'Bringing Up Our Yorta Yorta Children', in *Contexts of Child Development*

References

Culture, Policy and Intervention, eds G Robinson et al., Charles Darwin University Press, Darwin, 2008.

Atkinson, W, '"Not One Iota" of Land Justice: Reflections on the Yorta Yorta Native Title Claim 1994-2001', *Indigenous Law Bulletin* 5, no. 6, 2001.

Attwood, B, *The Making of the Aborigines*, Allen & Unwin, Sydney, 1989.

———, *Rights for Aborigines*, Allen & Unwin, Sydney, 2003.

Attwood, B et al., *A Life Together, A Life Apart: A History of Relations Between Europeans and Aborigines*, Melbourne University Press, Melbourne, 1994.

Attwood, B and A Markus, *Thinking Black: William Cooper and the Australian Aborigines Advancement League*, Aboriginal Studies Press, Canberra, 2004.

Austin-Broos, D, *Arrente Present, Arrente Past: Invasion, Violence and Imagination in Indigenous Central Australia*, University of Chicago Press, Chicago, 2009.

Australian Council for Educational Research, *Review of Education in Australia 1955-1962*, Australian Council for Educational Research, Melbourne, 1964.

Ballantyne, T, 'Strategic Intimacies: Knowledge and Colonisation in Southern New Zealand', *Journal of New Zealand Studies*, no. 14, 2013.

Bamblett, L, 'Aboriginal Australians: A History Since 1788', *Australian Aboriginal Studies*, no. 2, 2010.

Barcan, A, *A Short History of Education in New South Wales*, Martindale Press, Sydney, 1965.

———, 'The Transition in Australian Education', in *Australian Education in the Twentieth Century*, eds J Cleverley and J Lawry, Longman, Melbourne, 1972.

———, *Two Centuries of Education in New South Wales*, New South Wales University Press, Kensington, 1988.

Barwick, D, 'Changes in the Aboriginal Population of Victoria, 1863-1966', in *Aboriginal Man and Environment in Australia*, eds DJ Mulvaney and J Golson, Australian National University Press, Canberra, 1971.

———, 'Coranderrk and Cumeroogunga: Pioneers and Policy', in *Opportunity and Response: Case Studies in Economic Development*, eds TS Epstein and DH Penny, C Hurst, London, 1972.

———, 'Mapping the Past: An Atlas of Victorian Clans 1835-1904', *Aboriginal History* 8, part 2, 1984.

———, *Rebellion at Coranderrk*, eds LE Barwick and RE Barwick, Aboriginal History Monograph 5, Canberra, 1998.

Barwick, D, J Urry and D Bennett, 'A Select Bibliography of Aboriginal History and Social Change: Theses and Published Research to 1976', *Aboriginal History* 1, no. 2, 1977.

References

Beresford, Q, 'Separate and Unequal: An Outline of Aboriginal Education', in *Reform and Resistance in Aboriginal Education*, eds Q Beresford, G Partington and G Gower, UWA Publishing, Perth, 2012.

Bessant, B, 'Rural Schooling and the Rural Myth in Australia', *Comparative Education* 14, no. 2, 1978.

Bielefeld, S, 'History Wars and Stronger Futures Laws: A Stronger Future or Perpetuating Past Paternalism?', *Alternative Law Journal* 39, no. 1, 2014.

Billot, CP (ed.), *Melbourne's Missing Chronicle*, Quartet Books, Melbourne, 1982.

Bin-Sallik, M, 'Cultural Safety: Let's Name It!', *Australian Journal of Indigenous Education* 32, 2003.

Bingham, HL and M Wallace, *Muhammad Ali's Greatest Fight: Cassius Clay vs. the United States of America*, Robson Books, London, 2004.

Biskup, P, *Not Slaves Not Citizens: The Aboriginal Problem in Western Australia, 1898-1954*, University of Queensland Press, Brisbane, 1973.

Boddy, K, *Boxing: A Cultural History*, Reaktion Books, London, 2008.

Booth, D and C Tatz, *One Eyed: A View of Australian Sport*, Allen & Unwin, Sydney, 2000.

Bowe, H, L Peeler, and S Atkinson, *Yorta Yorta Language Heritage*, Department of Linguistics, Monash University, Melbourne, 1998.

Boyce, J, *1835: The Founding of Melbourne and the Conquest of Australia*, Black Inc., Melbourne, 2011.

Boym, S, *The Future of Nostalgia*, Basic Books, New York, 2001.

Bracknell, C, 'Kooral Dwonk-katitjiny (listening to the past): Aboriginal Language, Songs and History in South-western Australia', *Aboriginal History* 38, no. 1, 2015.

Branagan, DF and TG Vallance, 'David, Sir Tannatt William Edgeworth (1858-1934)', in *Australian Dictionary of Biography*, vol. 8, Melbourne University Press, Melbourne, 1981.

Briggs, M, J Lydon and M Say, 'Collaborating: Photographs of Koories in the State Library of Victoria', *The La Trobe Journal*, 85, 2010.

Broome, R, 'Professional Aboriginal Boxers in Eastern Australia, 1930-1979', *Aboriginal History* 4, no. 1/2, 1980.

——, *Treasure in Earthen Vessels: Protestant Christianity in New South Wales Society 1900-1914*, University of Queensland Press, Brisbane, 1980.

——, *Aboriginal Australians: Black Response to White Dominance, 1788-1980*, George Allen & Unwin, Sydney, 1st edn, 1982.

——, *The Victorians: Arriving*, Fairfax, Syme & Weldon, Sydney, 1984.

——, *Coburg: Between Two Creeks*, Lothian, Melbourne, 1987.

——, 'The Struggle for Australia: Aboriginal-European Warfare, 1770-1930', in *Australia: Two Centuries of War & Peace*, eds M McKernan & M Browne,

Australian War Memorial/Allen & Unwin, Canberra, 1988.

——, 'Tracing the Humanitarian Strain in Black White Encounters', *La Trobe Library Journal*, 1989.

——, *Aboriginal Australians: Black Responses to White Dominance*, Allen & Unwin, Sydney, 2nd edn, 1994.

——, 'Aboriginal Victims and Voyagers: Confronting Frontier Myths', *Journal of Australian Studies* 18, no. 42, 1994.

——, 'Aboriginal Workers on South-Eastern Frontiers', *Australian Historical Studies* 26, no. 103, 1994.

——, 'Victoria', in *Contested Ground: Australian Aborigines under the British Crown*, ed. A McGrath, Allen & Unwin, Sydney, 1995.

——, 'Theatres of Power: Tent Boxing circa 1910–1970', *Aboriginal History* 20, 1996, pp. 1–23.

——, 'The Australian Reaction to Jack Johnson, Black Pugilist, 1907-9', in *The Best Ever Australian Sports Writing: A 200 Year Collection*, ed. D Headon, Black Inc., Melbourne, 2001.

——, 'The Statistics of Frontier Conflict', in *Frontier Conflict: The Australian Experience*, eds B Attwood and SG Foster, National Museum of Australia, Canberra, 2003.

——, *Aboriginal Victorians: A History Since 1800*, Allen & Unwin, Sydney, 2005.

——, 'Entangled Histories: The Politics and Ethics of Writing Indigenous Histories', *Melbourne Historical Journal*, 33, 2005.

——, '"There were Vegetables every Year Mr Green was Here": Right Behaviour and the Struggle for Autonomy at Coranderrk Aboriginal Reserve', *History Australia* 3, no. 2, 2006.

——, 'Not Strictly Business: Freaks and the Australian Showground World', *Australian Historical Studies* 40, 2009.

——, *Aboriginal Australians: A History Since 1788*, Allen & Unwin, Sydney, revised 4th edn, 2010.

——, 'Changing Aboriginal Landscapes of Pastoral Victoria, 1830-1850', *Studies in the History of Gardens & Designed Landscapes* 31, no. 2, 2011.

——, *Fighting Hard: The Victorian Aborigines Advancement League*, Aboriginal Studies Press, Canberra, 2015.

Broome, R with A Jackomos, *Sideshow Alley*, Allen & Unwin, Sydney, 1998.

Broome, R and C Manning, *A Man of All Tribes: The Life of Alick Jackomos*, Aboriginal Studies Press, Canberra, 2006.

Bunce, D, 'Australasiatic Reminiscences', in *Travels with Dr Leichhardt*, Oxford University Press, Melbourne, 1979 [1859].

Burney, L, 'An Aboriginal Way of Being Australian', *Australian Feminist Studies* 9, no. 19, 1994.

Butler, J, 'Precarious Life, Vulnerability, and the Ethics of Cohabitation', *Journal of Speculative Philosophy* 26, no. 2, 2012.

Butlin, N, *Our Original Aggression*, Allen & Unwin, London, 1983.

Campbell, C and H Proctor, *A History of Australian Schooling*, Allen & Unwin, Sydney, 2014.

Carlson, B, *The Politics of Identity: Who Counts as Aboriginal Today?*, Aboriginal Studies Press, Canberra, 2016.

Carter, P, 'Dark with an Excess of Bright: Mapping the Coastlines of Knowledge', in *Mappings*, ed. D Cosgrove, Reaktion Books, London, 1999.

Cato, N, *Mister Maloga: Daniel Matthews and His Maloga Mission*, University of Queensland Press, Brisbane, 1976.

Chesterman, J and B Galligan, *Citizens without Rights: Aborigines and Australian Citizenship*, Cambridge University Press, Melbourne, 1997.

Christie, MF, *Aborigines in Colonial Victoria 1835–86*, Sydney University Press, Sydney, 1979.

Clark, ID, *Scars in the Landscape: A Register of Massacre Sites in Western Victoria, 1803–1859*, Aboriginal Studies Press, Canberra, 1995.

Clark, CMH, *A Short History of Australia*, Mentor Books, New York, 1963.

Clements, T, *From Old Maloga (The Memoirs of an Aboriginal Woman)*, Fraser & Morphet, Melbourne, n.d.

Clendinnen, I, *Tiger's Eye: A Memoir*, Scribners, New York, 2000.

——, *Dancing with Strangers*, Text, Melbourne, 2003.

——, 'Reading Mr Robinson' in *The Cost of Courage in Aztec Society*, Cambridge University Press, Cambridge, 2010.

Close-Barry, K, 'Land, Labour and Ambivalence: Lutheran Missionaries Managing Land Disputes at Cape Bedford Mission', *Journal of Religious History* 41, no. 2, 2017.

Cole, A, 'Unwitting Soldiers: The Working Life of Matron Hiscocks at the Cootamundra Girls Home', *Aboriginal History* 27, 2003.

Connell, RW, 'Working-class Families and the New Secondary Education', *Australian Journal of Education* 47, no. 3, 2003.

Corris, P, *Aborigines and Europeans in Western Victoria*, Australian Institute of Aboriginal Studies, Canberra, 1968.

——, *Lords of the Ring: A History of Prize-fighting in Australia*, Cassell, Melbourne, 1980.

Critchett, J, *Untold Stories, Memories and Lives of Victorian Kooris*, Melbourne University Press, Melbourne, 1998.

Crosby, A, *Germs, Seeds and Animals: Studies in Ecological History*, ME Sharpe, New York, 1994.

References

Crowley, FK (ed.), *A New History of Australia*, Heinemann, Melbourne, 1974.

Dawson, J, *Australian Aborigines. The Languages and Customs of Several Tribes of Aborigines in the Western District of Victoria, Australia*, Melbourne, George Robertson, 1881, reprinted AIATSIS, Canberra, 1991.

Diamond, J, *Guns, Germs and Steel: A Short History of Everybody for the Last 13,000 Years*, Vintage, London, 1998.

Dlamini, J, *Native Nostalgia*, Jacana, Johannesburg, 2009.

Dodson, M, 'The End in the Beginning: Re(de)finding Aboriginality', in *Blacklines: Contemporary Critical Writing by Indigenous Australians*, ed. M Grossman, Melbourne University Press, Melbourne, 2003.

Driscoll, C, *The Australian Country Girl: History, Image, Experience*, Ashgate, Farnham, 2014.

Dunn, M, 'Aboriginal Guides in the Hunter Valley, New South Wales', in *Brokers and Boundaries: Colonial Exploration in Indigenous Territory*, eds T Shellam, M Nugent, S Konishi and J Cadzow, ANU Press, Canberra, 2016.

Einfeld, M, J Killen and K Mundine, *Toomelah Report: Report on the Problems and Needs of Aborigines Living on the New South Wales–Queensland Border*, Human Rights Australia, Belrose, Sydney, 1988.

Evans, R, K Saunders and K Cronin, *Exclusion, Exploitation and Extermination: Race Relations in Colonial Queensland*, Australia and New Zealand Book Co, Sydney, 1975.

Farhood, S and S Weston (eds), *Ring Chronicle of Boxing*, Hamlyn, London, 1993.

Fels, M, *Good Men and True: The Aboriginal Police of Port Phillip District 1837–1853*, Melbourne University Press, Melbourne, 1988.

Ferguson, WC, 'Mokare's Domain', in *Australians to 1788*, eds DJ Mulvaney and PJ White, Fairfax, Syme and Weldon, Sydney, 1987.

Flannery, T, 'Introduction', in *The Life and Adventures of William Buckley: Thirty-Two Years a Wanderer amongst the Aborigines of the then Unexplored Country round Port Phillip*, Text, Melbourne, 2002.

Fletcher, JJ, *Clean, Clad and Courteous: A History of Aboriginal Education in New South Wales*, J Fletcher, Melbourne, 1989.

Foley, D, 'Indigenous Epistemology and Indigenous Standpoint Theory', *Social Alternatives* 22, no. 1, 2003.

Foucault, M, 'The Ethics of the Concern for Self as a Practice of Freedom', in *Ethics: Subjectivity and Truth*, The New Press, New York, 1997.

Fox, K, 'Globalising Indigeneity?: Writing Indigenous Histories in a Transnational World', *History Compass* 10, no. 6, 2012.

Fradetta, S, *Jack Johnson*, Branden Publishing Company, Boston, 1990.

Fredericks, B, '"We Don't Leave our Identities at the City Limits": Aboriginal and Torres Strait Islander People Living in Urban Localities', *Australian Aboriginal Studies*, no. 1, 2013.

Gammage, B, *The Biggest Estate on Earth: How Aborigines Made Australia*, Allen & Unwin, Sydney, 2011.

Genovese, ED, *Roll Jordan Roll: The World the Slaves Made*, Pantheon Books, New York, 1974.

Ginibi, RL, *Don't Take Your Love to Town*, Penguin, Melbourne, 1988.

Goodall, H, *Evans Head History Report for the Application for a Native Title Determination*, Report, No NG 6034.

——, 'Land In Our Own Country: The Aboriginal Land Rights Movement in South-Eastern Australia 1860 to 1914', *Aboriginal History* 14, nos 1/2, 1990.

——, 'New South Wales', in *Contested Ground: Australian Aborigines under the British Crown*, ed. A McGrath, Allen & Unwin, Sydney, 1995.

——, *Invasion to Embassy: Land in Aboriginal Politics in NSW, 1770–1972*, Allen & Unwin, Sydney, 1996.

Government Statistician, *The Official Year Book of New South Wales*, Bureau of Statistics, Sydney, 1947–61.

Green, N, 'King George's Sound: The Friendly Frontier', in *Archaeology in ANZAAS 1983*, ed. M Smith, Western Australian Museum, Perth, 1983.

Greig, AW, 'Some New Documentary Evidence Concerning the Foundation of Melbourne', *Victorian Historical Magazine* 12, no. 4, 1928.

Guiness, C, 'What Motivates the High School Student?', in *Aboriginal Education: The Teacher's Role*, ed. T Roper, National Union of Australian University Students, North Melbourne, 1969.

Haag, O, 'From the Margins to the Mainstream: Towards a History of Published Indigenous Australian Autobiographies and Biographies', in *Indigenous Biography and Autobiography*, eds P Read, F Peters-Little and A Haebich, ANU ePress, Canberra, 2008.

Hagen, R, 'Ethnographic Information and Anthropological Interpretations in a Native Title Claim: the Yorta Yorta Experience', *Aboriginal History* 25, 2001.

Hancock, WK, *Australia*, Ernest Benn, London, 1930.

Harris, J, *One Blood: 200 Years of Aboriginal Encounter with Christianity: A Story of Hope*, Albatross Books, Sutherland, 1990.

Harris, JW, 'The Education of Aboriginal Children in New South Wales Public Schools since 1788: Part 1', *Aboriginal Child at School* 6, no. 4, 1978.

——, 'The Education of Aboriginal Children in New South Wales Public Schools since 1788: Part 2', *Aboriginal Child at School* 6, no. 5, 1978.

Hasluck, P and Department of Territories, Australia, *The Policy of Assimilation: Decisions of Commonwealth and State Ministers at the Native Welfare Conference, Canberra, January 26th and 27th, 1961*, AJ Arthur, Commonwealth Government Printer, Canberra, 1961.

References

Hennessy, G, 'Character Above Colour: Fast Track to Assimilation? Margaret Tucker MBE and the Politics of Assimilation', *Social Alternatives* 21, no. 1, 2002.

Hinkson, M, 'In the Name of the Child', in *Coercive Reconciliation: Stabilise, Normalise, Exit Aboriginal Australia*, eds J Altman and M Hinkson, Arena Publications, Melbourne, 2007.

——, 'Media Images and the Politics of Hope', in *Culture Crisis: Anthropology and Politics in Aboriginal Australia*, eds J Altman and M Hinkson, UNSW Press, Sydney, 2010, p. 230.

Howard-Wagner, D and B Kelly, 'Containing Aboriginal Mobility in the Northern Territory: From "Protectionism" to "Interventionism"', *Law Text Culture* 15, 2011.

Howitt, AW, *The Native Tribes of South-east Australia*, Aboriginal Studies Press, Canberra, 1996 [1904].

Huggonson, D, 'Towards a History of Aboriginal Education in New South Wales', *Aboriginal Child at School* 12, no. 5, 1984.

Hughes, J, 'The Development of the Comprehensive School in New South Wales: The Influence of Harold Wyndham and the 1957 Wyndham Report', *Education Research and Perspectives* 28, no. 2, 2001.

Isenberg, A, *The Destruction of the Bison: An Environmental History, 1750–1920*, Cambridge University Press, Cambridge, 2000.

Johnson, J, *Jack Johnson: In the Ring and Out*, National Sports Publishing, Chicago, 1927.

Johnson, W, 'On Agency', *Journal of Social History* 37, no. 1, 2003.

Jones, J, 'Indigenous Life Stories', *Life Writing* 1, no. 2, 2004.

——, 'As Long as She Got her Voice: How Cross-cultural Collaboration Shapes Aboriginal Textuality', *Altitude* 5, 2005.

——, *Country Women and the Colour Bar: Grass Roots Activism and the Country Women's Association*, Aboriginal Studies Press, Canberra, 2015.

Keen, I, 'The Interpretation of Property on the Australian Colonial Frontier', in *Indigenous Participation in Australian Economies: Historical and Anthropological Perspectives*, ed. I Keen, ANU ePress, Canberra, 2010.

Kociumbas, J, 'Introduction', in *Maps, Dreams, History: Race and Representation in Australia*, ed. J Kociumbas, Department of History, University of Sydney, Sydney, 1998.

Koorie, Koorie Cultural Heritage Trust, Melbourne, 1991.

Kowal, E, 'Responsibility, Noel Pearson and Indigenous Disadvantage in Australia', in *Responsibility*, eds G Hage and R Eckersley, Melbourne University Press, Melbourne, 2012, p. 48.

Langton, M, *"Well I heard it on the Radio and I saw it on the Television...": An essay for the Australian Film Commission on the politics and aesthetics of filming* by and about Aboriginal people and things, Australian Film Commission, Canberra, 1993.

——, 'Trapped in the Aboriginal Reality Show', *Griffith Review* 19, 2008.

Lattas, A and B Morris, 'The Politics of Suffering and the Politics of Anthropology', in *Culture Crisis: Anthropology and Politics in Aboriginal Australia*, eds J Altman and M Hinkson, UNSW Press, Sydney, 2010.

Lear, J, *Radical Hope: Ethics in the Face of Cultural Devastation*, Harvard University Press, Cambridge, Massachusetts, 2006.

Lee, I, *The Logbooks of the 'Lady Nelson' with the Journal of her First Commander Lieutenant James Grant*, Grafton & Co, London, 1915.

Lester, A and Z Laidlaw, 'Indigenous Sites and Mobilities: Connected Struggles in the Long Nineteenth Century', in *Indigenous Communities and Settler Colonialism: Land Holding, Loss and Survival in an Interconnected World*, eds A Lester and Z Laidlaw, Palgrave Macmillan, Basingstoke, 2015.

Loos, N, *White Christ, Black Cross: The Emergence of a Black Church*, Aboriginal Studies Press, Canberra, 2007.

Lorcin, PME, 'Imperial Nostalgia; Colonial Nostalgia: Differences of Theory, Similarities of Practice?', *Historical Reflections* 39, no. 3, 2013.

Lydon, J, 'The Experimental 1860s: Charles Walter's Images of Coranderrk Aboriginal Station, Victoria', *Aboriginal History* 26, 2002.

——, 'Imagining the Moravian Mission: Space and Surveillance at the Former Ebenezer Mission, Victoria, Southeastern Australia', *Historical Archaeology* 43, no. 3, 2009.

Maddison, S, *Beyond White Guilt: The Real Challenge for Black-White Relations in Australia*, Allen & Unwin, Sydney, 2011.

——, 'Indigenous Identity, "Authenticity" and the Structural Violence of Settler Colonialism', *Identities: Global Studies in Culture and Power* 20, no. 3, 2013.

Manne, R, 'The History Wars', *The Monthly*, November 2009.

Martin, D, 'Reforming the Welfare System in Remote Aboriginal Communities: an Assessment of Noel Pearson's Proposals', in *Competing Visions*, eds T Eardley and B Bradbury, Social Policy Research Centre, University of New South Wales, Sydney, 2002.

Maxwell, W, *F.B. Eyes: How J. Edgar Hoover's Ghostreaders Framed African American Literature*, Princeton University Press, New Jersey, 2015.

Maynard, J, *Fight for Liberty and Freedom*, Aboriginal Studies Press, Canberra, 2007.

——, 'Fred Maynard and Marcus Garvey: Storming the Urban Space', in *Exploring Urban Identities and Histories*, eds C Hansen and K Butler, AIATSIS, Canberra, 2013.

References

McBryde, I, 'Wil-im-ee Moor-ring: Or, Where do Axes Come From?', *Mankind* 11, 1978.

McClintock, A, *Imperial Leather: Race, Gender and Sexuality in the Colonial Contest*, Routledge, New York, 1995.

McConnochie, KR, *Realities of Race: An Analysis of Race and Racism and their Relevance to Australian Society*, ANZ Book Co, Sydney, 1973.

McGrath, A, 'Aboriginal Women Workers in the Northern Territory, 1911–1939', *Hecate* 4, no. 2, 1978.

——, *Born in the Cattle*, Allen & Unwin, Sydney, 1987.

——, 'The State as Father: 1910–60', in P Grimshaw et al, *Creating a Nation*, Penguin Books, Melbourne, 1994.

McKenna, M, *From the Edge: Australia's Lost Histories*, Miegunyah Press, Melbourne, 2016.

McKenzie, M, *The Road to Mowanjum*, Angus & Robertson, Sydney, 1969.

McKinnon, C, 'Indigenous Music as a Space of Resistance', in *Making Settler Colonial Space: Perspectives on Race, Place and Identity*, eds T Banivanua-Mar and P Edmonds, Palgrave Macmillan, New York, 2010.

McLisky, C, 'The Location of Faith: Power, Gender and Spirituality in the 1883–84 Maloga Mission Revival', *History Australia* 7, no. 1, 2010.

——, 'Managing Mission Life, 1869–1886', in *Settler Colonial Governance in Nineteenth-Century Victoria*, eds L Boucher and L Russell, Aboriginal Studies Press, Canberra, 2015.

Mendes, P, 'Welfare Reform and Mutual Obligation' in *Howard's Second and Third Governments: Australian Commonwealth Administration, 1998–2004*, eds C Aulich and R Wettenhall, UNSW Press, Sydney, 2005.

Mitchell, IS and JE Cawte, 'The Aboriginal Family Voluntary Resettlement Scheme: An Approach to Aboriginal Adaptation', *Australian and New Zealand Journal of Psychiatry* 11, no. 1, 1977

Mitchell, J, *In Good Faith? Governing Indigenous Australia Through God, Charity and Empire, 1825–1855*, ANU ePress, Canberra, 2011.

Mitchell, R and A James, *Maps: Their Untold Stories – Map Treasures from the National Archives*, Bloomsbury and the National Archives, London, 2015.

Moore, GF, *The Millendon Memoirs: George Fletcher Moore's Western Australian Diaries and Letters, 1830–1841*, Hesperian Press, Perth, 2006, 25 January 1833.

——, *Diary of Ten Years Eventful Life of an Early Settler in Western Australia; and also a Descriptive Vocabulary of the Language of the Aborigines*, M Walbrook, London, 1884.

Moreton-Robinson, A, *Talkin' Up to the White Woman: Aboriginal Women and Feminism*, University of Queensland Press, St Lucia, 2000.

Mulvaney, DJ and N Green (eds), *Commandant of Solitude: The Journals of Captain Collet Barker*, Melbourne University Publishing, Melbourne, 1992.

Nakata, M, *Disciplining the Savages, Savaging the Disciplines*, Aboriginal Studies Press, Canberra, 2007.

——, 'Introduction to the Special Issue: Engaging with Indigenous Knowledge, Culture and Communities', *Australian Academic and Research Libraries* 45, no. 2, 2014.

Nakata, M et al., 'Decolonial Goals and Pedagogies for Indigenous Studies', *Decolonization: Indigeneity, Education & Society* 1, no. 1, 2012.

Nance, B, 'The Level of Violence: Europeans and Aborigines in Port Phillip, 1835–1850', *Historical Studies* 19, no. 77, 1981.

Nanni, G and A James, *Coranderrk: We Will Show the Country*, Aboriginal Studies Press, Canberra, 2013.

Neale, T, 'Staircases, Pyramids and Poisons: The Immunitary Paradigm in the Works of Noel Pearson and Peter Sutton', *Continuum* 27, no. 2, 2013.

Oates, JC, *On Boxing*, Harper, New York, 2006.

O'Brien, A, *Philanthropy and Settler Colonialism*, Palgrave Macmillan, Basingstoke, 2015.

Pearson, N, 'Mabo: Towards Respecting Equality and Difference' in *Voices from the Land: 1993 Boyer Lectures*, ABC Books, Sydney, 1994.

——, '*Guugu Yimidhirr* History: Hope Vale Lutheran Mission (1900–1950)', in *Maps, Dreams, History: Race and Representation in Australia*, ed. J Kociumbas, Department of History, University of Sydney, Sydney, 1998.

——, *Our Right to Take Responsibility*, Noel Pearson and Associates, Cairns, 2000.

——, 'On the Human Right to Misery, Mass Incarceration and Early Death', *Arena Magazine* 56, 2001–2.

——, 'White Guilt, Victimhood and the Quest for a Radical Centre', *Griffith Review* 16, 2007.

——, *Up from the Mission: Selected Writings*, Black Inc, Melbourne, 2009.

Pitty, R, 'A Poverty of Evidence: Abusing Law and History in *Yorta Yorta v Victoria* (1998)', *Australian Journal of Legal History* 5, no. 1, 1999, pp. 41–61.

Povinelli, EA, 'Indigenous Politics in Late Liberalism', in *Culture Crisis: Anthropology and Politics in Aboriginal Australia*, eds Jon Altman and Melinda Hinkson, UNSW Press, Sydney, 2010.

Price, R, *The Making of Empire: Colonial Encounters and the Creation of Imperial Rule in Nineteenth Century Africa*, Cambridge University Press, Cambridge, 2008.

Rademaker, L, '"We want a good mission not rubish please": Aboriginal Petitions and Mission Nostalgia', *Aboriginal History* 40, 2016.

References

Ramsland, J, 'The Aboriginal Boys' Training Home, Kinchela, 1924-1970, and the Development of a Culture of Physical Fitness and Sport', *Journal of Educational Administration and History* 38, no. 3, 2006.

Read, P, *The Stolen Generations: The Removal of Aboriginal Children in New South Wales 1883 to 1969*, New South Wales Ministry of Aboriginal Affairs, Sydney, 1984.

——, *Charles Perkins: A Biography*, Viking, Melbourne, 1990.

Read, P, F Peters-Little and A Haebich (eds), *Indigenous Biography and Autobiography*, ANU ePress, Canberra, 2008.

Reece, RHW, *Aborigines and Colonists: Aborigines and Colonial Society in New South Wales in the 1830s and 1840s*, Sydney University Press, Sydney, 1974.

Report on the Select Committee on Aborigines (British Settlements), with the Minutes of Evidence, F Cass, London, 1968 [1837].

Reynolds, H, 'The Other Side of the Frontier: Early Aboriginal Reactions to Pastoral Settlement in Queensland and Northern New South Wales', *Historical Studies, Australia and New Zealand* 17, no. 66, 1976.

——, *The Other Side of the Frontier*, James Cook University, Townsville, 1981.

——, *Forgotten War*, New South Publishing, Sydney, 2013.

Rigney, LI, *Indigenist Research and Aboriginal Australia*, Ashgate, Hampshire, 2006.

Robinson, F and B York, *The Black Resistance*, Widescope, Melbourne, 1977.

Rowley, CD, *The Destruction of Aboriginal Society*, Penguin Books, Harmondsworth, 1972.

——, *Equality by Instalments: The Aboriginal Householder in Rural New South Wales, 1965 and 1980*, Australian Institute of Aboriginal Studies, Canberra, 1982.

Rowse, T, *Rethinking Social Justice: From 'Peoples' to 'Populations'*, Aboriginal Studies Press, Canberra, 2012.

Russell, L, *Roving Mariners: Australian Aboriginal Whalers and Sealers in the Southern Oceans 1790-1870*, SUNY Press, New York, 2012.

Ryan, L, 'Settler Massacres on the Port Phillip Frontier, 1836-1851', *Journal of Australian Studies* 34, no. 3, 2010.

——, *Tasmanian Aborigines: A History Since 1804*, Allen & Unwin, Sydney, 2013.

Sahlins, M, 'The Original Affluent Society' in *Stone Age Economics*, Routledge, London, 2nd edn, 2004.

Salmans, Rev LB, 'Some Reasons for Prayer for Missionaries', in *The Gospel in All Lands*, Journal of the Methodist Episcopal Church Missionary Society, 1899, vol. 20, 537.

Sanders, Rev CS, 'The Training of a Native Ministry on Foreign Missionary Ground', in *The Hartford Seminary Record*, eds. WS Pratt and AL Gilbert, Hartford Seminary Press, Hartford, 1901.

Santos, B De Sousa, *Epistemologies of the South: Justice Against Epistemicide*, Paradigm, Boulder, CO, 2014.

Schilling, K, 'Mister Maloga (Book Review)', *Australian Aboriginal Studies*, no. 2, 1994.

Scott, E, 'The Early History of Western Port, Part One', *Victorian Historical Magazine* 6, no. 1, September 1917.

Scott, K, 'From Drill to Dance', in *Decolonising the Landscape: Indigenous Cultures in Australia*, eds K Schaffer & B Neumeier, Brill Academic Publishers, Amsterdam, 2014.

——, 'Not so Easy: Language for a Shared History', *Griffith Review* 47, 2015.

Scott, R and A Heiss (eds), *The Intervention: An Anthology*, Concerned Australians, Sydney, 2015.

Secretariat of National Aboriginal and Islander Child Care Inc, '"Ending Paternalism: New Leadership, New Partnerships" SNAICC Welcomes Appointment of Jenny Macklin, MP to Indigenous Affairs Portfolio', *Aboriginal & Islander Health Worker Journal* 32, no. 3, 2008.

Seidel, P, 'Native Title: The Struggle for Justice for the Yorta Yorta Nation', *Alternative Law Journal* 29, no. 2, 2004.

Shellam, T, *Shaking Hands on the Fringe: Negotiating the Aboriginal World at King George's Sound*, UWA Publishing, Crawley, WA, 2009.

——, 'Manyat's "sole delight": Travelling Knowledge in Western Australia's Southwest, 1830s', in *Transnational Lives: Biographies of Global Modernity, 1700–present*, eds D Deacon, A Woollacott and P Russell, Palgrave Macmillan, Basingstoke, 2010.

South West Aboriginal Land and Sea Council, J Host and C Owen, *"It's still in my heart, this is my country": The Single Noongar Claim History*, UWA Publishing, Crawley, WA, 2009.

Spivak, GC, *A Critique of Postcolonial Reason: Toward a History of the Vanishing Present*, Seagull Books, Calcutta, 1999.

Stannage, CT, *The People of Perth: A Social History of Western Australia's Capital City*, City of Perth, Perth, 1979.

Stanner, WEH, *After the Dreaming: Black and White Australians – An Anthropologist's View*, Australian Broadcasting Commission, Sydney, 1969.

——, 'The History of Indifference Thus Begins', *Aboriginal History* 1, no. 1-2, 1977.

——, *White Man Got No Dreaming: Essays 1938–1973*, Australian National University Press, Canberra, 1979.

Stephens, M, *White Without Soap: Philanthropy, Caste and Exclusion in Colonial Victoria, 1835–1888: A Political Economy of Race*, University of Melbourne Custom Book Centre, Melbourne, 2010.

Taffe, S, *Black and White Together: FCAATSI: The Federal Council for the Advancement of Aborigines and Torres Strait Islanders 1958–1973*, University of Queensland Press, Brisbane, 2005.

Tate, F, 'Rural School Administration', in *The Rural School in Australia*, ed. PR Cole, Melbourne University Press, Melbourne, 1937.

Tench, W, *A Complete Account of the Settlement at Port Jackson in New South Wales*, G Nicol, London, 1793.

Themelis, S, 'Meritocracy through Education and Social Mobility in Post-war Britain: A Critical Examination', *British Journal of Sociology of Education* 29, no. 5, 2008.

Thomas, W, *The Journal of William Thomas, Assistant Protector of the Aborigines of Port Phillip & Guardian of the Aborigines of Victoria 1839–1867*, Volume two: 1844 to 1853, ed. M Stephens, Victorian Aboriginal Corporation of Languages, Melbourne, 2014.

Thompson, RC, *Religion in Australia: A History*, Oxford University Press, Melbourne, 2002.

Townsend, H, *Serving the Country: The History of the Country Women's Association of New South Wales*, Doubleday, Sydney, 1988.

Tucker, M, *If Everyone Cared: Autobiography of Margaret Tucker*, Ure Smith, Sydney, 1977.

Turnbull, D, *Maps are Territories: Science is an Atlas*, Deakin University Press, Melbourne, 1989.

Van Toorn, P, 'Wild Speech, Tame Speech, Real Speech', *Southerly* 67, nos. 1-2, 2007.

Walden, I, '"That Was Slavery Days": Aboriginal Domestic Servants in New South Wales in the Twentieth Century', *Labour History*, no. 69, 1995.

Ward, GC, *Unforgivable Blackness: The Rise and Fall of Jack Johnson*, Pimlico, London, 2006.

Watt, E, 'The Implementation of the Capabilities Approach in Cape York: Can Paternalism be a Pre-condition for Participation?', *Development Bulletin*, no. 75, 2013.

Watts, BH, *Aboriginal Futures: Review of Research and Developments and Related Policies in the Education of Aborigines*, Education Research and Development Committee, Canberra, 1981

Widders, T, 'What Education Means to Me: An Aboriginal's Perspective', *The Aboriginal Child at School* 2, no. 1, 1974.

Wild, R and P Anderson, *Ampe Akelyernemane Meke Mekarle*, 'Little Children Are Sacred': *Report of the Northern Territory Board of Inquiry into the Protection of Aboriginal Children from Sexual Abuse*, Department of the Chief Minister, Darwin, 2007.

Williams, R, *The Country and the City*, Oxford University Press, New York, 1973.

Windschuttle, K, 'The Myths of Frontier Massacres in Australian History, Parts I, II and III', *Quadrant* 44, nos. 10–12, 2000.

Wolfe, P, 'Nation and MiscegeNation: Discursive Continuity in the Post-Mabo Era', *Social Analysis: The International Journal of Social and Cultural Practice*, no. 36, 1994.

Wootten, JH, *Royal Commission into Aboriginal Deaths in Custody: Report of the Inquiry into the Death of Malcolm Charles Smith*, Australian Government Publishing Service, Canberra, 1989.

Wyndham, HS, 'Statistics', in *The Rural School in Australia*, ed. PR Cole, Melbourne University Press, Melbourne, 1937.

Young, M, *The Rise of Meritocracy 1870–2033: An Essay on Education and Equality*, Penguin, Harmondsworth, 1958.

Websites

Altman, JC, 'The Howard Government's Northern Territory Intervention: Are Neo-Paternalism and Indigenous Development Compatible?', Centre for Aboriginal Economic Policy Research, Topical Issue 16/2007, viewed 1 December 2016, <http://caepr.anu.edu.au/sites/default/files/Publications/topical/Altman_AIATSIS.pdf>.

Atkinson, W, 'The Cummera Walk Off and the Return to Base Camp Politics', 2009, viewed 11 January 2017, <https://waynera.files.wordpress.com/2010/10/cummerawalkoff-doc.pdf>.

Campbell, C, 'Comprehensive Government High School, Australia 1950–2010', *Dictionary of Educational History in Australia and New Zealand (DEHANZ)*, 2014, viewed 20 January 2016, <http://dehanz.net.au/entries/comprehensive-government-high-school/>.

Cato, N, 'Matthews, Daniel (1837–1902)', *Australian Dictionary of Biography*, 1974, viewed 11 January 2017, <http://adb.anu.edu.au/biography/matthews-daniel-4170>.

Merriam Webster dictionary online, accessed 5 July 2016, <http://www.merriam-webster.com/dictionary/hams>.

Roe, M, 'Morgan, John (1792–1866)', *Australian Dictionary of Biography*, 1967, viewed 18 February 2016, <http://adb.anu.edu.au/biography/morgan-john-2479/text3331>.

The Federation of Aboriginal & Torres Strait Islander Languages & Culture Corporation, 'October 1998: Aretha Briggs and David Wirrpanda', viewed 11 December 2017, <http://archive.li/N7ajA>.

'The Lyrics to Bura Fera', We Want to Walk With You, 2016, viewed 11 January 2017, <http://towalkwithyou.com/the-lyrics-to-bura-fera/>.

References

'The surrender of Joseph', *Harper's Weekly* 21, no. 1090, 17 November 1877, p. 906, viewed 25 February 2016, <https://content.lib.washington.edu/aipnw/surrenderofjoseph.html>.

Thwaites, M, 'For Yarmuk, Elder of the Ulupna Tribe', viewed 11 January 2017, <http://thwaites.com.au/wp/for-yarmuk-elder-of-the-ulupna-tribe/>.

Victorian Aboriginal Health Service, 'History – pre 1967', viewed 19 December 2016, <http://www.vahs.org.au/history-pre-1967/>.

Films

Blair, W, *The Sapphires*, motion picture, Hopscotch Entertainment, Sydney, 2012.

Morgan, A and G Bostock, *Lousy Little Sixpence*, motion picture, Sixpence Productions, Canberra, 1984.

Index

Note: page numbers in bold refer to photographs and illustrations; page numbers in italics refer to figures.

Abbott, Tony 49, 55-6, 61
    and Noel Pearson on paternalism 55-6, 57, 60, 61
Aboriginal Australians 8-10, 18, 19, 20
    first edition 8-10, 18, 20, 29, 37, 39, 43
    Memmi's 'usurper complex' 33, 34
    and race relations model 18-21, 23, 31-4, 36
    subsequent editions 9, 16, 18
    and Wolfe's 'logic of elimination' 33, 34
Aboriginal Family Education Centres 137
Aboriginal Family Resettlement Scheme 137
Aboriginal history *see* history, Aboriginal
Aboriginal people 91-3, 170-2
    as agents 19, 20-6, 27, 31-3, 35-6
    as victims 19, 27-9, 30, 32, 35-6
        statistics of deaths 27, 30-2, 34
    as voyagers 19, 27-30
Aboriginal Secondary Grants Scheme (ABSEG) 138-9
Aboriginal Study Grant Scheme (ASGS) 138
Aboriginal Victorians 32-4, 45-6

Aboriginal, new ways of being 3, 5, 11, 15, 127, 166-7
    accepting Christianity 14, 29, 109, 154
    adaptive strategies 127, 137, 149-50, 151, 154
    balancing continuity and change 14, 151, 153-4, 156-7
    beyond mere survival 142, 158
    building cultural capacity 165-6, 170-2
    creative adaptation 170-2
    embracing change 11, 83, 90, 92-3, 158
    and farming 109-11, 151, 154-5, 158
    and leadership 13, 146, 149-50, 154-5, 157
    and radical hope 144-5, 154, 156, 158
    requests for land 13-14, 110-11, 151-7, 160
    in response to cultural devastation 143, 144
    retaining Aboriginal identity 150, 153-4, 156, 157
    see also Billibellary
Aborigines Advancement League (Victoria) 5, 14-15, 140, 157-8, 163
    see also radical hope
Aborigines Progressive Association 111, 156
Aborigines Protection Board (previously Central Board for the Aborigines; later

229

Aborigines Welfare Board)
108, 111-13, 116-18, 154-8
and education 122-4, 131-5
Aborigines Welfare Board (AWB)
see Aborigines Protection
Board
activism 8, 10, 14, 71, 102, 108,
111, 156-7
  Aboriginal organisations
  5, 14-15, 68, 111, 137, 140,
  156-8, 163
  Richard Broome on 131-2
  and demands for land 109-10
  and radical hope 5, 140
  see also Cummeragunja
agency 11, 12, 16, 40-1, 61, 71, 140
  Aboriginal people as agents
  19-27, 31-3, 35-6
  and boxing 64
  Richard Broome on 19-21,
  23, 27-30, 36-7
  critique of concept 45
  and *Koorie* exhibition 27-9
  and missions 44, 46-8, 50-1
  and paternalism 39, 60, 62
  within race relations
  framework 19-21
  re-framing of definitions 41,
  43-4, 46-8
  see also Clements, Theresa;
  Johnson, Jack
Ali, Mohammad 65, 72, 79
Andrews, Leah (née Briggs) 98,
  100, 103, 104, **117**
archives 6, 101-02, 161
  Richard Broome on 4, 5, 7,
  95, 169
  disproving notion of terra
  nullius 169, 170
  importance of 4-7, 95, 169,
  170
  inaccuracies in 101-02,
  115-16

role in teaching Aboriginal
history 159-61, 164-9, 170
Armstrong, Francis Fraser 91, 92,
93, 95
assimilation policy 29, 49, 52, 53,
62, 157, 161
  and education 162-5
  and loss of identity 163-5
  see also *From Old Maloga*;
  paternalism
Australian Aborigines' League 156,
157
Australian history see history,
Australian
AWB (Aborigines Welfare Board)
see Aborigines Protection
Board

Bamblett, Esme 158
Barak, David, 154-5
Barak, William 147-8, 158
  activism 153, 154, 155-6, 157
  and Maloga Mission 110,
  154-5
Barker, Captain Collet 81, 87, 89,
90, 92
Batman Treaty 30, 145, 147, 154
Batman, John 30, 145
Bebejan 146
Benbow 151-2
Billibellary 5, 146-9
  and Aboriginal identity
  147-8, 150-1, 156
  adaptive strategies of 149-50,
  151, 154
  authority of 147-8, 149
  and friendship with William
  Thomas 148-51
  and radical hope 154, 156, 158
  and self-sufficiency 151, 155,
  156
Boggabilla Aboriginal Station 128,
133, 134, 137

Boonwurrung 148, 149, 151-2, 154
  first contact 1-2, 16-17
  population crash 145-6, 148
  see also Coranderrk
    Aboriginal Station; Kulin
Borrunupton 146
Bourke, Governor Richard 145
boxing 4, 7, 64
  Aboriginal boxers 65-6, 71-2
  and Johnson defeat of white
    boxers 68, 69-72
  as means of escaping poverty
    64, 67, 71
  and racism 63-79
  source of inspiration 64, 65,
    68-9, 71-2
  source of pride 66-7, 69-71
  see also Johnson, Jack
Bradbury 22, 25
Briggs, Evelyn (née Clements) 98,
  115, 117
Briggs-Walsh, May 162-3
Briggs, Geraldine (née Clements)
  98, 104, 108, 113-14, **115**
Briggs, Hartley 162
Briggs, Hyllus 104
Briggs, Leah see Andrews, Leah
Broome, Richard **8**, 38-48, 61-2,
  80, 131, 159, 170
  on activism 131-2
  approach to research 1-2,
    6-13, 37
    and importance of
      archives 4, 5, 7, 95, 169
    and assessments of death
      statistics 28, 30-1, 32-4, 36-7
    attitude to Aboriginal people
      2, 9-12, 16, 27-9, 127
    attitude to term 'massacre'
      27-9, 32, 35-6
    and boxing 8, 63-4, 68, 78
    and colonialism 2-3, 16-17

evolution of concept of
  paternalism 39, 41, 45-7, 62
  rethinking term 31-4, 36,
    38, 45-6
history as complex and
  nuanced 10-11, 17
and importance of Aboriginal
  perspective 3, 9-11, 19
influence of work 3, 37, 47-8,
  166, 170
and *Koorie* exhibition 10-11,
  27-9
and Marxist model 30, 34
and mission paternalism 3-4,
  39, 45-7
and race relations model
  18-21, 23, 31-4, 36
and reciprocity 46-7
relationships with others 6, 7,
  78, 80, 95
and 'right behaviour' 15, 46,
  47, 110
and 'two-way dynamic' 38, 46,
  48
see also *Aboriginal Australians*;
  radical hope
Brough, Mal 56, 57-8
Bungaree, John 16
Burney, Linda 166-7
Burra Ferra 107-8

Calma, Tom 56, 57
Carl McGrady Scholarship 133
  recipient's response 135-6,
    139
  recipient's results 135, 137-8,
    139
Carnac Island 83-4, 85, 91, 93, 94
cattle stations 44
Central Board for the Aborigines
  see Aborigines Protection
  Board
Cheyenne 141, 143

children, Aboriginal
    protecting 52, 55, 57-9
    removal of 5, 16, 97, 114, 116-19, 123
    see also education of Aboriginal children
churches 47, 167-8
    Aboriginal attitude to Christianity 14, 16, 29, 108-09
    see also missions
citizenship 51-2, 156-7, 166
    and Aboriginal ways of being Australian 166-7
citizenship rights 124-5, 157
Clay, Cassius see Ali, Mohammad
Clements, Margaret see Tucker, Margaret
Clements, Theresa (née Middleton) 4-5, 96, **97**, **98**, **104**, **115**, **117**
    attitude to Christianity 108-09
    background 104-06, 115-17, 121
    descendants 96, **98**, **114**, 116-21, **117**
    education 107-08, 114, 119
    father's background 101, 105, 109-10, 112-13
    and importance of culture 107-08, 109
    and importance of family 103-05, 116-21
    letters from 103-05, 117-19
    removal of daughters 116-19
    strength in face of adversity 99, 116, 119, 121
    see also Cummeragunja; *From Old Maloga*; Maloga Mission
Clements, William 98, 115-16
Cocknose 22, 25
Collie, Alexander 81
colonialism 1-3, 12-13, 16-17, 19-21, 32, 36, 49
    and Aboriginal agency 19, 29, 37
    and Batman Treaty 30, 145, 147, 154
    challenged by Johnson 74-5
    Marxist model of 19-20, 30, 34
    Memmi's paradigm of 29-31, 33-4
    and notion of terra nullius 166-7
    ongoing effects of 17, 30, 98-9, 165-7
    see also frontier wars
Coloured Progressive Association 68
connection to country 80-1, 89-90, 91, 93, 94-5
    narrating own country 90-3, 95
constitutional recognition 172
Cooper, William 155-8
Cootamundra Aboriginal Girls Training Home 117
Coranderrk Aboriginal Station 13-15, 38, 46, 110, 153, 155
    desire for self-sufficiency 155, 156
    and farming success 154, 155
    government inquiry 152, 155-6
Coranderrk Reserve see Coranderrk Aboriginal Station
Country Women's Association see CWA
CPP see Cultural Permission Program
Crow people 141-3
    and alliance with US Government 141, 144, 149-50
    loss of traditional lifestyle 141-2, 143-4
    response to rapid change 143, 149, 158
    and traditional enemies 141, 149-50
    see also Plenty Coups

Culpendure 149
cultural devastation 142-3, 145-6, 148, 161
  adaptive strategies for survival 143, 144, 149-50, 151, 154
  desire to remain Aboriginal 150, 153-4, 156, 157
  and life of mere survival 142, 144
  and population crashes 145-6, 148, 152
  and radical hope 144-5, 154, 156, 158
  responses to 141, 142, 145-8
  see also Aboriginal, new ways of being; Billibellary
Cultural Permission Program (CPP) 160-1
culture, Aboriginal 29, 46, 52, 146-7, 159
  and identity 99, 102, 127, 135-7, 165, 166, 170
  maintaining 6, 107-09, 160-1, 168
  and oral history 161, 162, 171
  and social contract 166, 167
  telling own story 161-2, 164
Cummeragunja 5-6, **106**, 110-14, 161-2
  and Aborigines Protection Board 112, 113
  and education 114, 162-3
  employment of residents 114, 162-3
  and farming 109-13
  and land 110-11, 155
  move from Maloga Mission 110-14
  paternalism of managers 112-14
  and traditional life 114, 162, 165

CWA (Country Women's Association) 5, 122, 123, 134, 135
  disappointment at recipients' responses 129, 130-1, 132, 139
  encouragement of recipient 129, 130-1
  and exercise of agency by recipients 127, 132
  expectations of recipients 123, 129
  lack of understanding of structural inequalities 127, 130
  see also Carl McGrady Scholarship; Susie McGrady Scholarship
CWA Aboriginal branches 128, 137
  Gwydir CWA Group 128, 133, 134-5, 136

Daungwurrung (Taungwurrung) people 147-8, 152-3, 154
  and revenge for Billibellary's death 150-1
  see also Billibellary
Davis, Ben 95
Dawson, James 146-7
Day, David 33-4
Day of Mourning 156
deaths in custody 16-17
disadvantage, Aboriginal 51-2, 60, 148
  in education 122-7, 129-30, 132-9, 163
  and self-determination 49, 53, 55-6, 58
disease 28, 31, 145, 167
  and Billibellary 150-1
  smallpox 143, 145, 167
  tuberculosis 154, 155
Donmera 83-4
Duffy, Charles 153

education 133-4, 138-9
  and Wyndham Scheme
    124-5, 131
education of Aboriginal children 5,
    139, 164-5, 166
  Aboriginal Secondary Grants
    Scheme 138-9
  and agency 123, 127, 132,
    136-7
  and AWB 122, 123-4, 129, 132
  and Carl McGrady Scholarship
    133, 135, 137-8, 139
  early school leaving 122, 124,
    126-7, 132, 136-7, 139
  and high school 122-7, 132,
    163-4
  and hostility to white values
    127, 135-7
  on missions 162-3
  obstacles to 122-7, 129-30,
    132-9, 163
  reforms of 123, 124-6, 133-4,
    137-8
  and scholarships 122, 123-4,
    132
  Susie McGrady scholarship
    123, 128-32, 134, 135, 139
  see also history, Aboriginal,
    teaching of
environmental history 80
  Aboriginal land management
    80, 81
  and connection to country
    80-1, 89-90, 91, 93, 94-5

farming 29, 109, 108, 111, 114
  Aboriginal ownership of
    farms 109-10, 112-13
  as adaptation to change
    109-11, 151, 154-5, 158
  Yorta Yorta land claim and
    1887 petition 110-11
Fawkner, John Pascoe 145, 147

Ferguson, Bill 111, 156
Fighting Hard 140
firearms 26, 35
  limitations of 22, 26, 28, 30,
    34-6
first contact 1-2, 7, 16-17, 161
  and moments of common
    humanity 2-3, 15-16
Fort Laramie Treaty 141
From Old Maloga 96-8, 100, 102,
    103, 119
  discrepancies in 96, 108-09,
    111, 121
  external influences on 96,
    102-03, 111
  further documentation by
    descendants 99, 108-09
  and oral history 96, 121
  and other historical
    documents 101, 102, 115-16
  value of 101, 102, 120, 121
  see also Clements, Theresa
frontier 10, 11, 27-9
  complexity of 10-11, 27-8,
    144, 149
frontier wars 3, 18-19, 24, 26-7, 33,
    36-7, 145
  Aboriginal combatants as
    British subjects 22-3, 26
  Aboriginal leadership 22, 25
  adaptation of fighting tactics
    21-22, 25
  context of 32-3, 34
  and economic warfare 20, 22, 33
  estimates of casualties 20,
    22-3, 27
  and firearms 22, 26, 35-6
  and guerrilla warfare 20, 24,
    26-7
  increasing numbers of settlers
    20, 22
  and Native Police Corps 22,
    25-6, 28, 29, 149

and power relationships
20-21, 26
    settler tactics 21-6, 35-6
    statistics of deaths 27, 28,
    30-2, 34, 36-7
    at Swan River 83, 86-7
    traditional fighting practices
    21-5, 35
    in Victorian 3, 18-37
    see also massacres; violence

Garvey, Marcus 75
geographies 81, 85, 87, 91-3, 95
    depth of knowledge 87, 89-90
    and networks 82, 85
    reasons for recording 91-2, 95
    see also maps
Ginibi, Ruby Langford 124
Great Australian Silence 7, 165-9
Green, John 15, 154-6
Gunai (Kurnai) people 149, 154
Gunditjmara people 145
Guugu Yimidhirr 50-1
    see also Hope Vale Mission;
    Pearson, Noel
Gwydir CWA Group 133
    and Carl McGrady
    Scholarship 133, 134-5, 136
Gyalliput 4, 82, 84, 85-9, 92-3, 95
    diplomacy at Swan River 82,
    84-5, 90, 93-4
    map by 4, 80-2, 87-9, **88**, 90, 95
    and mobility 82, 84, 93-5
    and naming of country 84-5,
    90
    and Yagan 84-5, 90, 93-4

Hasluck, Paul 163-4
Henty brothers 145
history wars 31-2, 38-9, 169
history, Aboriginal 7-9, 11-12, 15,
81, 98
    centralising Aboriginal
    experience 2-13, 64, 78, 96-7,
    121
    and ethics 6, 13, 15-16
    Great Australian Silence 7,
    165-9
    when subject is family 97-8,
    119-20
    see also Clements, Theresa
history, Aboriginal, teaching of 3,
7-9, 159-61, 163-6, 168-9
    Aboriginal people driving
    process 170-2
    and Aboriginal worldview
    170-2
    following cultural practice
    161-2, 164, 171
    and notion of terra nullius
    161, 165, 166-7, 169, 170
    and role of archives 159,
    160-1, 169, 170
    shared history since white
    settlement 167, 169
history, Australian 6-10, 13, 81,
161, 168, 170
    Great Australian Silence 7,
    165-9
    and moments of common
    humanity 2-3, 15-16
    need to centralise Aboriginal
    experience 2-6, 8-13, 15
    and notion of terra nullius
    161, 165, 166-7, 170
    and race relations model 19,
    20, 31, 32, 33
    see also frontier wars; history,
    Aboriginal
history, frontier see frontier wars
Hope Vale Mission 50-4
    complexity of legacy 50-1, 52-3
    as home 46, 50, 52-4, 61
    interplay between 'village' and
    'mission' lives 50-1, 60, 61

Howard Government 38, 169
   and paternalism 54-5, 59, 61
   and Noel Pearson 54-5, 58-9, 60, 61
Howard, John 49, 57-8
Howitt, Alfred 147-8

identity 99, 102, 127, 135-7, 165, 166, 170
   see also Aboriginal, new ways of being
Inquiry into the Protection of Aboriginal Children from Sexual Abuse, NT 57
Intervention, Northern Territory 57-8
   and defence of 58-9

Jaga Jaga *see* Billibellary
James, Thomas Shadrach 107-08, 114
Jerome, Jerry 71
Jika Jika *see* Billibellary
Johnson, Jack 4, 67-9, 72-3, 74, 76-7, 78
   and Aboriginal boxing 63, 69, 71-2
   background 67-8, 71, 72, 76
   boxing exploits 68, 69, 70-2, 77-8, 79
   challenge to racial hierarchy 67, 74, 75-6
   cultural interests 68-9, 72-5
   defeat of Tommy Burns 68, 69, 72, 77
   defeat of Jim Jeffries 70-1, 72, 74, 76
   influence on oppressed peoples 63, 68-72, 76
   master of own destiny 63, 67, 71, 72, 78, 79
   personal attributes 67-9, 72-4
   political beliefs 74-5, 76, 78
   responses to racism 75, 76-7
   white fears of influence 68, 69, 76, 78
Jupiter 22, 25

keeping places and knowledge centres 168, 172
King George Sound settlement 81-5, 87, 93
Koorie exhibition 10-11, 27-8, 29
   Richard Broome's response to 10-11, 27-9
Kulin 13-14, 15, 110, 147
   population crash 145-6, 148, 152
   see also Boonwurrung; Daungwurrung; Wathaurung; Woiwurrung
Kurnai (Gunai) people 149, 154

Langton, Marcia 13, 61
languages, Aboriginal 84-5, 107, 109, 166
   prohibition against speaking 99, 168
   white settlers learning 83-4, 91
leadership, Aboriginal 21, 32, 34, 50, 146-8, 154, 157
   and new ways of being Aboriginal 13, 146, 149-50, 154-5, 157
Linderman, Frank B 142, 150
logic of elimination 33, 34
Lousy Little Sixpence 109-10, 113-14
Lyon, Robert Menli 83-4, 91, 93, 95

Mabo 29, 168, 170
Maloga Mission 4-5, 106, **106**, 107-11, 155-8
   and Aboriginal culture 107, 108, 109, 114
   and attitudes to Christianity 108-09, 111

and Coranderrk Aboriginal
  Reserve 110, 112, 154-5
education and training
  106-07, 111
and farming 108, 154-5
and Thomas Shadrach James
  107-08, 114
and Daniel Matthews 106, 107
move to Cummeragunja 110,
  112, 113, 114
Manyat 84-5, 94
maps 82, 87, **88**, 91-2, 95
  as acknowledgement of
    occupation 90, 92, 93, 95
  by Gyalliput 4, 80-2, 87-9,
    88, 90, 92
  by Maragnan 87, 92, 93, 95
  by Mokare 80-2, 90, 95
  as tools of dispossession 92, 93
  by white settlers 91-3
Maragnan 87, 92, 93, 95
massacres 19-20, 22, 24, 26, 35-6,
  167
  Richard Broome, and
    evidence of 20, 22, 24, 29,
    31-3, 35-6
  and introduction of disease
    20, 167
  and *Koorie* exhibition 10-11,
    27, 29
  and limitations of firearms 22,
    26, 28, 30, 34-6
  poisoning 22, 26, 167
  in retaliation for killing of
    settlers 20, 24, 26-7
  statistics 28, 30-2, 34
  of white settlers 24
  and Windschuttle debate 31-2
  see also frontier wars; violence
Matthews, Daniel 106, 108, 110,
  112, 155
  harsh treatment by 109, 111, 112
  and Maloga petition 110, 111

Matthews, Janet 108, 155
Matthysson, Frances (née Briggs)
  105-06
Mayers, Naomi 117
Maynard, Fred 67-8, 77
Maynard, Merv 66
McGrady, Carl 133, 134, 137-8
  response to scholarship
    135-6, 139
  see also Carl McGrady
    scholarship
McGrady, Susie 128, 133
  see also Susie McGrady
    scholarship
McIntosh, Ron 137
memoir 5, 102-03, 162-3
  and external influences 96,
    102-03
  see also *From Old Maloga*
Miago 91
Middleton, George 98, 109-10,
  112-13
  background 101, 105, 109-10,
    112-13
Middleton, Theresa *see* Clements,
  Theresa
Milius, Pierre Bernard 1-2, 6,
  16-17
Mineng Nyungar 81-3
  and King George Sound
    settlement 81-5, 87, 93
  Mokare's map 80-2, 90, 95
  see also Gyalliput
missions 42, 43-4, 48, 100, 107,
  116, 168
  and agency 44, 46-8, 50-1
  attitudes to missionaries 44,
    46, 47, 48, 51
  cultural cost of 99, 107, 167-8
  and decline of 51-3
  experiences of 161-3, 164-5
  as home 46, 52-4, 61

as means of domination 38, 47, 48, 56
nostalgia for mission life 3-4, 51, 53, 54
and paternalism 3-4, 38, 39, 40-8, 50-3
and reciprocity 44, 46-8, 60
and rights 52-3
as safe havens 99, 167-8
support for by whites 152, 153, 154
see also Cummeragunja; Hope Vale Mission; Maloga Mission
mobility 82, 87, 91, 93, 94-5
and Gyalliput 82, 84, 93-5
and Manyat 84-5, 94
and Maragnan 87, 92, 93, 95
and networking 81, 85, 87, 94
Mokare 80-2, 90, 95
Molloy, Georgina 82, 94
Moonahcullah Mission 116
Morgan, John 85-6, 90, 92
   scribing for William Buckley 85-6
   scribing for Gyalliput 85, 86-90, 92
Munday 91
Mundine, Tony 65
Muni see Schwarz, Father George
Munnering, Tommy 152
Murray, John 1
Murrumwiller (Charles Never) 12, 16
'mutual obligation' 49, 54-5, 60

Native Americans 141-3
Native Police Corps 22, 25-6, 28, 29, 149
native title 101, 167, 168, 172
neoliberal policy 49-50
   and 'mutual obligation' 49, 54-5, 60

see also paternalism, new; Pearson, Noel
Never, Charles (Murrumwiller) 12, 16
new ways of being see Aboriginal, new ways of being
Nicholls, Doug 157, 163
Ningina 83-4
Noongar see Nyungar
nostalgia 49, 51-3, 55-6, 61
   for mission life 3-4, 51, 53, 54
   see also Pearson, Noel
Nyungar 92
   language of 83-4, 85, 91

Onus, Bill 157
oral history 96, 99, 101-02, 116
   and inaccuracies in official records 101-02, 115-16
   see also *From Old Maloga*

parenting 52, 55, 58
   and new paternalism 57, 58
paternalism 38, 41-5, 48, 50, 54, 58
   and cultural practices 41, 43, 44, 46, 48
   and agency 3, 39, 40, 41, 44-5, 53, 60-2
   attitudes to, negative 38, 42-3, 44, 47, 56, 59
   attitudes to, positive 38-9, 43-4, 48-9, 52-3, 60, 62
   basis of 38-9
      Christian tradition 39, 42-5, 46-50
      community 53, 55-7, 59-61
      family 38-9, 42, 52-3
      race 42-3, 52-3, 50, 56
   breakdown of 46-7, 51-2
   and Richard Broome 38, 45-8
   changes in attitudes to 38, 47, 52-3

definitional differences 38-9, 60
as domination 38, 47, 48, 49, 56
enabling self-determination 41, 53, 56, 61
and history wars 38-9
and reciprocity 44, 46-7, 48, 61
and right behaviour 15, 46, 47
as site of negotiation 47, 53
state 50, 55, 56
as system of relationality 3-4, 38, 41, 43, 46
as 'two-way system' 38, 44-6, 48
and welfare dependency 46-7, 51-2, 60
see also missions
paternalism, 'new' 38, 49-51, 54
calls for 49, 55-6, 58-9
as community-based 53, 55-7, 59-61
and Howard Government 38, 54-5, 58-9
and 'mutual obligation' 49, 54-5, 60
as solution for poverty 59-60
see also Pearson, Noel
Patten, Christina (née Middleton) 103-04, **104**
Patten, Jack 111
Pearson, Noel 3, 38-40, 46, 50, 51-4, 58, 61-2
advocating for paternalism 38, 41, 49, 60
white interpretations of 41, 49, 54-5, 60, 61
on causes of Aboriginal disadvantage 49, 51-2, 55, 60
Christian mission paternalism 39, 41
on community versus state paternalism 53, 55-7, 59-61
criticism of ideas 54-5, 57-9
and Howard Government 54-5, 58-9, 60, 61
and 'mutual obligation 49, 54-5, 60
and 'native nostalgia' 49-53, 54, 60, 61
on parenting 52, 55, 57, 58
on paternalism enabling agency 60, 62
on paternalism and reciprocity 54, 60, 61
on paternalism and self-determination 41, 53, 56, 61
on personal responsibility 49, 54, 60, 61
and politics 49-50
and rescuing children 52, 55, 57-9
on welfare reform 40, 51-2, 54, 57, 60, 61
petitions for land 153, 155-7
see also Coranderrk mission; Cummeragunja
Phillip, Arthur 3, 34
Pilbara strike 14
Pindan Mining Company 14
Pindan Mob *see* Pindan Mining Company
Pinjarra massacre 91
Plenty Coups 142-4, 150
and adaptive strategies 144-5, 149-50
bravery of 141-2, 144
and loss of land 142, 148
and loss of traditional role 143, 144
and spiritual dream 143-4
and radical hope 144-5, 158
re-imagining being Crow 144, 151, 156-7, 158
policies affecting Aboriginal people 55, 62, 171

assimilation policy 49, 52, 53, 62, 102, 157-8, 161-5
the Intervention 49, 57-9
and mission nostalgia 3-4
'mutual obligation' 49, 60
self-determination 41, 49, 53, 55-6, 58, 61
'separate development' 58
see also paternalism; Pearson, Noel
Port Phillip District 145, 148

race relations 18, 23, 36, 37
race relations model 19-21, 31, 32-4, 36, 37
   abandoning of 33, 34
   and Richard Broome 18-21, 23, 31-4, 36
   ineffectiveness of 32, 34
racism 66, 71, 78-9, 99, 123
   and boxing 63-79
   enunciations of white superiority 68, 69, 71, 75
radical hope 5, 6, 13-17, 131, 144-5, 158
   and activism 5, 140
   and conceiving of a future 143-4, 156-7
reserves, Aboriginal see missions
resistance 29, 37, 97, 99, 108, 127, 131
   in education, and agency 123, 127, 132, 136-7, 139
   resistance literature 97
   see also activism; radical hope
right behaviour 15, 46-7, 110
   see also radical hope
rights of Indigenous people 41, 109, 168-9
   and assimilation policy 157, 163-4
   breaching of 52-3, 164
   and citizenship 125, 156, 157

and Intervention 58
land rights 109, 119, 167, 168
and missions 52-3
reclaiming 18, 19, 100, 131-2, 156-8
recognition of 19, 37, 164, 168-9
and retaining culture 131, 157, 164
traditional 84-5, 121
Robinson, George Augustus 93, 95, 147
Rose, Lionel 65-6, 71
Royal Commission into Aboriginal Deaths in Custody 16

Sands brothers 65, 71
The Sapphires 108
scholarships for Aboriginal children 122-4, 127
   and ABSEG 138-9
   and AWB 122-4, 132-3
   conflicting priorities of recipients 123, 126
   and education reform 123-5
   expectations by sponsors 123, 129
   and pressure to assimilate 123, 129, 139
   see also Carl McGrady Scholarship; CWA; Susie McGrady Scholarship
Schwarz, Father George (Muni) 50, 52-3, 60
Scott, Helenus 95
Scott, Robert 94
self-determination 45, 49, 53, 58
   as cause of Aboriginal disadvantage 49, 55-6, 58
   enabled by paternalism 41, 53, 56, 61
   and 'mutual obligation' 49, 60
   and nostalgia for time before 49, 52, 53

Shortland, Edward 91-2
Sioux tribe 141, 143
Smith, Malcolm 16-17
State Library of Victoria 160-1
    Koori librarian role 159, 160-1
Stirling, Governor James 82, 91
Strickland, Reverend 155
Susie McGrady scholarship 123, 128-32, 134, 135
    AWB intervention 129, 132
    optimism of recipient's teachers 129, 130, 131
    recipient's resistance 131-2, 139
    sponsors' disappointment 129, 130-1, 132, 139
    sponsors' encouragement of recipient 129, 130-1
    sponsors' expectations 129-30, 139
    see also Carl McGrady Scholarship
Swan River settlement 82, 83-4, 91, 92
    and Gyalliput's diplomacy 82, 84-5, 90, 93-4
    and treatment of Whadjuk Nyungar 82-4, 86-7
    see also Morgan, John

Taroom Aboriginal settlement 71
Taungwurrung 159, 162
    see also Daungwurrung
Te Huruhuru 91-2
Tench, Watkin 3, 167
terra nullius, notion of 5, 160, 161
    archival evidence refuting 169, 170
    and teaching of Aboriginal history 161, 165, 166-7, 169, 170
Thomas, William 147, 151-2
    and friendship with Billibellary 148-51

Thompson, Hector 65
Toodle, Maggie 98, 100
tourism, and survival of cultural practices 168
travellers, Aboriginal *see* mobility
treaties 172
    Batman Treaty 30, 145, 147, 154
    Fort Laramie Treaty 141
    at Swan River settlement 82
Tucker, Margaret (née Clements) 98, 103, 109-10, **115**, 116-18, **117**

Ulupna people 105, 110, 121
Ulupna Station 105, **106**, 106, 115
'usurper complex' 33-4

Victorian Aborigines Advancement League *see* Aborigines Advancement League (Victoria)
violence 3, 18, 36
    and abduction of Aboriginal women 21, 22, 32-3
    against Aboriginal people 31, 33, 35-6, 167
    by Aboriginal people 24, 33, 36, 167, 169
    initiators of 32-3, 36, 169
    and introduction of disease 20
    on frontier 10, 27-8, 149
    and poisoning of Aboriginal people 22, 26, 167
    see also frontier wars; massacres; Native Police Corps

Walker, May (née Clements) 98, **115**, 116-18
Warangesda Mission 116
warrior culture 141-2, 143
    and radical hope 144-5, 158

wars *see* frontier wars
Wathaurung 147-8
welfare 46-7, 54, 61
   and 'mutual obligation' 49, 54-5, 60
   'passive' 54, 60
   reform of 40, 54-5, 57, 61
   see also Pearson, Noel
Wellard, Reverend Colin 133, 134
Whadjuk Nyungar 82-4, 86-7, 91
White Australia 68, 167
Windschuttle, Keith 31
Wiradjuri 162
Wirrpanda (née Briggs), Margaret **117**
Woiwurrung 13-15, 146, 148, 149
   population crash 145-6, 148
   and requests for land 151-4
   and revenge for Billibellary's death 150-1
   see also Billibellary; Coranderrk Aboriginal Station; Kulin
Wonga, Simon 149, 152-3, 157
   and Coranderrk 152-3, 154
Wurundjeri clan 146
Wurundjeri-Willam sub clan 146, 147
   see also Billibellary
Wyndham Scheme 124-5, 130, 131
Wyndham, Harold 122, 124-5

Yagan 83-4, 91, 93-4
   and Gyalliput 84-5, 90, 93-4
Yanner, Murandoo 59
Yarmuk *see* Clements, Theresa
Yellagonga 84-5, 90
Yorta Yorta 101, 107, 108, 110
   and 1887 petition 110-11
   see also Cummeragunja; Maloga Mission